Global Decisions, Local Collisions

Global Decisions, Local Collisions

Urban Life in the New World Order

David Ranney

TEMPLE UNIVERSITY PRESS

PHILADELPHIA

For Pat Wright

Temple University Press, Philadelphia 19122
Copyright © 2003 by Temple University
All rights reserved
Published 2003
Printed in the United States of America

⊗The paper used in this publication meets the requirements of the American
National Standard for Information Sciences—Permanence of Paper for
Printed Library Materials, ANSI Z39.48–1984.

Library of Congress Cataloging-in-Publication Data

Ranney, David C.
    Global decisions, local collisions : urban life in the new world order
/ David Ranney.
        p.   cm.
    Includes bibliographical references and index.
    ISBN 1-59213-000-3 (cloth : alk. paper) — ISBN 1-59213-001-1 (pbk. :
alk. paper)
        1. Chicago (Ill.)—Economic conditions.   2. Urban policy—Illinois—
Chicago.   3. Labor—Illinois—Chicago.   4. Globalization.   5. Urban
economics.   I. Title.
    HC108.C4 R35   2003
    330.9773'11—dc21   2002070252

Contents

Acknowledgments

The reader will see that this book is the product of work I have been doing for nearly twenty-five years. It is based not only on my academic research but also on my association with a variety of people through my courses and seminars over the years and work in several Chicago area factories, community organizing activities, popular education workshops with labor unions and community groups, and work to develop an alternative vision to the new world order with colleagues and friends in a number of other countries in this hemisphere, particularly Canada and Mexico. In many ways this book is the story of all of these people as seen through my eyes. I am grateful for the many insights these associations have given me.

I am also specifically grateful to a number of people who read all or parts of various drafts of this book and offered helpful comments. These include: Sarah Anderson, Larry Bennett, Robin Broad, John Cavanagh, Peter Daniels, Beth Gonzalez, Darlene Gramigna, Karen Hansen-Kuhn, James Jennings, Lou Kushnick, Peter Marcuse, David McBride, Wayne Orthwein, David Perry, Neil Shadle, Snigdha Srivastava, Shari Stone-Mediatore, Nik Theodore, Jessica Tulloch, Kelly Vaughan, Don Wiener, and Mary Zerkel. Adolph Reed Jr. read the entire manuscript and offered detailed comments that were particularly helpful. My editor, Peter Wissoker, not only offered many useful comments on the substance of the book, but also responded promptly to my many questions about the status of the review and publication process. Pat Wright, my partner and co-author of Chapter 6, has discussed and helped sharpen many of the ideas in this book for the past several years. During the year in which the book was written, she not only read and commented on several drafts of the entire manuscript, but also talked to me about the project every single day. No acknowledgment is sufficient for such a contribution.

Several case studies appearing in this book were updated and adapted from earlier published versions. I am grateful to the original publishers for their permission to use this material. The case of the closing of Wisconsin Steel in Chapter 4 was adapted from David C. Ranney, "The Closing of Wisconsin Steel," in Charles Craypo and Bruce Nissen (eds.), *Grand Designs: The Impact of Corporate Strategies on Workers, Unions and Communities*, pp. 65–91, Copyright © 1993 by Cornell University Press. Used by permission of the publisher, Cornell University Press. Two cases, "The Chicago White Sox Get a New Stadium," and "Gentrifying the South Loop" appearing in Chapters 5 and 6, respectively, were adapted from David C. Ranney, Patricia A. Wright and Tingwei Zhang, *Citizens, Local Government and Development of Chicago's Near South Side,"* United Nations Research Institute for Social Development (UNRISD) Discussion Paper #90, Geneva, 1997. "The Destruction of Public Housing: The Case of Cabrini Green" that appears in Chapter 6 was adapted from David C. Ranney and Patricia A. Wright, "Race, Class and the Abuse of State Power," *Sage Race Relations Abstracts* 25, no. 3 (August 2000), pp. 3–32.

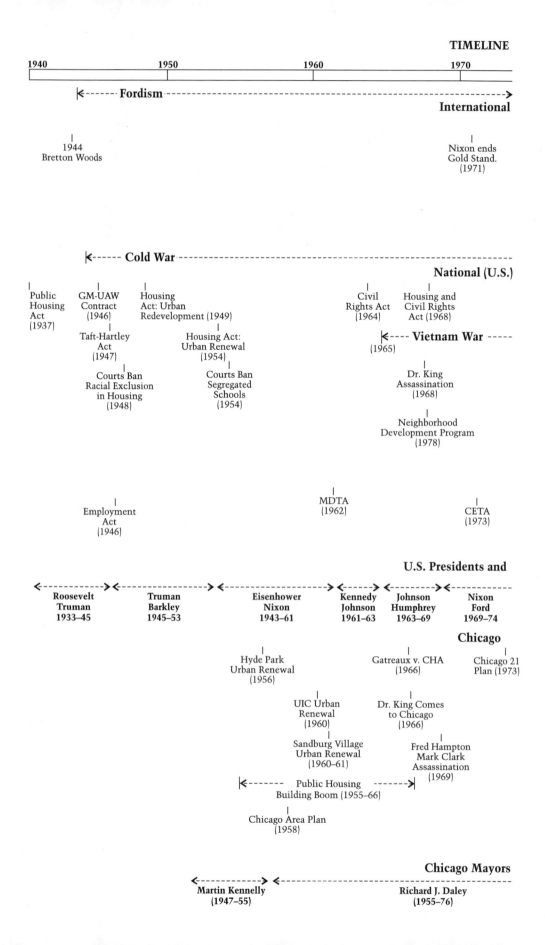

TIMELINE

| 1940 | 1950 | 1960 | 1970 |

|←------ Fordism --→|

International

1944
Bretton Woods

Nixon ends
Gold Stand.
(1971)

|←------ Cold War --

National (U.S.)

Public
Housing
Act
(1937)

GM-UAW
Contract
(1946)

Housing
Act: Urban
Redevelopment (1949)

Civil
Rights Act
(1964)

Housing and
Civil Rights
Act (1968)

Taft-Hartley
Act
(1947)

Housing Act:
Urban Renewal
(1954)

|←---- **Vietnam War** -----
(1965)

Courts Ban
Racial Exclusion
in Housing
(1948)

Courts Ban
Segregated
Schools
(1954)

Dr. King
Assassination
(1968)

Neighborhood
Development Program
(1978)

Employment
Act
(1946)

MDTA
(1962)

CETA
(1973)

U.S. Presidents and

|←----------→|←----------→|←----------→|←---→|←-------→|←----------

| Roosevelt Truman 1933–45 | Truman Barkley 1945–53 | Eisenhower Nixon 1943–61 | Kennedy Johnson 1961–63 | Johnson Humphrey 1963–69 | Nixon Ford 1969–74 |

Chicago

Hyde Park
Urban Renewal
(1956)

Gatreaux v. CHA
(1966)

Chicago 21
Plan (1973)

UIC Urban
Renewal
(1960)

Dr. King Comes
to Chicago
(1966)

Sandburg Village
Urban Renewal
(1960–61)

Fred Hampton
Mark Clark
Assassination
(1969)

|←------- Public Housing -------→|
Building Boom (1955–66)

Chicago Area Plan
(1958)

Chicago Mayors

|←-----------→|←---|
Martin Kennelly
(1947–55)

Richard J. Daley
(1955–76)

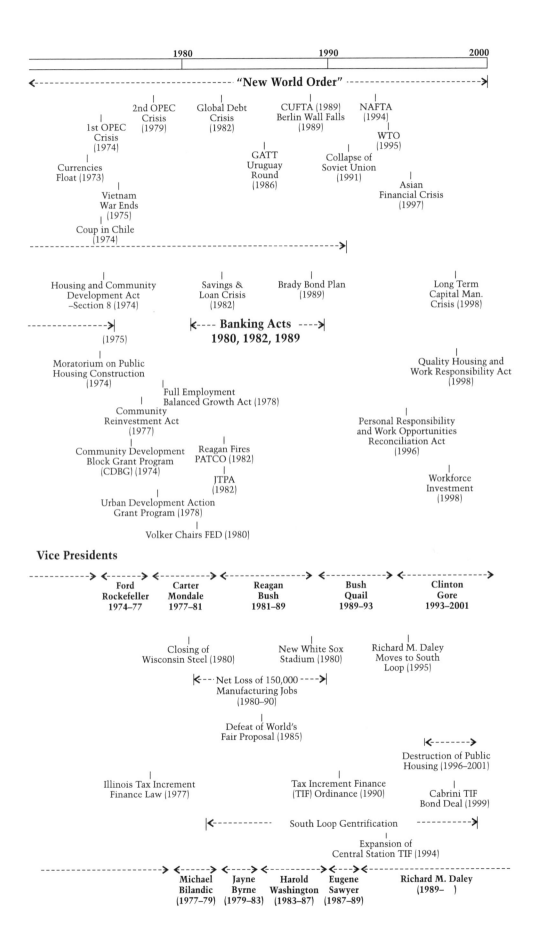

1980 · 1990 · 2000

←-------------------------------------- "New World Order" --------------------------------→

2nd OPEC
Crisis
(1979)

1st OPEC
Crisis
(1974)

Global Debt
Crisis
(1982)

CUFTA (1989)
Berlin Wall Falls
(1989)

NAFTA
(1994)

WTO
(1995)

Currencies
Float (1973)

GATT
Uruguay
Round
(1986)

Collapse of
Soviet Union
(1991)

Asian
Financial Crisis
(1997)

Vietnam
War Ends
(1975)

Coup in Chile
(1974)

←---→

Housing and Community
Development Act
–Section 8 (1974)

Savings &
Loan Crisis
(1982)

Brady Bond Plan
(1989)

Long Term
Capital Man.
Crisis (1998)

←-------------→
(1975)

←---- **Banking Acts** ----→
1980, 1982, 1989

Moratorium on Public
Housing Construction
(1974)

Quality Housing and
Work Responsibility Act
(1998)

Full Employment
Balanced Growth Act (1978)

Community
Reinvestment Act
(1977)

Personal Responsibility
and Work Opportunities
Reconciliation Act
(1996)

Community Development
Block Grant Program
(CDBG) (1974)

Reagan Fires
PATCO (1982)

JTPA
(1982)

Workforce
Investment
(1998)

Urban Development Action
Grant Program (1978)

Volker Chairs FED (1980)

Vice Presidents

-----------→ ←------→ ←----------→ ←----------------→ ←----------→ ←----------------→

Ford
Rockefeller
1974–77

Carter
Mondale
1977–81

Reagan
Bush
1981–89

Bush
Quail
1989–93

Clinton
Gore
1993–2001

Closing of
Wisconsin Steel (1980)

New White Sox
Stadium (1980)

Richard M. Daley
Moves to South
Loop (1995)

←---·Net Loss of 150,000 ----→
Manufacturing Jobs
(1980–90)

Defeat of World's
Fair Proposal (1985)

←------→
Destruction of Public
Housing (1996–2001)

Illinois Tax Increment
Finance Law (1977)

Tax Increment Finance
(TIF) Ordinance (1990)

Cabrini TIF
Bond Deal (1999)

←------------ South Loop Gentrification ------------→

Expansion of
Central Station TIF (1994)

-------------------→ ←------→ ←----→ ←----------→ ←----→←------------------------

Michael
Bilandic
(1977–79)

Jayne
Byrne
(1979–83)

Harold
Washington
(1983–87)

Eugene
Sawyer
(1987–89)

Richard M. Daley
(1989–)

CHAPTER I

Introduction

The history of people living and working in the global capitalist system since the fourteenth century can be divided into distinct periods or eras. These periods are defined in part by the broad strategy used by the system as a whole to accumulate a social surplus that is used to keep the system going. They are also defined by the social struggles of ordinary people who find the specific rules that define this strategy to be contradictory to their own development as human beings. Historically, each period has ended in crisis and has ushered in a new strategy for the accumulation of surplus. Each period has also generated the need for people to find new ways to struggle for their humanity by contesting the terms of the new era.

We entered a new period in the mid-1970s. Both aspects of the period—the global rules that define its strategy and the character of social struggles contesting its terms—have been evolving since then. I call this period a "new world order," using the phrase originally coined by U.S. President George H. Bush. This book traces the impact of this shift on urban public policies and on the lives of the people who are affected by those policies. It also looks critically at current efforts to organize against the abuses of this new world order, offering an alternative organizing strategy better suited to the present era.

The Dawn of a New Era

In the late 1970s, I lived and worked in Southeast Chicago. At the time the neighborhood was a vibrant, mixed-race, working-class community of solid single-family homes and manicured lawns. Its economic anchor was the steel industry. U.S. Steel Southworks, Wisconsin Steel, Republic Steel, and Acme Steel employed over 25,000 workers. Southeast Chicago was also teeming with businesses that used steel or that sold products to the steel mills: steel fabrication shops, industrial machinery factories, plants that made farm

equipment, and railroad cars. There were also firms that sold the mills industrial gloves, shoes, tools, nuts and bolts, and welding equipment. The commercial strip had retail stores, bars, and restaurants. Many of these, like the
steel mills, were open twenty-four hours a day, seven days a week. Not only
were the community and its economy vibrant, there was a system in place
that looked to future generations. The mills and many of the related firms
had strong unions. Through the union you could get your children into the
steel mills to learn a trade or get a well-paying job that would allow them to
save and go on to college.

Some of the nostalgic accounts of these times, however, leave out important
considerations that are critical for understanding today's realities and possibilities. One is that in the 1930s and 1940s workers fought for the good pay
and benefits of the heavy industrial economy. The formation of the Congress
of Industrial Organizations (CIO) and its union constituents, like the United
Steel Workers of America (USWA), was bitterly contested by corporate management. On Memorial Day 1937, police in the employ of steel mill owners
attacked a peaceful protest of workers and their families in front of Chicago's
Republic Steel mill. Ten workers died and dozens were badly wounded. The
living wage jobs enjoyed by workers in the 1970s did not come easily.

The multiracial character of the steel mills was also the result of struggle—
often among co-workers as well as with the corporations. International Harvester's Wisconsin Steel Company, for example, was racially integrated only
after being forced to do so by President Roosevelt's executive order in 1940.
But racism in and around the mill persisted. During this period, the white
workers living near the mill fought the integration of their community and
the mill by systematically stoning the cars of black workers as they traveled to
and from work. Despite protests to management and city of Chicago officials,
this practice persisted for two years.[1] Up to the early 1980s, struggles against
racism in the workplace continued. Inspired by the civil rights movements
of the 1960s and 1970s, all of the major steel mills had black, Latino, and
women's caucuses that operated in the mills and the union. The caucuses
struggled to modify work rules that kept members of their group in the worst
jobs with the lowest pay.

In addition, not all people of color and women workers had access to the
better-paying union jobs that dominated the Southeast Chicago economy. For
those who lacked access to the better workplaces, there were many smaller
firms, which had either corrupt unions or no unions at all. The bulk of workers
at these firms were African Americans, Latinos, and sometimes women. Pay
and benefits were relatively meager. Working conditions were often dangerous
and dirty. I worked at two such plants during the late 1970s and early 1980s.
I was fired from both for organizing for better pay and working conditions.

One of these, the Chicago Shortening Company, employed forty male production workers. All but three were African American or Latino. Basic pay

was half of what was available in the steel mills and benefits were poor. The working conditions were dangerous; there were many accidents. U.S. Department of Agriculture inspectors frequently shut the plant down because of unsanitary conditions. Also, the union was corrupt. Workers believed that contract ratification votes were routinely fixed. In 1978, following a suspect ratification vote, we took our own poll and found that nearly all of the workers claimed to have voted against the contract while the company and union (who counted the votes together without workers present) maintained that an overwhelming majority voted for it. So we went on strike.

The wildcat strike was undertaken with a certain confidence that if things didn't work out we could get work elsewhere. There seemed to be plenty of jobs; and even though pay, benefits, and working conditions were bad in many of them, a worker could still make a living that supported a family. And there was also a sense of militancy and optimism that had grown out of the civil rights movement and the related social justice movements of the late 1960s and 1970s. We all believed that worker solidarity could improve our lives. During the strike both the anger at injustice and the optimism that things could change for the better were summed up by one worker when he joked, "There ain't no justice, there's just us."

We lost the strike and the company fired nearly all of us. While the loss of the strike and our jobs was hard to take, there was still a strong sense of optimism. As one of the workers said after the firings were announced and we watched scab replacements walk into the plant, "If I had known what would happen when we started this I would have still done it. These were the proudest days of my life."

But this sense of optimism and the militancy that went with it were about to come to an abrupt halt. During the 1980s, the Chicago steel industry collapsed and took down with it much of the related industrial and service economy that depended on it. Both Wisconsin Steel and U.S. Steel Southworks eventually closed. Republic Steel was bought out by a conglomerate and was greatly downsized. Steel jobs in Southeast Chicago declined from about 25,000 workers to less than 5,000 in a decade. And the decline in manufacturing extended far beyond steel. The Chicago metropolitan area suffered a net loss of 150,000 manufacturing jobs during the 1980s. People's lives were torn asunder in the wake of massive layoffs. Divorces, alcoholism, even suicides were on the rise. Industrial unions were decimated and union membership declined throughout the United States The new jobs created in the wake of this decline paid far less than the jobs that had been lost. Many were temporary or part-time and usually lacked benefits like health care. Workers taking these jobs no longer made enough to live on. So they worked two or sometimes three jobs to make what they had previously made at one. Many of the dislocated workers never worked again. This turn of events hit people of color and women the hardest. The struggle over civil rights in the workplace and within the union was over because the workplace itself no longer existed. And a certain nostalgia emerged for the previous life in the mills or even that at plants like Chicago Shortening.

A New World Order

In the 1960s and 1970s, when African American, Latino, and women workers struggled for justice within their unions and workplaces and workers generally continued to push for better pay and working conditions, certain aspects of the society we lived in were considered to be permanent. The manufacturing-based economy with jobs that paid living wages were seen this way. The gains that had come out of social struggle were also seen as permanent. Not only better pay, benefits, and decent working conditions, but also social gains for women, African Americans, and Latinos were viewed as conditions that, once established, acted as a social ratchet. They could be improved upon, but they also provided a floor that we could never go below again. The large industrial workplaces of the period also played an important role in the creation of a widespread faith in the efficacy of social struggle. The interdependence of workers in their places of work revealed the reality of social power based on class.

Government was viewed as the protector of these conditions. If you had a labor dispute, you could go to the labor board for relief. If you were discriminated against by your company or union based on your race or gender, you could file a complaint with the Equal Employment Opportunities Commission. If you were laid off, you could pick up your unemployment compensation and find another job through the Department of Employment Security Jobs Service. If unemployment became prolonged, there was always the social safety net—food stamps, Medicaid, public housing, and welfare. If government agencies treated you unfairly, you organized to protest with the expectation that justice would be done.

It was the sense of permanence of such conditions combined with the social character of the manufacturing workplace that produced the militancy and optimism that marked our strike at Chicago Shortening—even when we lost it. The fact was, however, that there were social processes under way even before the strike occurred that were undermining the stability of all of these "permanent" features of U.S. society. Global decisions were being made that propelled us into a period of transition to what former U.S. President George H. Bush called a new world order. But at the time, we didn't have any idea we were in such a transitory state. And when the collapse of manufacturing jobs came to Chicago, we were unprepared to understand it and to figure out what to do about it. Very quickly a new set of permanent conditions replaced the old ones. The new world order required each individual and every firm to be globally competitive. The new workplaces and the state of unemployment lacked the social character of the old job. Individualism, fueled by President Reagan and his British sidekick Prime Minister Margaret Thatcher, prevailed. A global economy that favored deregulation and a high degree of mobility for capital, goods, and services was developing. And in this world, improved conditions, it seemed, would not come through social action and government programs but from individual effort and free markets. And those who did not fit in, who wouldn't conform to the standards of the new world order, were categorized and demonized as part of a pathological "underclass."

To many workers, and especially to people of color, the new world order has meant lower living standards and, in many cases, abject poverty. This has certainly been true in the developing world, where not only job security, but even food security has been destroyed. But it has also been true in the United States and specifically in Chicago, the focus of much of this book. Many are searching for a solution to their plight that is constrained by the new sense of permanence. They take for granted the institutions and values of the new world order, which appear as permanent attributes of society to which they must adapt. The discipline of the market is increasingly being accepted as the highest arbiter of social concerns. Each individual must make himself or herself "competitive." Having a job is seen primarily as a form of behavior rather than as a source of income. A job is something that provides the worker with "discipline and regularity," which is key to being competitive.[2] This means that holding a job—any job, even if it is dangerous and doesn't pay enough to live on—is considered critical to survival in today's permanent reality. The issues of the Chicago Shortening strike are now passé. The concerns of the African Americans, Latinos, and women who formed caucuses in the mills are not only outmoded but condemned as having been wrongheaded to start with.

During a television debate in the early 1990s, that I had with an economist in the employ of Citicorp she talked about the tragedy of her family—mother, father, brothers and sisters—who had all been autoworkers in Detroit. We were debating the merits of the North American Free Trade Agreement (NAFTA) and a simultaneous proposal then before Congress to raise the minimum wage. She was for NAFTA and against raising the minimum wage. The tragedy of her family, in her view, was not that they lost their jobs as General Motors and Ford shifted production to low-wage/high-productivity plants in Mexico or that they were forced to take low-wage jobs that didn't pay enough to live on. The tragedy was that the high pay they had received as autoworkers in the past had destroyed their jobs and undermined their incentive to get more education, which would have made them more competitive in today's world. None of them would ever be economists in the employ of Citicorp because they had been misguided by their high pay and decent living standards. Essentially, she argued that decent living standards had distorted or masked the market signals that would have led them in a more fruitful direction. To the extent that one agrees with this view, any social action to improve conditions is pointless, silly, and self-defeating. Such a line of reasoning is part of the new world order.

Philosophical Perspectives

The new world order has been evolving for more than two decades. Yet, throughout the developing world, peasants whose labor once fed their nations and themselves are forced to export cash crops while they go hungry. Some eventually have to abandon their lands. They come to the cities, where they live in poverty through the informal economy. Others go to work in the export-processing zones, where firms from Chicago and throughout the developed world pay poverty wages and workers toil long hours to survive in squalid shantytowns. Still others come to the developed world in search of work. Here they are often met by racist hysteria from workers suffering under the new world order in their own nation. In the United States they are met by the militarization of the U.S. border with Mexico, new laws that violate their civil rights, and vigilantism.

In the developed world, and specifically in the United States, workers have felt the pain of the elimination of hundreds of thousands of living wage manufacturing jobs. Many have been unable to find comparable work, and their sons and daughters are facing the prospect of either no work at all or jobs that are temporary or part-time and that pay below what it takes to live a decent life. Government is more interested in balancing its budget and getting smaller (except when it comes to going to war) than in offering protection to workers caught in the fallout of the new world order. The U.S. government is destroying publicly subsidized housing and shrinking housing subsidy programs as the ranks of the homeless soar. In Chicago, a program is under way to eliminate over 18,000 units of public housing at a time when there is a shortage of affordable housing—more than two families looking for every unit that is available. Public funds for basic subsistence living (food, clothing, and medical care)—programs won by workers' struggles of the past—are being eliminated and people are being told to find nonexistent jobs. In the Chicago area during the height of the 1990s economic expansion, there were over thirty people available for every entry-level job that paid a living wage.

I describe and begin a critique of this period in Chapter 3. However, it is not enough simply to condemn this state of affairs or to argue about exactly what the new world order is. A key point of this book is to seek ways to organize to improve social conditions for everyone. If we are to find a direction forward that can truly improve the lives of the millions of people who are presently hungry and without adequate housing and health care, we need to initiate a discussion that is grounded in the experience of real people. Summarizing that experience with numbers is important, and this book does so. But change comes about when people are able to bring their experiences together and connect them to the bigger picture. That process is necessarily social in nature. A book can serve the purpose of initiating dialogues to stimulate such a social process. Toward that end, this book combines social science research on the new world order and its impacts with a memoir that includes reflections on my own experiences—my recollections of countless encounters with other people and more deliberate personal interviews.

My perspective on the nature of the new world order, its impacts on urban life, and the implications for approaches to social change—the subject of this book—are necessarily grounded in philosophy. Philosophy is the method through which all of us comprehend the world around us. It is also the basis of action. Everyone, in this sense, is a philosopher. Thus in initiating a dialogue, which is the purpose of this book, it is important to lay out the philosophic ground each of us brings to that dialogue. Chapter 2 formally presents the philosophic ground of this book. There are three philosophic themes that are central to the analysis in the remainder of the book: value and its relation to broader values; space, place, and time; and social change.

Value and Values

A full understanding of the issues analyzed and discussed in the following chapters requires us to delink the concept of value from values. Marx argued that under capitalism money becomes the community because it is the basis for survival and the outcome of society's production process. In such a system, value becomes expressed as the price of a commodity or a service—in other words, money. All other values of life—people's needs, the development of various capacities (loving, learning, creating), and their means of enjoyment—become subsumed under the money form of value. Broader values in most modern economic analysis are reduced to the abstract concept of utility, which is expressed as the choices one makes as an individual consumer in the markets society has constructed for this purpose.

The dominant culture's tendency to reduce all values to their expression as monetary bids in markets is nothing new. But the historical primacy of the money form of value takes on a specific character in the new world order. One aspect of this character is the individualization of everyday life. The credo of the new world order—markets make the best decisions; individuals must be competitive; social action to improve your life is silly and ultimately self-defeating—has reduced all meaningful human activity to individual consumer choices expressed in money terms. The combination of this credo with the material fact of the destruction of workplaces where production was social in both appearance and essence means that the social dimension of everyday life is masked or obscured. This makes the development of a social movement whose goals are based on the betterment of classes and groups difficult to achieve. I argue in this book that an understanding of individualism in social terms—the notion of the *social individual*—is a philosophic prerequisite of such a movement. And it is crucial to our approach to organizing in this age.

Second, if value is reduced to money price, needs—even survival needs like food, clothing, shelter, health care, and a toxic-free environment—can only be met or expressed as needs if the people whose needs are not being met can pay for them. The very notion that there are universal human rights such as those contained in the United Nations Declaration of Human Rights or the International Labor Organization's (ILO) protocols becomes relegated to the trashcan of history. During his administration, President Clinton blocked international resolutions that declared housing and enough to eat to be human rights rather than manifestations of individual consumer sovereignty. In doing so, the Clinton administration essentially declared the fifty-year-old UN Declaration of Human Rights null and void. This book not only looks at the implications of this in terms of the housing of the poor and employment opportunities, it also demonstrates the importance of reestablishing fundamental human rights as the ground for organizing.

A third aspect of the primacy of the money form of value in the new world order is its global dimension. The extension of global rules for unimpeded capital and commodity mobility through the International Monetary Fund (IMF) and World Bank structural adjustment programs and multilateral free trade agreements like NAFTA has enhanced the political power of a handful of global corporations. Simultaneously, it has reduced political accountability at the national and local levels.[3] Establishing a global-local link is thus critical to organizing in the present period.

Chapter 2 develops these ideas in greater detail and also presents an alternative conception of value that offers a framework for considering the tension between money price and other values.

Space, Place, and Time

The dimensions of space, place, and time are key features of the new world order. Many have observed that falling transportation costs and the elimination of constraints on the flow of goods and capital around the world have given economic enterprises great mobility. But this observation is treated as an independent and permanent reality in much urban socioeconomic analysis. Some analysts have concluded that in these circumstances it is necessary to adapt to this new spatial reality by becoming more "competitive."[4] I make two basic arguments to the contrary. One is that our conception and use of space is no more permanent than any other feature of social life.[5] Social forces have given the mobility of capital, goods, and services the *appearance* of permanence. However, definitions of time, space, and place change. When they do, the place-based foundation of militant movements (such as the strike at Chicago Shortening being grounded in the Southeast Chicago manufacturing economy) is undermined.[6] I use this line of reasoning to critique the spatial dimension of the new world order. A key to social change in this new world order of high capital, commodity, and service mobility is to broaden the perspective of place-based social movements to include other places where people are also struggling with aspects of the new world order. The practical importance of this will be developed in Chapters 2 and 9, where I use notions of the social construction of space and place to discuss the importance and practicality of a global movement based on conditions and perceptions in multiple places—making the global-local link.

Social Change

My research and teaching in an urban planning graduate school and my experiences as a factory worker in the 1970s and early 1980s, along with the subsequent collapse of manufacturing in Chicago, has led to an insight that informs this book. Much traditional economic analysis treats permanence as the natural state of things. Economic models often begin by defining a state of equilibrium as a price where the amount of goods or services that suppliers are willing to produce and those that consumers are willing to purchase are equal. Analysis attempts to discover why or how things get out of balance when supply is either more or less than demand. Yet, when I think back to the Chicago Shortening strike, the general attitudes of industrial workers in the 1960s and 1970s, and the cataclysmic events that followed, I am compelled to turn this type of analysis on its head. From the perspective of my experiences and reflection on this period, change is the natural state of things and analysis should attempt to explain the appearance of stability.

Why is this so important? If permanence is only the appearance of our present circumstances, then a study of the underlying forces that both create this appearance and at the same time undermine it can yield insights into how change can come about. Part of the new world order involves a perception about "the way things are." Markets make the best decisions! Individuals must be competitive! Government must not interfere! Social action to improve your life is silly and self- defeating! Treated as permanent, these ideas place limits on change by failing to consider alternatives that fall outside the prescriptions of the new world order. Unwittingly, the acceptance of these prescriptions also contributes to their political legitimacy. On the other hand, if we choose to study the historical forces from which the new world order emerged, and which continue to sustain the system, then we can see that these permanent structures are historically contingent. And we can then envision many new paths forward.

Ordinary people play a key role in either maintaining the appearance of permanence or destabilizing it. Much of social discourse attempts to undermine such a notion. When the subject of economics is discussed in the newspapers or on television, commentators talk about markets being "happy" or "unhappy"; or they reduce economic events to abstract concepts like gross domestic product, the federal funds rate, and the strength (or weakness) of the dollar. But rarely is economics associated with human beings. It is as if economics has a life of its own apart from the people who work, go to school, and enter into all sorts of relationships with other human beings. In the words of President Bill Clinton: "It's the Economy, stupid!"

Thus we are told that we must give up important health- and safety-related work rules on our jobs because of "competition." We can't find decent housing because of "the market." If we don't cut government social programs and balance the budget, we might have inflation, which will "upset the financial markets." Even much of the left falls into this trap by accepting many of the conditions we face as permanent, urging "practical" strategies that take these things into account.

What is the meaning of Marx's famous statement in his preface to *Critique of Political Economy*: "It is not the consciousness of men that determines their existence but their social existence that determines their consciousness"?[7] Does it mean (and do we agree) that consciousness is determined by the material structures in which people work and live? A more dialectical view is in order. As people come up against material conditions that adversely affect their own development, they develop new ideas about how to get rid of the old and create the elements of something new.[8] The practical implication of such a view is that the road to change lies with ordinary people who are fully informed about their own situation. The tendency to see the role of people in a social movement as "bodies" at a demonstration or as "votes" to convince congresspeople of the wisdom (or lack thereof) of a particular piece of legislation will not lead to meaningful changes in today's new world order. What is missing in this approach to social change is the subjective element—the need and possibility of changing the basic perception of permanence. Again, these views of the nature of change inform the critique of much of today's organizing strategies and the approach taken in Chapter 9.

Global Decisions

Chapter 3 argues that in the mid-1970s there was a basic shift in the way global capitalism functions. The previous Fordist era had been in force since the end of World War II. It was a regime that was grounded in U.S. supremacy among capitalist nations. And it was fueled initially by the rebuilding of Europe after World War II. In the United States workers were essentially offered a share of the benefits derived from U.S. hegemony. In return, organized labor agreed to a set of rules that ensured a degree of labor peace. Labor leaders also agreed to support U.S. foreign policy, which was focused on competition with the Soviet bloc nations for world supremacy and the exploitation of the developing world. Yet, by the late 1960s, this system was beginning to un-ravel. This evolving crisis manifested itself in both economic and political terms. Economically, the world was experiencing stagflation—simultaneous unemployment and inflation. Politically, there was growing unrest at home and abroad. In the United States people of color were demanding a fair share of the largess of the Fordist era. In addition, there was a militant anti-war movement that challenged the assumptions of U.S. cold war foreign policy. And many nations in the developing world began to resist and contest U.S. hegemony, which began its decline with the Vietnam War.

The evolution of the present period eased the economic and political crisis that marked the end of the Fordist era. Chapter 3 argues that the new world order combines global deregulation of business with high mobility of goods, services, and capital that is fueled by expanded credit and speculation. More-over, the system has become institutionalized, with public policies grounded in specific ideologies that feed socioeconomic theory and politics. I refer to these developments as "global decisions." The new world order's hegemonic grip on the world presently seems awesome.[9]

Local Collisions

The present system has produced a growing polarization of income and wealth both between and within nations.[10] Polarization is the result of the local colli-sions resulting from new world order practices and policies. In the developing world, despite some periods of economic growth, there has been growing pov-erty and an enormous increase in debt. In developed nations like the United States, the early days of the new world order brought with it terrible social dis-location. In the 1980s, hundreds of thousands of workers were displaced from living wage jobs. Chapter 4 examines this dislocation in Chicago through de-tailed case studies that include interviews with workers who talk about what this period did to them and their families. Some of these workers and their children were permanently removed from the labor force. Others found work at lower pay in the service sector or in the temporary and part-time work industry. In the United States generally, the consolidation of the new world order also brought about major shifts in urban policy. Chapters 5–7 look at these shifts and their impact on people from the middle to the lower end of the polarization as local collisions. The focus is on Chicago, but combines lo-cal data and case studies with trends in the United States. Chapter 5 discusses local politics as they apply to urban development strategies. City government not only provides public services, but helps organize production and distribu-tion at a local level. Thus, it must deal with contradictions and conflicts that the broader system of each era generates. These roles shape local politics and place limits on what local government can accomplish for city residents. The chapter contrasts the regime of Mayor Richard J. Daley, whose administration coincided with the previous Fordist era, to that of Mayor Harold Washington, who attempted reform at a time when the new world order was beginning to take hold. Case studies of citizen efforts to contest development strategies during the Washington years that had carried over from the previous regime are used to discuss the limits of local government itself.

This theme is further developed in Chapter 6, which first shows how shifts in U.S. policies in the 1980s and 1990s that affect housing the poor are linked to the new world order. I then examine how this has played out in Chicago under the regime of the present mayor, Richard M. Daley. Two cases, one on gentrification and another on the destruction of public housing, show how citizens are trying to fight back. Chapter 7 focuses on employment, including the theories and policies that govern welfare "reform," job training, free trade, and labor rights. Again, there have been policy shifts that are linked to the evolving new world order. Because employment, wages, and their distribution profoundly influence urban development possibilities and housing, the lens of employment policy shifts and the theories and ideologies behind them are an appropriate way to sum up the link between global decisions and local collisions.

That link also has profound implications for what people can do about the polarization that marks the new world order. Chapters 8 and 9 include a discussion of how to organize to combat the ill effects of this period. While Chapters 5–7 include case studies of citizens organizing against various local collisions, Chapter 8 discusses the growing movement against institutions and programs that generate global decisions. Since the Seattle demonstrations in 1999, opposition to the World Trade Organization (WTO), IMF, World Bank, NAFTA, and related institutions and programs has been growing. In the chapter I offer insights into the origins and conduct of part of this movement through a detailed case study of the anti-NAFTA effort that began in 1991 and continues to this day. A major point of this chapter is that there is a disconnect between the struggles against the new world order that generated local collisions in cities like Chicago and those against the global decisions themselves. The root of this disconnect lies in both the practice of the anti-globalization movement and the approach to organizing used at both global and local levels. Approaches to organizing used during the Fordist era cannot simply be readapted to the new era. I develop these points first through the case study of the anti-NAFTA work and then through a return to the philosophic discussion of Chapter 2. Thus, in Chapter 9, which is the conclusion of the book, the concepts of value, space/place, and social change are used to sum up the limitations of current organizing to combat both global decisions and local collisions and to offer a framework for alternative approaches to organizing that can make the needed global-local link.

CHAPTER 2

Philosophical
Perspectives

Philosophy is the method through which we comprehend the world around us. It is also a basis for action. Often the philosophic premises of both thought and action lie beneath the surface and go unexamined. This is a mistake. There are many different philosophic premises that underlie how we try to understand and comprehend the world we live in and how we act on this understanding. And many of these premises are in conflict. The purpose of this chapter is to establish the philosophic ground that will become the method of this book.

That ground can be illuminated through a personal experience.

On a warm early spring day in 1980, I was sitting outside at a picnic table in a small, rectangular concrete area adjacent to a cinder block factory building. The concrete slab was fully enclosed on three sides by a chain-link fence; there was no way in or out except through the factory. The place was the Solo Cup Company's area for employee breaks on warm days. I was on break from my job as a maintenance mechanic. I was alone, since the break schedule of maintenance people was based on times when everything was running properly. Soon, however, a small group of Latino material handlers arrived for their regularly scheduled break. They were talking rapidly and with considerable agitation. Unabashed eavesdropping revealed two facts: "Mucho policia acerca de Wisconsin Steel" (There are a lot of police around Wisconsin Steel); and "Cerrado!" (Closed). Knowing a number of workers at Wisconsin Steel, I went and sat with the other Solo Cup Company workers in order to learn more.

What I learned was this. In the dead of night, the Chase Manhattan Bank Corporation of New York City flew a planeload of security guards to this Southeast Chicago steel mill to secure their assets. Wisconsin Steel had gone bankrupt. The private security force entered the mill, escorted workers inside to the plant gates, and placed a bilingual sign there: Closed/Cerrado. Workers arriving for the next shift found the mill surrounded by Chicago police. A mill that for nearly 100 years had been a mainstay of the Chicago economy was gone in a period of less than an hour, 3,500 living wage jobs were lost instantly. Personal chaos ensued. Workers' paychecks bounced; pension funds were unavailable; eventually, homes, cars, and other possessions were lost; alcoholism, drug abuse, divorces, and even suicide among the displaced workers were on the rise. This was the beginning of more that was to come. During the following decade, the Chicago area suffered a net loss of over 150,000 living wage manufacturing jobs.

How can we comprehend this incredible event? Some analysts of the loss of manufacturing jobs have tended to step back from the lives of the individual workers, focusing their attention instead on the economic shift away from manufacturing.[1] Others have focused on changes in steel and other manufacturing process and product technologies.[2] In Chapter 3, I situate the Wisconsin Steel closing as part of a major shift in the organization of global capitalism. In Chapter 4, I focus on the causes of plant closings in Chicago and on what happened to the people who used to work at Wisconsin Steel and other factories and to their standard of living. The analysis of Chapters 3 and 4 and the remainder of the book is based on three philosophic premises: the nature of value and values; space and place; and permanence and change.

Philosophy isn't really *applied* to concrete activities; rather, it is *recreated* or *worked out* through action and reflection on action. The chapters that follow are reflections on events I have studied or participated in. Thus, each chapter of this book is a further elaboration of the basic ideas that are presented in this chapter.

Value and Values

I recently had a conversation with two friends about the rising price of property. We were in a remote area of rural Wisconsin that had begun to attract summer residents from surrounding urban locations like Chicago. The price of land was skyrocketing. I remarked to my friends that the land was now priced way beyond what it was worth.

"What do you mean? It's worth whatever people want to pay for it," one friend vigorously asserted.

"Maybe," said the second friend, who was a permanent resident of the area and living on a modest fixed income. "But if the price keeps going up, it will mean that people like me won't be able to afford to live here."

This exchange represents a key philosophical issue that is critical to answering some important questions: What is something worth? How is that value determined? How do you measure it? My friend who was so clear that land (or anything else, for that matter) is worth whatever people will pay expressed the prevailing view on the subject. This view is predominant in the minds of most people because it reflects their own experience. The question raised by my second friend is generally separated from a discussion of value. Value is seen in terms of money price. The issue of whether my friend on a fixed income will be able to afford his home is generally not considered to be part of the question of what his property is worth. Yet the two issues—what the land sells for and who can afford to live there—are connected in real life.

Similarly, the dynamics that caused the shutdown of Wisconsin Steel are usually separated from what that plant closing did to the lives of the workers who suddenly lost their jobs. The causes of the shutdown are seen strictly in money price terms. Was the steel produced there competitive pricewise with comparable-quality steel? Were the costs of producing steel, especially labor cost, competitive with those of other steel mills in other parts of the world? The *social* value of the living wage jobs workers had there—not only the economic impact of higher wages, but the value of stable families and children who looked forward to a decent life—is generally considered to be a separate issue. Not only that, but even people who are concerned about the welfare of the workers tend to accept the fact that the positive social effects of the jobs that Wisconsin Steel provided are necessarily constrained by the money price considerations that keep plants like Wisconsin Steel competitive.

The equation of value with money price is reinforced by the dominance of a philosophy that makes this identity seem like the natural state of things. It is backed by "scientific" economic theory, enabling sober-faced economists to justify massive job dislocation by going on television and yammering on about "the power of the market." Economics textbooks often start with a section on "economic man." This person (who could be a woman, too) is above all an individualist who is well informed, is rational, and has insatiable wants and needs. Because societies can't possibly satisfy wants and needs that can't, by this rendition of human nature, be satisfied, a mechanism is needed to allocate "scarce resources." That mechanism is the market. This perspective on human nature and motivation and the role of the market has gained wide acceptance in today's world. Modern economic man pursues his self-interest by competing with other individuals to gain the money required to meet his needs in the market successfully. Economists in this tradition argue that this "sovereign consumer" ultimately determines value by bidding in an open market. The bid is based on how much utility or pleasure you can get out of what you are bidding on, constrained only by how much income or credit you have.

This philosophy has gained popular acceptance because it describes what can be observed in everyday life. The money price of commodities and the social and political power of those who can pay that price explain a lot of what we see. We are paid in money. We need money to get what we need. Money is the only universally accepted measurement of what everything is worth. It is also a form of political and social power.

Market theory based on individualism and utilitarianism also becomes the political rationale for removing social restrictions on the functioning of markets. If the value of everything is determined by its money price, and if the money price is determined by individual households and firms competitively bidding in an unrestricted market, how can we really know what things are worth if we try to regulate how the market functions? Moreover, if the government offers subsidies to individuals by giving them welfare payments or subsidized housing, what possible incentive is there for these individuals to compete to meet their needs? How can the market give them the necessary signals that will tell them what they need to do to purchase the things they want and need? If Wisconsin Steel closed because it was no longer competitive, the market has spoken.

It should be stressed, however, that this logic is premised on the philosophical perspectives relating to individualism and utilitarianism. If human behavior boils down to the individual pursuit of pleasure through the market, it becomes possible to separate value, as the prices individuals will pay (for steel or for land), from the values that are implied by the consequences. Some schools of thought in modern economics would argue that limits should be placed on markets in order to achieve other values. Based on such considerations and the demands of people who are unable to meet their needs through markets, we have developed public programs that subsidize housing, food, and basic living allowances. But even proponents of these views and these programs do not usually question either the nature of economic man or the separation of value from values.

The notion that economic man determines value through the market establishes a hierarchy of concerns that makes money price the ultimate arbiter of all other concerns. As we will see throughout this book, acceptance of this hierarchy affects our understanding of the period we presently live in and also limits perceived possibilities for change. There are, moreover, alternative views of human nature that do not place money price in such a lofty position, leading to a more unified theory of value that opens up broader avenues to change.

It is beyond the scope of this book to enter into a lengthy engagement with alternative philosophies of human nature and value. I will, however, lay out my own premises, which I concretize in the remainder of the book. Historically, human societies have created social institutions—government, an economic system, an educational system, a family structure, and so on—to meet certain social goals. These goals are derived from a basic human drive for self-development. What is central to human nature, therefore, is not the individual pursuit of pleasure, but an effort to develop oneself to one's full potential as a human being. Moreover, because we live in a society rather than as isolated individuals, that effort is social. The drive of "social individuals" for self-development is the essence of human freedom.[3] Furthermore, the pursuit of human freedom in this sense is what moves history. The social construction of the basic institutions that define a society may systematically thwart the human development of groups of people in similar ways. When that happens, people band together to remove the obstacles to their self-development and in the process develop a vision of something new, which becomes the substance of social change. What is valued in a society in this perspective is self-development. Wealth is not gold, money, or even stock options, but what Marx termed "an absolute movement of becoming."[4]

The social process of an absolute movement of becoming occurs through labor. Labor, from this perspective, is not solely a way to make money, but is more generally a form of self-development. Labor can involve all sorts of things—from creating beautiful works of art, to raising children, to making things that other people can use. But the labor process takes different forms in different social structures. Marx argued that in a capitalist society, labor is alienated and exploited through the elevation of production for exchange (to make money) over labor for human self-development. Commodities in our society thus have a dual value. They are useful (have a use value) in the sense that they can aid the self-development process, and they have a value based on how much they can be exchanged for. Use values make labor a meaningful, creative social process. But this is truncated by the need of workers to sell their labor to produce exchange values.

The elevation of exchange value can be clarified by thinking about the nature of housing. A home has value as a place of shelter—its use value. But it also has value as a way to gain profits for those who have the legal authority to sell it—its exchange value. The dominant political view of housing at this time is defined in terms of exchange value. The exchange value dominates a house's dual character. If land prices in northern Wisconsin get bid up by rich vacationers, my friend who lives there on a modest fixed income may have to abandon his home. The value of steel that was once produced at Wisconsin Steel Works is viewed strictly in terms of its price—*not* in terms of its value to the workers who produce it or the fact that it could be used to build infrastructure in Chicago that will benefit others. Thus, there is a conflict or contradiction between use value and exchange value. In this way the "price" of joblessness can be separated from the value of steel. The elevation of exchange value to simply value is the elemental expression of the primacy of money price.

If labor is valued primarily in terms of the capacity of people to produce exchange values, the broader function of labor as a vehicle for the pursuit of self-development is truncated. The domination of exchange value over use value reduces human beings to commodities whose value to society is measured in terms of their contribution to commodity production. The value of noncommodity production such as housework is seen solely in terms of its contribution to the bread winner's capacity to produce exchange values for someone else. The social significance of any effort to develop one's self is judged in terms of its contribution to making a person competitive. A good education is learning that adds to an individual's human capital development. In other words, human activity that enhances one's ability to produce exchange values is given priority over everything else. Anything else is either a waste of time, or downgraded to a hobby. Hobbies and so-called leisure time activities include all possible forms of self-development—art, reading, and various forms of creative expression. Ultimately, the social expression of value is money price alone.

The reduction of labor to a commodity that produces surplus exchange values is the basis of capitalist competition. Capitalists compete for surplus value produced by their workers. The economy is organized to accumulate surplus value. But valuing labor in terms of its ability to generate surplus values is also the basis for both alienation (the truncation of human self-development) and exploitation (the requirement that you work more for someone else than for your own reproduction or self-development). I can recall working as a maintenance mechanic at the Foseco Corporation. Foseco was a plant that made chemical products used in the production of steel. By union contract, we were required to work eight hours a day. But we could be forced to work more than that if the company paid us one and a half times our regular wages. By helping to keep the machines running, I was producing value. I probably produced enough exchange value in three hours to generate the amount of money (through sales of the product) which the company paid me for eight hours of work. In a sense, I worked five hours for the company and three hours for myself. The exchange value I produced in the next five hours (*surplus value*) went to management. When production was high or when things were not working well, we were required to work overtime. We were compensated by being paid time and a half.

Some workers needed the money so badly that despite the fact that the work was very hard and the conditions were very harsh they were forced to allow the job to dominate their lives. I can recall going to the locker-room after my shift and starting to clean up when the foreman would come up behind me, grab my arm, and say, "Not so fast, Dave!" It was not a good feeling. It was alienating because I was forced to neglect other aspects of my life. Also, most of the value of work I did beyond the first three hours was going to someone else. The process of production, therefore, is inherently a process of *exploitation* and *alienation*. Exploitation and alienation are part and parcel of the process of extracting surplus value from human beings.

Alienation comes not only by having your life dominated by your job, as my example of forced overtime at the chemical plant illustrates. Alienation is also inherent in work itself. My life in the factory was governed not by self-development, but by the factory clock and management's need to use my labor to make profits. Exploitation is not limited to the factory. With the advent of cell phones and laptops, people are always working. The triumph of exchange value over use value is visible everywhere. Go to any airport and you will see commuters talking on their phones with great intensity while banging away on their laptops. Riding the commuter highways from the Chicago suburbs to the Loop, you will see about three out of every five drivers is on the phone. Much of that driving-while-yakking is related to work. Walk down a busy Chicago street, and you will be treated to a cacophony of beeper "music" and the sorry sight of harried businesspeople on their phones as they hurry to or from the office. Stephen Roach, chief economist for Morgan Stanley/Dean Witter, put it this way:

> The dirty little secret of the information age is that an increasingly large slice of work goes on outside the official work hours the government recognizes. Courtesy of laptops, cell phones, home fax machines and other appliances, knowledge workers are now online in cars, planes, trains and homes, virtually tethered to their offices. The "24/7" culture of nearly round-the clock work is endemic to the wired economy.[5]

But alienation in the process of production is most obvious in the factory. While working at Foseco, I was part of a team that installed new machines. These machines processed special panels that both insulated and helped to purify steel in its molten state. Silicone and other ingredients were mixed in huge blenders, pressed into molds, and then baked in enormous ovens. The panels that came out of the ovens were about 3 feet long and 2 feet wide. Before we installed the new machines, about fifteen workers were involved processing materials for each oven. The new machines, largely controlled by a computer, were now assigned to a single operator. But that operator had to take the panels and stack them as they came out of the oven and then haul the stacks away with a forklift. When he returned with the empty forklift, he had to rush to his workstation, as new panels were already starting to pile up. He had no control over the rate of production, and was driven by the computer program at a furious pace. There was, however, a panic button on the machine that could stop production altogether in an emergency. The harried operator began to use it frequently, as panels piled up at his workstation each time he drove off on the forklift. Whenever he stopped production, a loud alarm would sound and soon his area would be crawling with white shirts, who berated him for not keeping up. After pushing the panic button a number of times and hearing a number of threats that he would lose his job if he continued to stop the monster machine, the young man lost his temper, pulled a knife, and threatened to cut the foreman's throat. He was immediately dragged off by security. This prompted a brief but effective wildcat strike. All of us on the shift were unanimous about two things. First, we demanded that the foreman and company drop charges and give the guy his job back. Second, we insisted that he have a helper. It soon became clear that production would be delayed for some period of time unless our demands were met. But it was also evident to the management that the pace of the computer program was too much for anyone. So they gave in.

The fact that everyone in the plant was willing to strike over the issue demonstrates that factory workers instinctively understand both alienation and exploitation. While these contradictions exist in all forms of production, their relationship to work is clearest on a shop floor, where everyone's work and the toll that it takes is visible to all and where work itself is by necessity more social than at other kinds of workplaces. Interestingly, maintenance workers led the wildcat strike at the chemical plant. Yet, we had the most privileged jobs. We had the highest pay and were the least susceptible to the pace of production dictated by the computer programs. We, after all, had installed the computer-based machinery to begin with. But we were the first to object to any effort to subject any worker to the pace set by that machinery.

I can remember one time when one of the big machines broke down. Railroad cars carried the raw panels in huge trays into the ovens. On this occasion, the oven door that would let the cars out when the panels were sufficiently cooked failed to open. The computer signaled the conveyor to pull the cars out anyway. The result was a huge mess. The cars smashed into the door, damaging it beyond repair. The cars became derailed inside the oven, spilling panels of product everywhere. A rail was bent in the disaster. Maintenance workers from all three shifts were called in to get the machine back into production. We had to shut down the oven and let it cool enough so we could go inside. We had to replace an oven door (which was about 20 feet high and 10 feet wide). We had to straighten one of the rails, get the cars back on the track, and pick up all the panels that were strewn about inside the oven. It was a big job.

We went about our task with cool deliberation. There were ten of us. The foremen and a gaggle of white shirts fidgeted nervously as we sat in the lunchroom planning our approach to the project and dividing the responsibility (none of the white shirts had a clue about what to do). We then strolled out onto the shop floor and went to work. All the while the white shirts stood around, pacing back and forth and occasionally gathering for a few moments of hushed conversation. Eventually, a foreman came over and asked the guy who had emerged as the leader of our group when he estimated we would be finished. "We will be finished when we are finished," he replied. The foreman returned to the white shirt crowd and relayed the news. They didn't look happy.

Much of our work was inside the oven. Despite the fact that we imposed an hour of cooling time before we began, it was extremely hot. Everything was so hot that if you took off your gloves and touched anything you would get burned. After about an hour of work we were terribly overheated. So we decided as a group to take a break and get some water. We didn't ask permission; we simply went to the lunchroom. Within seconds our foreman came in and demanded to know what we were doing. We told him we were taking a break. Our leader also told him that he thought the job would take longer with all of the white shirts standing around. It was making us nervous. The foreman was furious and stormed out of the cafeteria, and we all had a good laugh. He presumably reported our insolence to the men of power who were assembled around the disabled machine. When we returned to work, a few of them had returned to their offices. When we took our second break, about an hour later, the foreman stopped us and ordered us back to work. Our lead man told him that it was hot and dangerous without the breaks. The foreman replied that they would decide when we could take a break. At that, we all threw our tools to the ground and walked off the shop floor. Some of us sat in the lunchroom while others went to the locker-room and began to dress in their street clothes. The wildcat strike lasted a matter of minutes before management gave in.

Of course, this circumstance put us in a tremendous position to contest the pace of work desired by the white shirts. But we used the occasion to push our advantage, not just to be contrary, but to strike a blow against the exploitation and alienation that we saw every day and which we helped to construct by installing the computer-based machines. This is why we were so quick to support our knife-wielding comrade. Actually, he wasn't the most popular guy in the plant and was considered to be a bit of a hot head!

The separation of money price from other forms of value is at the heart of social conflict and hence social change. As we will see in the following chapter, capitalism has organized itself in different ways in various periods of history in order to accumulate the surplus value generated through the labor process. That organization establishes the basis for both exploitation and alienation, which in turn shapes movements for social, economic, and environmental justice, which are essentially manifestations of the quest of social individuals for self-development.

Space and Place

The accumulation of surplus values through the labor process is also a process that gives a social definition to space, place, and time. The prevailing definitions of these concepts are often starting points of conventional analysis. But many studies also support the view that space, place, and time are socially constructed and are thus subject to change.[6] When they do change, the reconstruction has a profound effect on the lives of countless people throughout the world.

The social construction of space, place, and time is closely linked to the issue of value and values. If I have to be at work at 8:00 in the morning, I am likely to go to bed at 10:00 or 11:00 at night in order to get enough sleep. In between, I talk to my wife and kids, go shopping, help clean the house or cook a meal, and watch television or read. In the morning, if I live about 10 miles from work, I either take the train, if one is available, or I get into my car and brave totally aggravating traffic jams to get to my destination. I repeat the process at the end of the day. Where I live is a place that is my neighborhood. Where I go each morning is another place, my workplace. No thought is given to the abstract conceptions of space and place that are behind this routine. They are simply considered a natural part of life.

People's lives generally are structured around a particular configuration of space, place, and the time dimension associated with that. During the period of massive deindustrialization, which in Chicago began in a major way with the closing of Wisconsin Steel, the character of space, place, and time changed rapidly for many people. Workplaces were gone; neighborhoods were gentrified or people lost the financial ability to stay in their neighborhoods. Labor unions, shop floor organizations, and community-based organizations that were geared to creating conditions in specific places that would lend themselves to self-development suddenly found themselves adrift. The place basis of their organizing was gone.

It is important to understand the social processes that create a particular configuration of space, place, and time. The traditional view is that production processes and urban development patterns that define these dimensions are the outcome of the choices of individual firms and households through the agency of the market. An alternative view is that politics plays a critical role in shaping the spatial organization of urban areas and hence the character of the places that make up those areas.[7] The Wisconsin Steel story, and the massive deindustrialization that followed, illustrate this point.

The McCormick Reaper Company (later known as International Harvester and, later still, as Navistar) built Wisconsin Steel at the turn of the twentieth century to produce steel for its farm machinery manufacturing facilities. Steel production during this period underwent massive technological changes. The result was a large-scale system of production in which coal and raw iron were combined in huge furnaces that required the use of an enormous amount of energy. Once started, the production process could not be stopped without considerable cost. This necessitated shift work—three groups of workers keeping the steel operation going around the clock. Shift work altered an important aspect of the concept of time for workers engaged in this work and for their friends and families. Previously, day had been a time for work, while night was the time you spent with your family and slept. Working 8:00 A.M. to 4:00 P.M. one week, 4:00 P.M. to midnight the next, and midnight to 8:00 A.M. the following week eliminated this concept of time. I did shift work for a while. It is amazing what it does to sleeping, eating, and social habits. Your life is geared to the needs of the job. You learn to sleep standing up, sleep at family gatherings as relatives and friends talk happily around you, and go days without seeing your spouse or children. Workers had no say in the institution of shift work. It was the most effective way to accumulate surplus values created by workers in the steel-making process.

Time was altered for workers in other ways. Mass production technologies were developed to increase productivity so that each worker would produce more every minute he or she worked. The assembly line replaced individuals, making an entire product. Because the assembly line was introduced by Henry Ford to make his automobiles, mass production is often referred to as "Fordist production." Fordist innovations were eventually accompanied by scientific management, which figured out, to the second, the time and motion required to do each task on the assembly line. This innovation took decisions on the pace and method of work away from the workers and forced them to adhere to the pace of the machine.

Mass production also meant that it was more efficient (less costly) to produce at a very large scale (called by economists "economies of scale") and in a location near firms that made related products ("agglomeration economies"). To achieve these economies (to gain more surplus value from the production process), public policies and public funds resulted in the construction of needed infrastructure—railroad lines, highways, bridges, waterways, docks, and cranes—that could link transportation innovations with the new mass production facilities. International Harvester found it cost efficient to produce its own steel. In the Southeast Chicago–northwest Indiana area where Wisconsin Steel once stood there were a number of other steel mills. In the city of Chicago alone there were four major mills employing up to 25,000 workers. The presence of needed infrastructure to move raw materials into the area and out to steel markets made Chicago a good location for the Wisconsin Steel mill.

In addition to the steel mills, there were hundreds of other factories that used the steel produced there—steel fabrication shops, industrial machinery factories, railroad car manufacturers, and farm equipment factories (including some owned by International Harvester). Also, there were firms that supplied the mills and all these factories—producers and distributors of gloves, shoes, tools, nuts and bolts, and welding equipment.

The innovations in production and the accompanying transportation and infrastructure development were part of a social process. While Ford's initial motivation for introducing the assembly line was to gain more profits for his company, the process of competition made this innovation systemic and mandated transportation and other infrastructure innovations so that entire cities and regions could be competitive.

These innovations, moreover, created a new spatial dimension for manufacturing activity. The location of these spaces was defined as the cheapest transportation link between raw materials and markets. But that point, too, was socially constructed, as public resources were used to stimulate the construction of the transport links and other infrastructure. Public resources also went into attracting supplier firms as well as buyers of the industrial commodities in order to ensure agglomeration economies that would make local firms more competitive. The construction of housing, roads, public transportation, schools, and other community facilities helped to ensure the existence of an adequate and trained labor supply.

Thus, the time and spatial dimensions of Fordist mass production created places where not only heavy manufacturing commodities were produced but also where people worked and lived. Southeast Chicago was a neighborhood of well-kept homes and manicured lawns. It had a commercial center with department stores, drug stores, good restaurants, and bars that operated twenty-four hours a day. The union hall for the United Steel Workers served not only as a place to do union business and hold union meetings, but as a community center. Weddings, bar mitzvahs, anniversary parties, and meetings of community and civic organizations were held there. The community was full of churches. Baptist and Methodist churches largely served the African American community. Roman Catholic churches held masses in Polish, Spanish, and English. There were two Eastern Orthodox churches, one for Croatians and one for Serbs.

The social dimension of this place created out of the time and spatial dimensions of the mass production era included educational programs and facilities. A massive vocational school in Southeast Chicago taught its children every imaginable trade. And, when the children grew up and were ready to work, the union provided them with access to the employment opportunities in the mills and factories. In the mills, young people could extend their education with apprenticeships on the job and either work in the mills and related factories for the rest of their lives or save money and go on to college.

The transformation of Southeast Chicago into both a space for production and a place for its workers did not come without contention. The very fact that the jobs there paid good wages was the result of bitter struggle. Industrial unionism was born, in part, in Southeast Chicago. It was born out of the bloodshed of the Republic Steel Massacre in 1938. In addition to wages, there were struggles over the form that mass production took. Conceptions of time that tied the worker to the pace of the machine were fiercely contested. Health and safety standards and union work rules were the products of these struggles. Workers also gained a say in the way in which different jobs were distributed and compensated. Health and vacation benefits were won. Unionized workers placed limits on the surplus value that the new production system could generate. Definitions of time, space, place, and even efficiency were thus social and the product of struggle. There were also struggles among workers—based largely on race—over who could work at these well-paying jobs as well as where African American and Mexican workers could live.

Yet, even as these struggles continued to shape the meaning of time, space, and place of the mass production era and before the demise of Wisconsin Steel signaled the beginning of the end of that era, there were destabilizing social forces at work. In the 1950s, industrial development within Southeast Chicago and the city of Chicago generally began to be constrained by urban development. Land for mass production within the city was getting scarce. This set off another round of innovations that changed both time and space dimensions of manufacturing production. A variety of public policy innovations opened up large suburban areas to both industrial and residential development, causing a decentralization of demographic and economic activity. Highways and mass transit lines were extended outside the city limits, and mortgages guaranteed by the federal government caused a suburban housing boom. The availability of relatively cheap land for industrial development combined with infrastructure construction (a very important one being O'Hare Airport) led to the decentralization of industry. These developments changed the cost economies of the city location and hence altered the spatial dimension of production itself. The driving force behind these developments was the constraints placed by dense urban development on the accumulation of surplus value. To achieve the potential economies of scale and agglomeration there was a need for land to expand the spaces of industrial development. Land adjacent to the industrial spaces was simply not available or was very expensive. Thus, a new definition of both space and place was generated and took the form of suburbia. Suburbia as a place was initially restricted to white workers and the growing ranks of the middle class. And it began to undermine places like Southeast Chicago.

But by the 1980s, even farther-reaching innovations would soon revolutionize the time and spatial dimensions of production and destroy the place called Southeast Chicago. These innovations will be discussed more fully in Chapters 3 and 4. Briefly, we can catch of a glimpse of the nature of the new era of production by looking at the closing of Wisconsin Steel. The hallmark of this new era is high capital mobility made possible by technological innovations in transportation and communications technology.

In the case of Wisconsin Steel, its parent company, then called International Harvester, began as early as the 1960s to diversify its production in order to compete with Caterpillar and John Deere, which had taken the bulk of market shares in farm equipment.[8] Harvester responded by moving its capital into other products. It began to expand the production of trucks, construction equipment, and steel. It also began a modernization program at Wisconsin Steel. But deep recessions in the late 1960s and mid-1970s found Harvester seriously overextended. New management decided to consolidate its capital in its most profitable areas. Since Wisconsin Steel was in the midst of major innovation and renovation, it wasn't a very profitable operation. Despite brisk sales of steel, the debt incurred in the innovation program made the mill a losing proposition. So the parent firm decided to move its capital out of steel.

Wisconsin Steel was a very early victim of the ravages of high capital mobility. Capital mobility itself became possible due to innovations in communications and transportation. Telecommunications technology facilitated rapid movement of money, inventory control, and better coordination of parts of the production process, among other things. Transportation innovations reduced shipping costs. Altogether, manufacturing industries became much more footloose. Moving capital from steel to trucks or even to the production of oil became infinitely easier. Also, production could be divided and produced in different parts of the world. The old economies of scale and agglomeration had broken down. These changes have been termed "post-Fordist."

The new production processes of the post-Fordist era radically altered the prevailing notions of time, space, and place as they became generalized throughout the capitalist system. As factory after factory went down, huge areas of cities, including Chicago, were abandoned by capital and designated a "rust belt." The places that had been generated by mass production industry were likewise destroyed. Throughout the city of Chicago, neighborhoods whose workers had once toiled at former economic mainstays like Western

Electric, Sunbeam, Westinghouse, General Electric, Stewart Warner, Oscar Mayer, USX, LTV-Republic, and Wisconsin Steel either collapsed or became a target for redevelopment and upscaling. The reason was that these factories had closed and workers no longer had the means to maintain their homes.

In Southeast Chicago, homes were abandoned; stores, bars, and restaurants closed. The union hall fell into disrepair and soon became covered with gang graffiti. With the homes and facilities declining, the social structure that defined Southeast Chicago as a place began to come apart. The vocational school cut back most of its programs, and the unions could no longer place young people in apprenticeships. The system that had been established to guide young people into the world of work was destroyed and nothing was on hand to replace it. Gangs began to do battle over drug turf. Meanwhile, at the abandoned Wisconsin Steel site, a million-dollar blast furnace that had been purchased during International Harvester's modernization program but had never been fired up was blown up with dynamite and sold for scrap.

I have used the story of Wisconsin Steel and the rise and fall of mass production industry in Chicago to demonstrate how the drive to accumulate surplus value reconstructs the meaning of space and place.[9] The contradictions in the categories of value and labor reappear in the social construction of space and place. Capitalism as a social system is driven by competition to seek new paths to the accumulation of surplus value. The domination of the money price form of value and its separation from contending concepts of value leads to a continual and restless search for new modes of accumulation. In the process, the system reinvents the meaning of time and space, which in turn destroys and then creates new places. Those who feel the impact of these changes, moreover, resist. New processes of accumulation intensify alienation and exploitation. Resistance brings to the surface the tensions inherent in the value form that separates value from human development.

Permanence and Change

On March 31, 1999, 6,700 people waited in line to get applications for about sixty sewage treatment jobs offered by the Chicago Metropolitan Water Reclamation District. The new jobs would pay about $15 an hour. Workers began arriving at 5:00 A.M. even though the office didn't open until 9:00. Four days later, The *Chicago Tribune* reported that the jobless rate nationally and locally was at its lowest point in twenty-nine years. Economists were quoted in the article as declaring the Chicago economy "strong."[10]

The line at the Chicago Metropolitan Water Reclamation District and the *Chicago Tribune* observation demonstrate that new paths to the accumulation of surplus value that redefine the meaning of space and place bring challenges to those who are limited by the new order. Interviews with those standing in line revealed that most of them were "employed." *But* they were employed in jobs that paid less than a living wage. Officially they were not "jobless," which accounts for the apparent contradiction between the *Tribune* report and the lineup for a few jobs. The lines for the sewage treatment jobs contradicted the dominant notion of joblessness. The workers in line were no longer challenging the conditions at their workplaces. Rather, they were in a desperate search for wages they could live on. Still, the conflict over conceptions of joblessness could be the beginnings of a broader challenge to the new regime. This vignette raises, therefore, important philosophic questions. What is the nature of social change? Are there aspects of society that should be considered as permanent? If so, how do we decide what can be changed?

Answering these questions after a shift to a new mode of accumulation is particularly difficult for two reasons. First, the people who are part of organizations that focus on economic and social justice have based their militancy on the conceptions of space and place that were part of the previous era.[11] The militancy of the workers at Chicago Shortening, Foseco, and Wisconsin Steel was based on conditions and relationships that were specific to these workplaces. Today, all these places are gone; they are part of the toll of the new regime. To adapt social change movements to new definitions of space and place requires a deeper understanding of how such movements contribute to social change itself.

Second, new modes of accumulation always appear as permanent features of our existence. Therefore, there is a tendency for would-be militants to take perceived permanence as a starting point in an effort to change society. For this reason, the presumption of permanence becomes a philosophic concept to discuss. David Harvey argues that the creation of the appearance of permanence is necessary to our existence. A sense of permanence helps us to find meaning in our lives.[12] Everything is subject to the construction of permanence. Workers in Chicago's manufacturing industries considered the prevailing mass production system to be permanent and conceived of their organizing activities within those limits. The Southeast Chicago community as a place, including the workplaces that maintained it, was also considered permanent. Even theories, once constructed, become what writer Raymond Williams (whom Harvey draws upon) calls "permanencies." This makes a great deal of sense. We have to have a starting point for everything we do. There have to be some agreed-upon boundaries to both thought and action. Yet, at times it becomes necessary to move beyond those boundaries. The assumption that boundaries are permanent places limits on what we are willing and able to do in life. And the limits themselves become a permanency. Thus there is always the issue of where the starting point will be. What are the givens in a social movement? Which aspects of social life should we treat as permanent, and which ones should we consider changeable?

Understanding the nature of change and what can be considered changeable involves two philosophical divides. One is whether change originates through institutions or people; the other is whether the natural state of things is permanence or change. Dominant forms of analysis and the public policies and organizing strategies that follow from analysis assume that change originates in institutions and that the natural state of social systems is permanent. On the other side of the divide is the proposition that change originates through the agency of human beings and that social systems are inherently unstable.

The Question of Agency: Institutions versus People

The question of whether change originates through the agency of institutions or people can focus on the role of markets and government relative to human beings. Analysis of the collapse of the steel industry has generally focused on markets. The prevailing point of view is that the closing of Wisconsin Steel and the general collapse of manufacturing in older U.S. cities were the result of global overproduction combined with the inability of the older Chicago mills to compete with the leaner and meaner corporations both in the United States and abroad. Markets for steel, in this view, are the agent through which the restructuring of the steel industry proceeds. Similarly, in my example of land values in Wisconsin, the market is the agent through which value is determined. Social justice advocates often point to the failure of markets to satisfy basic human needs and turn to the state or government to address these failures. Despite the current fashion of "reinventing government" by reducing its budget and delegating more and more things to the private market, liberals still insist that government has a responsibility to correct "market failures." Everyone should have proper housing, enough to eat, and adequate health care. Public housing, food stamps, and universal health care, it is argued, should be provided by the government and paid for with taxes.

Both sides offer a limited and one-sided view of the question of agency for social change. An implication of my earlier discussion about value and values is that markets mask the fact that there are human relationships embedded in the commodities that are the product of capitalist production. Those relationships involve both exploitation and alienation. Markets are constructed to perpetuate these contradictions. The limit of the "power of the market" thus lies in the fact that the accumulation of surplus values that are needed to maintain the system depends on the exploitation and alienation of human beings. An important political role of the market as it is presently constructed is to mask these human relationships through their appearance as a simple exchange of things.

A similar critique can be made of the contention of many liberals that we should seek redress through government. Marx once said that the state is the excrescence (meaning the waste material) of the capitalist system.[13] This was not intended merely to be vulgar. He meant that the state was created to preserve capitalism by getting rid of its unwanted by-products. This could involve anything from waging war to passing workplace safety and environmental laws so that the system does not totally destroy its workforce—its source of surplus value. But the role of the state is ultimately to preserve the system. That means that the state, like the market, participates in masking the human relations that lie at the heart of the system. But it does so in a different way. The division of social life between public and private sectors strengthens the alienating division of the worker into a creator of useful commodities and a producer of exchange values. In such a system, relations among people are relegated to and regulated by the public sphere. The private individual is left to develop stripped of his or her social being in the private sector, where each individual's development is a potential barrier to that of every other individual.[14] Marx argued that in such a social arrangement, individualism prevails over the social individual, meaning that domination through competition replaces self-development through cooperative human relationships. In the process, human development is distorted and alienated. While the market preserves the *appearance* that wealth comes from the exchange of commodities, the state must ultimately reinforce this appearance. As such, it is limited in its contribution to human development.

This does not mean that government should be ignored. But it does mean that it cannot be the *agent* of meaningful social change. I once saw a film of a speech given by Dr. Martin Luther King Jr. at Stanford University. He gave the speech in 1967, exactly one year before his assassination. There was a great deal of discussion during that period about whether government could be the vehicle for African American emancipation. After his speech he was asked about the role that the courts and congressional legislation could play. His response was: "Laws can not make you love me. But they can help prevent you from lynching me." For him, of course, they didn't even do that. But his general point was that while government and legislation were a necessary part of the civil rights movement, the fundamental need was for the movement to produce a different sort of human being. The gains that were achieved in the legislative arena, moreover, were only as strong as the mass social movement behind them.

The problem with the institutional view of social change is that the institutions available are designed to place limits on the direction and extent of change itself. Ultimately, both markets and government institutions are designed to preserve the contradictions that define the system. The workers who were dislocated as a result of the closing of Wisconsin Steel had some recourse from governmental institutions. They used the courts to sue the company and, after a nine-year battle, retrieved some money that was owed to them for wages earned before the closing, vacation time, and pension liabilities. However, it was strictly a defensive battle. It did not take the offensive and challenge the forces that had put them on the street to begin with. The government also offered some job training and placement in other jobs. This is more of the excrement of the system and not a vehicle to meaningful change. The market is even more limited. Dislocated workers must use government and private job training programs to become more competitive. They can then compete in the market with other workers for jobs in the "new economy." Unemployment generated by social forces becomes an individual matter and alienates all who are touched from one another. That is why 6,700 workers will line up for sixty jobs. The lineup demonstrates the limit of both the power of the market and the role that government plays in trying to correct market failures.

If the institutional approach to change is limited, what exactly is the alternative? What does it mean to say that change originates through "human agency"? Human agency as the basis for change is grounded in the notion that human relationships are at the heart of all societies. Social change comes from our drive to develop ourselves to our full potential. This drive is impeded by the basic division in society between the production of use and exchange values. Yet all social movements originate in this fundamental contradiction. Furthermore, this process of self-development is social in character. What Marx referred to as wealth—the "universality of needs, capacities, enjoyments, productive powers, etc., of individuals, produced in universal exchange"—is gained by people in relation to one another.[15] This is what Marx termed "the social individual."

Those of us who worked at the Foseco Corporation's chemical factory in Chicago, where a young worker threatened his foreman, came to a common understanding that concretely we could not allow ourselves to be tied to the pace of the new computer-based machines. The cooperative nature of our work there is what produced that insight. We experienced the changing working conditions collectively. While its impact hit us as individuals, we shared, as a group, the limitations that the new conditions placed on our "universal needs, capacities and enjoyments." And out of that sharing, we developed a certain consciousness of the nature of the social character of our individuality. Solidarity in this limited arena was the product of this consciousness. And we acted to change the conditions that placed limitations on our development.

Generalizing that experience to broader social movements brings meaning to the concept of human agency. The impetus for change comes not from institutions but from the collective sense of limit that the social order imposes on us. The objective of organizing, therefore, is not to change institutions (although we may try to do that along the way), but to connect people with one another and with the broader social forces that place limits on their development.

Thus, people should not be the objects of the organizing project, but its subjects. An organizer against the World Trade Organization was quoted as saying, "We organizers have an axiom we go by: We educate people in order to organize them. We don't organize them in order to educate them."[16] Education in this instance was about the evils of the World Trade Organization. It was intended to bring people into the streets to block the work of that organization. The people were the objects of the campaign. The whole point was to raise such a ruckus that "decision makers" would be forced to make different decisions. Such a campaign limits discussion and education to strictly what is necessary to meet the objectives of the campaign. But the point of organizing is not to educate either. If the people affected by the WTO are the subjects of the social movement, it means that what needs to be changed is them and their perception of themselves in relation to a larger society. Then through their agency—through their understanding of themselves as social individuals being stunted by the new world order—the terms for social change will emerge. The objective of organizing under this conception is not simply changed institutions (stop the WTO), but changed people with a new and social understanding of their own situation. The method of organizing is to provide an arena in which to share experiences and to draw on those experiences to create a focus and strategy for change.

What Is the "Natural" State of Things: Permanence versus Change?

Another important philosophic divide is whether the natural state of society, its institutions and people, is stable or unstable. As I noted earlier, we create permanencies as a way to organize our lives, as the bases on which we live our lives day to day. If we are married, for example, most of us assume, that the relationship is permanent. If we didn't, its dissolution would become a certainty and our personal relationships would be in a constant state of turmoil. We make similar assumptions about other relations as well. I teach at a university. As far as I am concerned, the university and its structure are permanent. And I behave accordingly. I usually adhere to university rules; I try not to offend my colleagues. I do most of the things expected of me: I try to be a good teacher, do public service, publish articles and books, raise money, and attend many meetings that are designed to keep the institution going. But there are times when personal development depends on the ability to break out of the various permanencies we have constructed for ourselves or society has constructed for us. That is why there are divorces, why university professors change jobs, and why workers have been willing to risk their livelihoods and even their lives to organize unions, go on strikes, and undertake other militant activities.

But when people decide to destroy certain permanencies, questions arise over what the limits of the change should be. What boundaries should we place, if any, on change? If we go beyond what people perceive can change, they will argue that the proposed activity is not practical. This pragmatic statement, however, assumes that, while external forces can be marshaled to make things a little better, the basic nature of social institutions, and even "human nature," is static. Thus, there are limits on what we can do, and these limits should circumscribe our behavior. Certain aspects of today's new world order have become a permanency that many people are not ready to challenge. In many strategic discussions about how best to change the character of the new world order or parts of its program, someone will inevitably make a limiting statement prefaced by "in today's political climate we can only expect..."

This tendency appears not only as a part of political discourse, it is a feature of most social science and public policy analyses as well. Traditional economic analysis, for example, defines or assumes a point of equilibrium that is considered a desirable norm. Research is then directed toward understanding or identifying the external forces that could destabilize the system, moving it out of its natural state of equilibrium. The analysis then assumes that the permanency of equilibrium in an economy is natural and desirable. Policy is directed toward avoiding or counteracting forces external to the economy that would upset this state.

Dialectical philosophy, to which I subscribe, takes an opposing view. Dialectics contends that society, its people, and its institutions (including markets) are in a constant state of change. Further, internal relations within markets (or whatever we are trying to understand) are responsible for this natural state of instability. Research, based on this philosophic ground, examines the internal processes that lead to instability and attempts to understand why there is the appearance of equilibrium. Economic analysis that takes equilibrium as the natural state of things contradicts the dialectical view that the economic system is based on exploitation and alienation, which is the basis for social change. It was the dialectical ground that produced the question posed at the beginning of this chapter: What is something worth? The idea that things are worth what people will pay stands in constrast to the notion that within every commodity there is a dialectical tension between use value and exchange value. The resulting truncation of human development, in this view, makes the economy inherently unstable.

In economic and even political terms, the 1990s economy did very well. Markets were in equilibrium, unemployment was at "an all time low," and those with the resources continued to buy stocks far above prices that would have been acceptable in the 1980s. Yet, 6,700 people still lined up at 5:00 A.M. to apply for sixty jobs. Dialectical philosophy directs us to ask: What are the specific internal processes that lead to such a situation? How are the contradictions inherent in the production process and thus in the markets for the commodities produced through that process destabilizing markets? Why is there an appearance of stability or equilibrium?

The dialectic can also illuminate questions about organizing. Much organizing today is based on the dominant view that everything is basically stable and can be changed primarily through external forces—persons, institutions, or events that are outside whatever is changing. The lives of people who are being exploited, for example, are changed, in this view, by a new law, through the agency of a political party, or by an organizer/leader rather than the people themselves. From this philosophic ground, people are the objects of organizing campaigns. People are organized by organizers to move institutions, which in turn are pushed to make things better for people. This is the basis of the organizer's axiom: "We educate people to organize them. We don't organize them to educate."

The dialectical outlook looks at people and organizing in a very different light. The key philosophic proposition is that within human beings there is a fundamental contradiction between the drive for self-development and the constraints the social order places on that drive. The Marxist dialectic views the resulting social change process in terms of a "dual rhythm."[17] Groups of people (a class, a race, a gender), whose self-development is similarly thwarted, will join together to combat and get rid of the thing that is holding them back. That is the first negation, which involves the tearing down of the old. Second, in the process of tearing down the old, people can begin to develop an alternative and participate in the creation of the new. That is the second negation. The tearing down of the old and the building of the new are vital to the entire social change project. The engine that drives the process is the contradiction within the human condition itself. The new is not limited to new institutions, but is founded on new human beings. Unless that happens, the movement is frozen before it begins to reach its potential. In this view, everything is basically unstable and change comes about through internal relations.

This is the basis for my critique of the notion of educate to organize. The impetus for change comes not from within human beings but from the organizer. And the only possible outcome is an institutional change. Congress may or may not pass a law. Action on a good or a bad piece of legislation can make the objects of the organizing project better off. But the contradictions remain. And, most important, the human potential to create something new is stymied.

Conclusions

This chapter outlines a number of philosophic perspectives that inform the remainder of the book. Philosophy is concretized in all activities of our lives, including social analysis. Three philosophic issues—value and values; space and place; and social change—can guide us in an understanding of what I am calling the "new world order," how that order affects people and what to do about it. There are two very general conclusions I wish to make at this point. One is that the choice of philosophic perspective influences our understanding of the world around us, and what we do in our day-to-day lives. I have made a very preliminary argument for the perspectives that guide my own work. But I want to stress that the argument is preliminary because philosophy must always be made concrete through further elaboration of the material world. Thus, the remaining chapters all seek to further concretize the argument developed above.

CHAPTER 3

The Evolution of a New World Order

The history of global capitalism is marked by a number of distinct eras or periods that are defined by the way the system as a whole accumulates surplus value. Shifts from one era to another have been occasioned by crisis. The specific nature of each crisis is beyond the scope of this book, but the topic has been the subject of much debate.[1] The mechanisms for accumulation include a variety of institutions and a political and ideological apparatus to support them. The currently popular term "globalization" is more accurately a distinct approach to accumulation that describes the present period. I have chosen to call this period the new world order.

A thesis of this book is that the new world order caused a shift in U.S. urban policy, which has had a negative impact on working people in the United States. That impact has come through the destruction of residential places and places of work. And in the wake of that destruction many have found themselves working harder for less pay and without a decent place to live. To understand the nature of the shift it is important to understand some key features of the evolution of the previous Fordist period and some aspects of its collapse in the early 1970s.

From Fordism to a New World Order

The early twentieth century was marked by global capitalist crisis, labor upheaval, and a major shift in the nature of the production process that resulted in greater worker productivity. Henry Ford initiated the technological basis of this shift when he instituted the assembly line. The concept and technique of mass production that evolved was thus termed Fordism. Fordism advanced by bringing more and more parts of the production process under one roof. Ford Rouge, for example, was a massive industrial complex in Detroit that produced automobiles in a process that also included the production of steel, glass, and practically everything that went into the final product. In addition to Fordism, the new mode of accumulation employed the principles of scientific management known as Taylorism after its founder Frederick Taylor. Taylorism examined every movement each worker in the production process made, measured the time these movements took, and devised more efficient movements that would increase productivity. The combination of Fordism and Taylorism literally turned workers into parts of a huge industrial machine.

The combination of crisis and the beginnings of the shift to the Fordist era also gave rise to militant unionism in the United States. That included formation of the Industrial Workers of the World (IWW), who attempted to organize the workers in entire industries and posed their vision of "one big union" as an alternative to capitalism itself.[2] During its existence many key leaders were assassinated, and during World War I the remaining leadership was imprisoned for their opposition to the war. This effectively destroyed the organization. But in the aftermath of the Great Depression another militant industrial union movement, the Congress of Industrial Organizations (CIO), founded an independent federation of unions. Their break from the more moderate American Federation of Labor (AFL), who organized their members by craft rather than industry, was preceded by a series of strikes that were often violent. President Roosevelt attempted to secure labor peace by instituting new labor legislation that affirmed the right of workers to organize, form unions, and bargain collectively. Employers' refusal to recognize these rights generated continued militant strikes that often resulted in the occupation of factories.

It wasn't until World War II that both economic crisis and labor militancy dissipated as workers supported the war effort. In the aftermath of World War II, new institutions were put in place that created the structure that would enable Fordism to become a global system. By the summer of 1944, the war was winding down. In July a conference attended by forty-four nations in Bretton Woods, New Hampshire, mapped out a strategy for postwar development. The United States was in a position economically, militarily, and politically to determine the terms of this strategy. The United States had both its industry and infrastructure intact. The nations of Europe were in shambles. The resulting Bretton Woods Agreement became the basis for the development of the capitalist world until the early 1970s. It was designed for the rebuilding of Europe on U.S. terms.

The U.S. dollar was established as the international medium of exchange. The value of the dollar was fixed relative to the currencies of other nations and backed by gold. Institutions were created (the IMF, the World Bank, and the General Agreement on Tariffs and Trade [GATT]) to facilitate this system. The IMF and the World Bank had well-defined roles in the rebuilding of Western Europe. The IMF's purpose was to maintain stable values for currencies to facilitate international trade. If shortages and development bottlenecks caused inflationary pressures, the IMF would provide short-term loans and technical assistance to resolve the problems. The World Bank was established as a financial intermediary between U.S. lenders and the countries of Europe and Great Britain, who needed dollars to buy exports and engage in long-term development projects. The funding of these two institutions came from member nations. Voting rights on IMF and World Bank policy was based on the size of each nation's financial stake. This arrangement enabled the United States to maintain political control over international development policy. The GATT was established to facilitate trade among nations by preventing costly trade wars.

These arrangements enabled U.S. corporations to expand their profitability and blunt the effects of cyclical crisis. The Bretton Woods Agreement had as its U.S. domestic counterpart government fiscal and monetary policies that used government powers to spend, tax, print money, and establish the terms of borrowing and extending credit. These powers were used to stimulate economic growth. The war effort had consolidated Fordism and Taylorism as the global method of production. Productivity growth was thus on the rise.

Organized labor in the United States initially attempted to use both the postwar prosperity and the favorable labor legislation that had been won during the clashes prior to the war to press its advantage. Militancy returned to the United States in the early years of postwar development. But it was short-lived. In order to gain a share of the growing U.S. pie, labor union leaders decided to accommodate their objectives to the new Fordist era. A share of the growing prosperity of U.S. business was traded for labor peace at home and support for U.S. foreign policy. The accommodation of an evolving "business unionism" emboldened big business to make a move on the legislative front that undermined past labor gains. The resulting Taft–Hartley Act of 1947 reinstituted strike injunctions, outlawed mass picketing and secondary boycotts, and facilitated lawsuits against unions. It was a serious setback for the union movement. U.S. foreign policy was directed toward the cold war with the Soviet Union, and access to cheap resources in the developing world was often the battleground. As a result, many unions expelled leaders suspected of being subversive. In 1955, the CIO merged with the AFL, creating the AFL-CIO. In the 1960s, the AFL-CIO established a series of overseas institutes in the developing world that were designed both to export business unionism abroad and to participate in destabilizing governments or unions that opposed U.S. foreign policy.[3]

The Fordist period in the United States benefited a broad spectrum of the population. World War II, the process of rebuilding Europe after the war, and the ability of U.S. corporations to extract natural resources from recently independent nations of the developing world brought great economic power to the United States. The terms of the accommodation with labor meant that the income derived from this power was shared with U.S. workers. Incomes rose, and many workers were able to buy cars, homes, and appliances and move into newly developing suburbs. But there were some contradictions. All workers did not benefit, and this fact touched off a major civil rights movement that began in the mid-1950s and exploded in the 1960s and into the early 1970s. Civil rights struggles not only moved from South to North but also confronted labor unions, where discrimination was rampant. In addition, many workers began to resist the increasing pace of work that was generated by the extension of Fordist production into automation. Throughout the 1950s, there were waves of wildcat strikes in the mining, auto, and steel industries. Black worker caucuses led many of these strikes.

A major sign that U.S. dominance under the Fordist regime was weakening was Vietnam. Between 1965 and 1975, the United States was bogged down in an unpopular war that it eventually lost. The war began to weaken the United States both economically and politically. As the anti-war and civil rights movements in the United States gained momentum, post–World War II growth began to falter. In the late 1960s and early 1970s, the United States suffered major bouts of inflation. Meanwhile, the falling profit rates of U.S. and other capitalist corporations, the economic and political impact of the Vietnam war, and the continued labor and general social upheaval inside the United States and in other developed nations brought on an economic crisis. In the early 1970s, the U.S. economy particularly began to show signs of weakness with major bouts of inflation. Also, the United States began to run a trade deficit (more foreign goods coming into the United States than U.S goods going out) and a balance of payments deficit (more money going out than coming in). The terms of the Bretton Woods Agreement had made the dollar the international reserve currency. Specifically, the exchange rates among currencies were all pegged to the value of the dollar and all currencies were readily convertible to dollars or gold at a value of $35 to one ounce of gold. The deteriorating economic and political conditions in the United States meant that other nations in the developed world had to adjust their domestic economic policies to conform to the fluctuating demand for dollars. In practice, that could mean restraining prices and employment at home.[4] In the political economic context of the early 1970s, faith in the U.S. economy and the strength of the dollar began to dissipate and led to efforts to convert currencies to gold. In 1971, President Nixon initially devalued the dollar and eventually took the dollar off the gold standard. Under considerable pressure from other capitalist nations, he also announced that the value of the dollar would be allowed to float based on market demand for dollars. That act constituted a cancellation of the Bretton Woods Agreement and essentially brought a formal end to the Fordist period. The scene was now set for a period of deep social, political, and economic crisis, which would either destroy capitalism altogether or give birth to a new mode of accumulation.

The economies of the developed capitalist world continued to decline. Two oil shocks added fuel to the fire. In 1973, in retaliation for the U.S. support of Israel in the Arab-Israeli War, a cartel of oil-producing nations based in the Middle East Organization of Petroleum Exporting Countries (OPEC) withheld oil production needed by the United States and other industrial nations. This created oil shortages that drove prices sharply upward. In 1979, there was a second oil shock related to the revolution in Iran. Both cases demonstrated that the post–World War II system of capitalist accumulation depended on the political-military control of the Middle East. As that dissipated, the system, which depended on an unlimited supply of oil at stable prices, was in jeopardy. Both shocks caused high levels of inflation. The industrial nations, including Japan, responded by instituting national economic policies that restricted industrial expansion and led to unemployment. The result was what was called stagflation—high levels of inflation and unemployment occurring simultaneously.

A New Strategy for a New World Order

The crisis had now become both economic and political and it had reached every capitalist nation. Without the Bretton Woods system in place, and with the strategy institutionalized by that system in disarray, there was a void. Between 1972 and 1977, high-level discussions about an alternative strategy occurred. These involved leading academics and politicians in much of the developed capitalist world. They occurred in many forums, including such influential institutions as the Trilateral Commission and the Organization for Economic Development and Cooperation (OECD). There had also been a significant experiment in the aftermath of a coup in Chile in 1973 in which the military dictator Augusto Pinochet overthrew a popularly elected socialist government and endorsed an economic program promoted by University of Chicago trained economists and their mentor, Professor Milton Friedman.[5]

The Chile economic program included tight money to end inflation, drastic reductions in government spending, currency devaluation, and the opening of markets for goods and capital to foreign investors.

The Chilean experiment provided the outlines of a broad alternative strategy for surplus value accumulation that was evolving between 1972 and 1977. Essentially the strategy was to cheapen the costs of production and expand markets. A key focus of the strategy was the cost of labor, but other kinds of production costs were also targeted. These included the cost of raw materials and other inputs into the production process; the cost of environmental controls and cleanup; and costs associated with the demands for worker and human rights. The second element of the developing strategy was mobility of capital, goods, and services. Mobility was at the heart of the effort to cheapen production costs while expanding markets. Mobility involved developing a capacity to produce goods and services in a more flexible way and with greater efficiency, meaning less cost for each item produced. Mobility included both the ability to produce things in different geographical locations and the ability to move out of one kind of economic activity into another. The cheapening of production costs was discussed at length in the early Trilateral Commission papers. The commission's discussion stressed the need for greater efficiency and competition through free markets. There were some statements made during this period that put the issue more bluntly. Jacques de Larosiere, chairman of the International Monetary Fund in 1984, for example, stressed the need to reduce labor's share of profits.[6] A decade later, the OECD argued that lack of "flexibility in labor markets" caused unemployment and poverty, and that a key to the solution was to lower real wages.[7] The 1990s call for flexibility extended to work hours as well as social welfare policies for the unemployed. The OECD strongly recommended that the developed nations take measures to lower production costs through flexibility, which included wages, benefits, working hours, and a reduction of public benefits to the unemployed.[8] The broad outlines of a new mode of accumulation emerged from these developments.

Jumpstarting the New World Order

A new mode of accumulation doesn't just start by itself when the old system has broken down. Nor can it simply be imposed by politically powerful people. Workers in the developed world were demanding a bigger share of a shrinking pie. They were essentially making greater claims on value production than the system was capable of producing. Adding to the crisis, liberation movements in the developing world were demanding independence and often embracing socialism. U.S. corporations backed by their government had been at the center of the dying order. But the United States had lost its economic and political ability to continue to play this role. Moreover, capitalist profit rates were falling.[9] The mechanisms through which surplus values could be accumulated and used to create even more surplus values were deteriorating or were gone altogether. To create a new mode of accumulation it became necessary both to destroy claims on the value that had been generated under the old regime and to gain some more capital to get something new going. Unlike the previous period, where two world wars had destroyed claims on value while creating a demand for the expansion of production, the new period lacked a start-up mechanism. There was a need for some new form of "primitive accumulation" through which new capital could be accumulated and demands on capital destroyed. The source of new capital turned out to be credit. Credit expansion served to jumpstart the new mode of accumulation and continues to play a critical role in its ability to function. The need to destroy claims on value was accomplished, as I detail below, by a massive deindustrialization and an attack on organized labor in the developed world and a regime of austerity (such as that imposed on Chile) in the developing world. It was only through these mechanisms that new institutions could be fully built to implement the envisioned new world order.

Credit Expansion

Credit is a form of fictitious capital—fictitious in the sense that it is not produced by living labor and thus contains no value. Credit has always been a key feature of capitalist development. But its use and role have varied in different periods. In the waning days of the Bretton Woods Agreement, international banks were active making loans in Eurodollars, U.S. dollars being held by foreign banks. These dollars were initially used to finance the international operations of the emerging global corporations. At one point *Business Week* complained that these huge corporations were creating an uncomfortable demand for "stateless money."[10] But even after President Nixon ended the gold standard in 1971 and Bretton Woods by agreeing to allow the value of international currencies to fluctuate in 1973, most international business was still conducted in dollars. The reason was simple: the old system had left dollars in the reserves of nations, corporations, and banks throughout the world. The world was literally awash with dollars.[11] And the OPEC oil crisis added even more because the oil-producing nations decided to take their windfall profits in dollars. These profits, which were the fruits of the OPEC-induced price increases of 1974–77, were deposited in international banks.

Massive dollar reserves caused the banks to seek new and expanded markets for their dollars. Financing the expansion of international corporations thus continued. By 1986, the debt of non-financial U.S. corporations stood at a staggering twenty-two times the value of after-tax profits.[12] But loans also went to the developing world. The sources of these loans included both the commercial banks that saw opportunities to make money and governments, whose motivation was political. Government loans to developing nations became a ticket to political influence. The United States and other capitalist governments began to compete with the Soviet Union, using loans to draw nations into their orbit. Developing nations, some newly free of colonial rule, were in dire need of loans for development. Friendly governments could be bought. Debt in these countries rose from $100 billion in 1973 to over $900 billion by 1984.[13] During 1977–82, net capital flows from developed to developing nations were, on average, US$30.5 billion a year. Loans accounted for over $29 billion in positive flows.[14]

The expansion of credit was not confined to the developing world. Credit was used inside developed nations to maintain markets for goods and services there. Domestic credit expansion in the United States can be seen in the rise of consumer debt relative to income. In 1949, debt as a percentage of personal income was 29.5 percent. But as early as the late 1960s, the percentage had climbed to 59 percent. As the old regime crumbled, people were already beginning to live beyond their means. But with the coming of a new world order, household debt began to climb rapidly. By 1979, the debt burden of U.S. households was up to 63 percent of total personal income.[15] And only about 30 percent of this burden was due to mortgage debt, which at least could provide a tangible asset. Seventy percent of the debt was consumer debt. Many people were accumulating interest and principal obligations faster than the means to pay them off. This was not true of everyone. Rich people go into debt to "invest" or speculate on the growing array of opportunities in the stock market or more high-risk ventures. But for poor people the story is different. A 1990 study concluded that U.S. families with lower incomes, who comprised 40 percent of all families, borrowed in order to make up for falling or stagnating wages.[16] And the trend continues as the new world order gains steam. Between 1979 and 1989, household debt as a percentage of personal annual income climbed from 63 percent to 76 percent. Estimates for 1997 put the figure at nearly 85 percent.[17] During the 1990s, the use of credit cards in the United States exploded. Between 1990 and 2000, credit card debt as a percentage of disposable income increased by 61 percent and the amount of such debt went from $432 billion to $1,173 billion.[18] Balances averaged more than $7,000, which meant that more than $1,000 per year was being paid out in interest and related fees.[19]

The expansion of credit in the developed world can also be seen in the debt incurred by governments. This has been particularly dramatic in the United States. Outstanding debt of the U.S. Treasury had been high at the end of World War II (61 percent of gross domestic product [GDP] in 1952). But the postwar expansion under the terms of the Bretton Woods Agreement had greatly reduced these obligations. By 1974, outstanding debt had dropped to only 23 percent of GDP. But then it began to shoot up again.[20] By 1996, it had reached 51 percent of GDP and interest payments on that debt were 17 percent of GDP. The expansion of government debt in the developed capitalist world was not confined to the United States. In 1996, debt in the European Monetary Union nations amounted to 59 percent of GDP, with interest payments of 11 percent.[21] Outstanding debt is the accumulation of annual budget deficits when the government spends more than it gets in taxes and other revenues. Budget deficits in the United States accelerated sharply under President Reagan in the 1980s. While Reagan slashed social spending, he greatly increased military spending and cut taxes for corporations and rich people. The result was huge budget deficits that virtually exploded beginning in 1982. The deficits continued well into the 1990s and caused the amount of debt held by private investors to triple over a decade.[22] In 2000, total outstanding government debt in the United States stood at $5.7 trillion. In the Fordist era deficit spending by governments of developed nations had been used as a positive policy tool to stimulate the economy and pursue a full employment policy. But deficits during the twenty-year period from the mid-1970s to the mid-1990s were accumulated in a context of shrinking social programs. As we discuss in Chapter 8, this sort of positive fiscal policy has been abandoned. So growing government debt has become simply a part of the expansion of credit that jumpstarted and now sustains the new world order.

Corporate debt is also part of the picture of credit expansion. Borrowing money to buy assets that will increase profits is considered good business practice. But some uses of corporate debt can have negative social consequences. U.S. corporate bond debt, which is one indicator of the size of credit expansion to U.S. corporations, stood at about $3.3 trillion in 1997. For non-financial corporations the debt grew from 13 percent to 18 percent of GDP between 1980 and 1997. The growth was more dramatic for financial corporations, where the debt went from 3 percent to 17 percent.[23] As noted earlier, some of this debt was used to move capital to other nations. Since the mid-1980s, the growth of U.S. direct investment abroad (which involves having at least a 5 percent interest in a firm) has increased faster than comparable investment in the United States.[24] Also during the 1980s, there was the rise in so-called junk bonds, which involved lending at very high rates of interest to risky ventures that did not have much in the way of collateral. Finally, much of corporate debt has been used to finance mergers. Between 1980 and 1997, U.S. non-financial firms spent $3 trillion on buyouts of one sort or another.[25] Records in the value of mergers are set year after year. In 1997, for example, that value was $828 billion, eclipsing the record of $626 billion set the previous year according to a report from Securities Data Company.[26] If one were to add the money borrowed for these mergers to the money paid out for stock dividends and interest, non financial-firms' distribution of funds to financiers was 5 percent more than their capital expenditures between 1985 and 1997. These funds were simply plowed back into the stock market, which contributed to the rise of stock prices but not production (more about that later).[27]

It should also be noted that a considerable amount of debt was acquired in the 1990s in order to invest in the stock market. A number of analysts, including the chairman of the Federal Reserve, Alan Greenspan, expressed great concern about this because a sharp adjustment in the stock market could lead to massive debt default. What is important to note, however, is that credit expansion drove up stock prices. During the 1990s, margin debt of New York Stock Exchange members, which is the money they borrowed to buy stocks, increased from about $50 billion to over $270 billion.[28] This happened despite the fact that since the mid-1970s investors were required to put down half of the initial cost of buying a stock. The size of margin debt accelerated in the latter half of the 1990s. It was estimated that between 1995 and 1999, margin debt of New York Stock Exchange members as a percent of their stocks' market value increased by 190 percent. The growth of debt incurred through online brokers was even more staggering—459 percent during the same period.[29] Using the Standard and Poor 500 Index, it is also believed that the rise in debt margin is outpaced by the rise in stock prices. Margin debt as a percentage of total consumer debt increased from 7 percent to over 16 percent. Between October 1999 and February 2000 alone, margin debt soared by $83 billion. That is more than the book value of the equity capital of the ten largest investment firms in the United States.[30] The fall in stock prices in response to possible recession has put the rise of margin debt on hold. But it is nonetheless a part of the credit expansion that jumpstarted and sustains the new world order.

The Destruction of Claims on Value

Workers need to purchase goods and services that are a prerequisite to self-development—food, housing, clothing, health care, education. These create claims on the value they produce that conflict with capital's need for surplus value to keep the system going. Moreover, there are social claims on value that include environmental cleanup, social services like public education, and entitlements that maintain a basic standard of living for those who are unable to work. There are public claims on value for public health and safety. And there are claims generated by the cost of military forces and weapons. During a crisis the conflict between these claims and the need to accumulate surplus value becomes very great. And in order to begin again with a new mode of accumulation, some of the claims from the old order must be destroyed. War is one path to the destruction of value. So is an economic depression, which destroys businesses and puts workers on the street. But war and depression can be system-threatening. The Fordist period was ushered in with the cataclysms of both depression and two world wars. And these crises did pose a threat to world capitalism.

The new world order could only come into being with a similar destruction of claims on value. But this time the mechanism was quite different. The costs of production were cheapened by moving capital and by limiting the ability of labor organizations or governments to resist. In the United States, the post–World War II deal with labor to trade labor peace for a share of world capitalism's surplus was brought to an abrupt halt. It came in two ways. One was an out-and-out attack on labor. In the United States, the opening round came in the early days of the Reagan administration. Air traffic controllers who were forced to work long, stressful hours under frightful conditions began organizing and demanding a better deal. Ultimately they went on strike, which was forbidden by special federal government laws. President Reagan refused to bargain and fired everyone, replacing them initially with military controllers and then training new employees. This action broke an informal, yet critical part of the postwar deal. No one was supposed to replace striking workers permanently. When President Reagan did, he gave a signal that the practice was now politically acceptable. And corporations from that point on began to replace their workers routinely.

Second, the industrialized nations, led by the United States, began to move their capital into places or other kinds of economic activity where costs were cheaper. These relocations were initially within the United States itself from unionized high-wage areas in the North to the South and Southwest, but eventually moved out of the United States altogether.[31] Factories and mines were closed wholesale. It has been estimated that in the 1970s, the United States lost 30 million jobs to capital mobility. And in the 1980s, the loss was from 1.5 to 2 million jobs a year.[32] Furthermore, this massive job loss ultimately meant that workers suffered a loss of income.[33] Eventually, much manufacturing production in the United States departed to other nations. Between 1966 and 1986, the U.S. share of manufacturing exports fell from 17 percent to 11 percent, while the share of foreign affiliates of U.S. corporations rose from 8 percent to 10 percent. Also, U.S. direct investment abroad has been outpacing U.S. investment in the United States.[34] It is hard to measure the net effect of this in a comprehensive way. But anecdotal evidence suggests that globally labor costs have been cheapened. For example, General Motors opened up a new plant in Mexico in order to expand production of their sport utility vehicle. The new Mexican facility was state of the art and productivity was as high or higher than at U.S. plants. But Mexican workers were paid $1.54, while U.S. workers got $18.96 per hour. After the move, the sticker price of the GM Suburban actually increased by 10 percent.[35] Then there is Nike corporation and its famous traveling sneaker. This corporation has consistently moved its production from nation to nation in response to demands from workers for living wages. It went from Japan in 1967, to South Korea and Taiwan in 1972, to China and Thailand in 1986, to Vietnam in 1994. Each time workers began to organize, Nike moved to yet a lower cost area.[36] Moving capital in this manner would be pointless if it did not result in the expropriation of more surplus. What is more, the mobility of capital also began to give U.S.-based companies an edge since they could and have threatened to move if their workforce would not work on their terms.[37] While incomes of poor people and even middle-income people in the United States declined or stagnated between the early 1970s and late 1990s, some people became very rich. I argue later that the rise of the fortunes of rich people throughout the world, not just in the United States, is in part the result of the acquisition of fictitious capital through speculation. My point here is that deindustrialization and the attack on labor in the United States contributed to the lowering of global social wage. And a similar thing began to happen in other developed nations.

Furthermore, as workers in these nations began to flounder, their political leaders shut the door on their claims to the global surplus value by cutting government spending. President Reagan and British Prime Minister Thatcher enforced austerity on their nations' workers by cutting social spending. Programs in housing, education, health care, and public welfare—programs that had been a part of the deal with labor in the 1940s—were gutted. And the carnage didn't end with Reagan and Thatcher. All subsequent administrations followed suit under various pseudonyms—"a contract with America," "reinventing government," "a third way."

Global credit expansion and the destruction of claims on value in the developed world established the necessary groundwork for a fuller implementation of the new world order. But the success of the strategy could not be complete without the participation of the developing world. Colonialism was over. As the newly independent nations struggled for independence, new forms of control were sought to make them a part of the evolving new world order. It started when the industrialized nations and their bankers spread money throughout the developing world and the major multinational corporations began to build production facilities and export platforms there. But as that was about to take off, the evolving new world order suffered a major setback in the form of a debt repayment crisis.

A Bump in the Road and an Opportunity

As the capitalist world began to recover from the deep recession of the mid-1970s, another shock came in the form of a second OPEC oil crisis. In 1979, OPEC nations again decided to gain higher prices for their oil by withholding production, and oil prices spiked once again. In the United States, France, Great Britain, and Italy, oil prices touched off another round of general price inflation. And as the increased prices lowered the demand for products, these countries plunged back into a recession, experiencing simultaneous inflation and unemployment. The response of the United States was to increase interest rates to stifle inflation. By 1981, the U.S. Federal Reserve had pushed interest rates up more than 60 percent over the 1977 level.[38] Some U.S. interest rates were over 20 percent. The high interest rates, while dampening inflation in the United States, drove the economy into a deep recession.

But it did not stop at the borders of the United States. As high interest rates and subsequent unemployment choked off the demand for the world's products, prices began to fall. The price of oil collapsed. While in the previous crisis of the mid-1970s, the recession was limited to the industrialized nations, this time the crisis spilled over into the developing world. The reason had everything to do with the lending frenzy that had preceded the most recent collapse. Developing nations were vulnerable in three ways now. The only way these nations could pay off their loans was to use revenues from exports. But the deep crisis in the industrialized nations, which had been buying these exports, meant that the markets for the products of developing nations were collapsing. As prices for their products collapsed along with demand, export revenues slowed to a trickle. Second, with interest rates so high in the United States, money from all over the world began to flow there to take advantage of the high returns. That meant that some flowed out of the developing world. This, in addition to the drastic drop in exports, meant that the demand for the currencies of the developing world also collapsed and a devaluation ensued. A devaluation in a nation dependent on the outside world for many products means that many things are suddenly very expensive. So inflation began to cut into the purchasing power of the people of the developing world. And the economies of these nations were thus plunged into deep recession accompanied by high inflation. To make matters worse, these nations were forced to pay higher interest rates on their flexible rate loans. As a result, the payments on these loans went sky high.

This turn of events plunged already poor nations into desperate poverty. Millions of people were without work and without homes and many starved. But what got the attention of the industrialized nations and their international banks was the wave of debt defaults that ensued. In August 1982, Mexico, which had been paying off massive loans with oil revenues, announced that it would have to default. Other big borrowers—Brazil, Argentina, Yugoslavia, Romania, and India—followed suit. And numerous small impoverished nations—Ghana, Zaire, Bolivia, Peru, Bangladesh, Sri Lanka, Somalia—also became insolvent.

The cost of the debt crisis in terms of human suffering in the developing world was enormous. But for the industrialized nations, despite creditor concerns about default, the crisis presented an opportunity. The threat of debt default offered a wedge through which some aspects of the vision of a new world order could be institutionalized. Expanded credit, mobile capital, and cheapened production costs could now become part of the economic development program of developing nations. The mechanism used was to offer "bridge loans" to insolvent nations through the International Monetary Fund. These loans enabled these nations to make their debt payments. The credit crunch in the United States and other developed nations was thus offset by a credit expansion in the developing world, enabling the emerging system as a whole to be sustained by credit even when some parts of the system were raising interest rates.

Moreover, in return for the bridge loans, the IMF imposed a number of conditions that amounted to wholesale restructuring of entire national economies. These conditions, known as structural adjustment programs (SAPs), did not come out of the blue. As noted above, there had been some earlier experimentation in Chile. The mid-1970s Chilean stabilization package included devaluation of the Chilean peso, privatization, and an end to price supports. It also refocused the economy toward exports and removed trade barriers. These provisions were replicated in the later IMF structural adjustment programs.

Another predecessor to these programs was far less dramatic than the Chilean coup, but nonetheless provided an important set of building blocks for the emerging new world order. In the late 1970s, the World Bank had identified four Asian economies—Hong Kong, South Korea, Singapore, and Taiwan—as models for economic development. They were given the designation of "newly industrialized countries" (NICs). Their rapid growth rates and rising export economies also earned them the nickname of the "Asian Tigers." By 1978, these four economies, along with Brazil, Mexico, and India, accounted for 70 percent of the manufacturing exports from the developing world.[39] In

1979, the former U.S. secretary of defense during the Vietnam War, Robert McNamara, announced a major policy shift on the part of the World Bank. McNamara was now the bank's president. At a meeting of the United Nations Conference on Trade and Development (UNCTAD), McNamara called on poorer developing nations to emulate the economic development policies of the NICs and announced that the World Bank would play a role in helping them do so. Developing nations throughout Africa and Latin America were the target for the World Bank's new venture. They were designated as "less developed countries" (LDCs), and the idea was for them to become NICs. In the past the World Bank had been the source of major development loans that were focused on infrastructure—highways, dams, and the like. The "plan of action" announced by World Bank President McNamara proposed "structural adjustment loans" (SALs) that would focus on major export sectors of LDCs and be conditioned on policies focused on the development of export markets, liberalized trade, privatization, and reduced public-sector expenditures. One of the first SALs was awarded to the Marcos government in the Philippines. The $200 million loan was focused on the Philippine industrial sector.

It was in this context that the IMF responded to the debt crisis with its own version of the World Bank's SALs. In 1982 the IMF instituted its "extended fund facilities," which were ten year, highly conditioned bridge loans. In 1982 the IMF granted twenty loans in excess of $50 million each. Twelve of these went to the LDCs that had been designated by the World Bank as potential NICs.[40] What is important to note here is that two key Bretton Woods Institutions, the World Bank and the IMF, had begun to change their mission in the wake of the collapse of the Bretton Woods Agreement. The World Bank had been created to provide long-term development loans for the rebuilding needed after World War II. The IMF was created to maintain fixed currency exchange rates through short-term adjustment loans. Now these institutions had become a key vehicle for opening the developing world to the program of the new world order. By the end of the 1980s, seventy-five countries in Africa, Asia, Latin America, the Caribbean, and Eastern Europe had received more than $41 billion and 187 loans from the World Bank and IMF that were conditioned with structural adjustment programs.[41] The debt repayment crisis was a bad bump on the road to a new mode of accumulation. But the U.S. government, the IMF, and the World Bank turned that bump into an opportunity.

Institutionalizing a New Mode of Accumulation

SAPs, the conditions for both IMF extended fund facilities and World Bank structural adjustment loans, are a part of the institutional structure of the global economy. SAPs vary from one nation to another, but tend to have some common elements.[42] A typical SAP from IMF includes two phases. The first is a stabilization phase, which is a program of severe austerity. Stabilization nearly always includes currency devaluation, which makes exports cheaper so the nation can gain revenues to pay off loans. But it also makes imports expensive, thus causing domestic inflation that cuts real wages. The practice of indexing wages to inflation is also outlawed so that wages are contained. Price supports and subsidies are eliminated so that the nation's products compete on the basis of world prices. Internal credit is often restricted. Government budgets must be balanced, which is generally done by cutting social programs. Once the stabilization program is in place, the second phase of structural reform is instituted. Reforms include the removal of tariffs and other barriers to trade, removal of barriers to the flow of capital in and out of the nation, and privatization of state enterprise. Development is then focused on export industries that can earn foreign exchange to pay off the loans. These programs have such a harsh effect on the populace that force is sometimes required to contain social movements against them. Thus, human rights and labor rights abuses are common. Negative effects on the environment due to the single-minded push on developing an export sector are also common.

The point of SAPs, in addition to paying back loans, is to open the developing world to foreign investment. As I argued earlier, this meets the objective of cheapening the costs of production, thus reducing claims on value. The rise of SAPs should be seen in conjunction with the expansion of credit and the destruction of living wage manufacturing jobs in the developed nations. They are a significant part of the institutionalization of the new world order.

The process of institutionalization also included the promotion of so-called free trade agreements. This development began in 1986 when negotiations over the restructuring of a third Bretton Woods institution, the GATT, began. The GATT was created as part of the Bretton Woods Agreement in order to facilitate trade among the nations of Europe, the United States, and Canada. Originally, the GATT had only eight members who met to establish a set of general guidelines that would be the basis for bilateral trade negotiations. Over the years, the membership of the GATT grew to include many of the nations of the world. These additions included new rounds of GATT negotiations, not only to add new members, but to agree on increasingly complex issues that came with new partners. Through seven rounds of GATT negotiations, however, the basic structure of the association remained unchanged. It was still a forum to seek consensus about the basic features of trade among nations. Its focus was primarily on tariffs and quotas on the goods that were being traded among its members. Enforcement of rules could only happen through consensus. Formal trade agreements were bilateral—nation to nation.

But the eighth round of GATT negotiations, known as the Uruguay Round, marked a sharp departure. A sweeping transformation of the GATT was proposed. By 1995, these negotiations resulted in a new organization, the WTO, which is charged with enforcing a broad set of global regulations. Majority vote rather than consensus makes these rules enforceable. Members, who now include 135 nations with thirty-two nations having observer status, can challenge the trade practices of one another. A panel of three "trade experts," whose deliberations are closed, adjudicates charges of rule violations. GATT rules are greatly expanded by including a variety of "non-tariff barriers to trade" that impact domestic food safety laws, product standards, and investment policy.

The GATT negotiations, involving so many nations, were contentious and many specific proposals governing investment, agriculture, and trade in services were voted down. These were taken up, however, in more limited bilateral and multilateral venues. In 1989, the United States entered into a bilateral agreement with Canada known as the Canadian-U.S. Free Trade Agreement (CUFTA). It was signed despite a vigorous opposition campaign from a coalition of Canadian trade unions, environmentalists, women, and human rights activists known as Action Canada. CUFTA contained many of the elements that were included in the negotiations for the WTO. After the signing of the CUFTA, President George H. Bush presented publicly in July 1990 his vision of a new world order that would proceed initially throughout the hemisphere with his "Enterprise for the Americas Initiative." Indicating that Mexico would be the next step, he initiated negotiations among the United States, Canada, and Mexico for NAFTA.

Negotiations for NAFTA concluded in 1993 and the agreement was signed by all three nations in 1994. This time there had been vigorous opposition from coalitions in all three nations. President Clinton, who defeated Bush and assumed office in 1992, never missed a beat in the pursuit of the vision of a new world order. He concluded the negotiations and made a series of deals with different factions to push NAFTA through Congress. The terms of NAFTA are important to understand because they were the most comprehensive institutionalization of the new world order to date.

Half of NAFTA's thousand-page text is devoted to tariff schedules—size of tariffs and a calendar for reduction—for individual products. The rest of it is a set of global rules that contain many of the elements of the IMF and World Bank SAPs. A key rule used throughout the document is the concept of "national treatment" that makes it illegal for a nation to give special treatment to any of its domestic firms. Thus, it is impossible to use subsidies, domestic buying regulations, marketing restrictions, or any other measures as an industrial policy to achieve domestic economic development objectives. Conversely, it is a way to open nations to foreign corporations, making capital on an international scale more mobile. There are also "rules of origin" provisions that specify for every single product traded a percentage of value of total output that has to be produced inside the area. The different percentages for different products reflect the prevailing political interests of various industries. What this does in practice is to allow large global corporations to source components of their product outside the three-nation area, to make it cheaper to produce and still qualify for NAFTA benefits when they sell it in North America or when they want to move some parts of the production process within the NAFTA region. NAFTA also limits the use of food safety standards by forcing advocates of high standards to prove that they are not needlessly denying market access.

A major innovation in NAFTA is detailed rules dealing with investment and financial services that deregulate flows of capital within the region. It is illegal to give inducements to investors to purchase from local suppliers. It is also illegal to require that businesses that operate locally have some minimum local ownership. There are bans on any local economic development strategy that is exclusively directed toward corporations that are locally or nationally owned. Restrictions on what any corporations can do with their investments are illegal. Among the prohibitions on the list of illegal performance requirements is the practice of using subsidies to promote the development of particular industries within the nation and local purchasing requirements to increase locally produced content. It is illegal to require restrictions on the transfer of profits out of the country by requiring corporations to hold a portion of revenues or retained earnings in national banks. There are very strict rules governing the expropriation of foreign investments that enable corporations to mount legal challenges to practices that they perceive restrict their profits. This includes real sanctions that enable corporations to sue governments. There are similar provisions governing the activity of banks and other financial service firms, including a ban on rules that might prevent or discourage speculators from rapidly moving portfolio investments in and out of nations.

The expansion of these basic features of NAFTA, built on the earlier efforts to institutionalize the terms of the new world order in Chile, SAPs, and the WTO, continues. As I write this, negotiations are well under way to expand the scope of the WTO and to turn NAFTA into a "Free Trade Agreement of the Americas" (FTAA). The FTAA would include the remaining nations of the hemisphere (except Cuba) in an agreement to include the basic provisions of NAFTA while expanding directions of investment and financial services liberalization and the trade in services generally. The terms of SAPs, NAFTA, and the WTO all promote an agenda of cheapening production costs through full capital mobility. Tremendous technological advances are supportive of this direction. Telecommunications, computer hardware and software, and transportation technologies make these changes feasible and give them momentum.

Consolidation: Credit as a "Permanent" Feature of the New World Order

The new world order is thus a strategy of capital accumulation that uses capital mobility to cheapen production costs and destroy claims on value. As the new system becomes institutionalized through SAPs and global "free trade" agreements, various features of the new world order act to consolidate it. Here credit continues to play a critical role. It has provided new but fictitious capital to make capital mobile and to open up markets that facilitate the cheapening of production. And it has financed related technological and institutional developments. But profits generated by credit are not a sustainable basis for ongoing capital accumulation unless they are gained through activity that employs and compensates human labor. Further, such profits are not sustainable unless the labor power used in the production process is compensated at wages that can sustain human life and that meet the needs of human self-development. This has not been the case. The new world order is a mode of accumulation that continues to destroy claims on value and cheapen the costs of production—particularly labor costs. Credit is being used to perpetuate a system that has become a vicious circle. Credit, in such a system, feeds upon itself. The new world order is not only jumpstarted with credit, it requires expanding credit to survive.

The system's ongoing need for expanded credit became evident in the United States during the economic slump of the late 1980s and early 1990s. At the time there was a collapse of a number of credit sources. One of these was the savings and loan industry, which became overextended with highly speculative loans. Another was the growing market for junk bonds (very risky instruments with high interest rates) and exotic derivatives, securities whose "prices are derived from the prices of other securities or even things."[43] High rolling financiers had been selling these bonds and derivatives, which were then used to finance highly questionable activities. Their high returns made them attractive to buyers. Orange County, California, was one of them. As many of the speculative ventures went down, the junk bond and derivative purchasers, including Orange County, and a few of the financiers went down with them. The New York Federal Reserve did a study of the economic downturn of the late 1980s and concluded that a credit crunch—especially the drying up of bank credit—was largely responsible.[44] In other words credit expansion needed a continuous flow of credit to hold up.

Evidence presented earlier also supports the view that credit needs more credit to sustain itself: the relation of debt to the rise in stock prices, the growth of consumer debt to meet life's necessities, and the growth in government debt as social services expenditures decline. Moreover, evidence that continually expanded credit is an integral part of the new world order is not limited to experience in the United States or the developed world. Debt in the developing world has also become an essential element in the ability of less developed and very poor nations to adhere to the new world order programs. The World Bank and the IMF have designated very poor nations who are deeply in debt "heavily indebted poor countries" (HIPC). The HIPC nations include much of Africa, Central America, and some countries in Latin America. Other LDCs that have high debt burdens include nations like Mexico, Brazil, and the Philippines. Between 1980 and 1997, the debt of both HIPC and LDC nations has increased from $580 billion to $2.2 trillion;[45] $387 billion of this debt is owed by the HIPC nations. The massive growth of debt in the developing world as a whole has been accumulated as these nations made nearly $3 trillion in debt payments. The payments on this debt have resulted in a net transfer of wealth from HIPC and LDC nations to the developed world. Over the past fifteen years, HIPC and LDC nations have paid $1.5 trillion more in debt service payments than they have received in the form of loans and investments. Debt has rolled over again and again. Mexico, for example, has had its debt "restructured" eight times since 1982. In the African nations, there have been over 8,000 debt renegotiations since 1980.[46]

Much of the face value of the debt is not repayable. That has given rise to a secondary market for debt itself, where private lenders package and sell debt at a price determined by what they think the new debt owner can collect. Each owner of debt gains a return from the payments made by the developing nation and from the sale of the debt to a new debt holder. This process was initiated in 1989 through a plan conceived by Nicholas Brady, who was then U.S. secretary of treasury. The private debt to twenty-nine LDC nations was written down through its conversion to so-called Brady bonds. The bonds were then traded in international markets. While this reduced the exposure of private lenders for debt incurred in the 1980s, they continued to extend credit to these nations in the 1990s by purchasing bonds issued on the international bond markets by individual nations. These bonds, like Brady bonds, are bought and sold by speculators.

Further Consolidation: Credit, Speculation, and the New World Order

Credit expansion has become a permanent feature of the new world order. This has caused an explosive growth of the finance industry and the potential profits that go with it. The critical role played by speculation in credit expansion and possibly even "Ponzi finance" is part of what makes ongoing credit expansion a permanent feature of the new world order itself. Economist Hyman Minsky argued that there are essentially three types of credit structures: hedged, speculative, and Ponzi.[47] A hedged structure means that the interest and principal due on a debt can be paid for out of current income. Most home mortgages or car loans, for example, are financed this way. You take out a loan and allocate a portion of your income to pay it off each month. If a corporation or a nation is able to meet both principal and interest obligations out of income or current revenues, the debt structure is "hedged." A speculative structure means that while you can pay off interest out of your income (or current revenues if you are a government), you need to raise additional money to pay off principal. As an individual, that might mean you would have to get a huge raise, sell some assets, or take out another loan to meet these obligations. If you get behind in your mortgage payments, for example, you might have to sell your car or go to some credit institution, which (at a very high price) will give you a loan to consolidate and begin to pay off your debts. Applying that to a national economy or to the international capitalist system, a speculative debt structure means new loans to pay off old ones. Ponzi finance is another matter. Minksy named this practice after a con man named Charles Ponzi. He would seek out investors and promise them big returns on some phony investment scheme. Since the scheme was fictitious, Ponzi could pay the investors off only if he found a second group of investors who agreed to invest an even larger amount. He used the second group's "investment" to pay off the first group (after taking a handsome profit for himself). The scam went on until he ran out of shills. In Minky's notion of a Ponzi credit structure, there is no income or even assets to pay off debt. Its repayment is fully dependent on finding new sources of money. This framework offers a useful way to look at the use of credit extension as a mechanism to both jumpstart and maintain the new world order.

The ongoing development of a new world order has moved the global credit structure to the brink of a Ponzi finance scam. The new world order is fueled by a credit system that is at minimum highly speculative in nature. Rapid expansion of debt gave rise to an acceleration in the business of buying and selling the debt itself. The development of a secondary market for private debt owed by developing nations is one example. But trading debt is now common with many other kinds of assets. A very large part of the business is U.S. government debt. U.S. government bonds (which mature anywhere between ten and thirty years), U.S. government notes (one to ten years), and T bills (three months to one year) are issued regularly by the federal government at various rates of interest. Their value to a purchaser is based on how much income in interest rate payments they will yield over the life of the asset. They are also valued because there is no risk of default. The U.S. government guarantees them. But holding these assets until they mature does not generate the big profits. Trading debt-based securities in a secondary market makes the most money. There is a secondary market for this debt because big players want safe havens to park their money as the yield and risk on alternative investments fluctuate. So U.S. government debt tends to be bought and sold. In fact, the average holding period of U.S. Treasury paper (bonds, notes, and bills) is only one month. Other kinds of debt instruments, not only foreign debt but U.S. municipal and state bonds, corporate bonds, foreign currencies, and home mortgages, are traded on the same principle. These developments have been extended to include so-called derivatives, financial "products" whose value is derived from the value of other things. Trading "futures" on government debt—a contract for a bunch of bonds at some future date or options to buy in the future—is an example. These developments can be illustrated by looking at the operations of two venerable Chicago institutions: the Chicago Board of Trade (CBOT) and the Chicago Mercantile Exchange (the Merc). Both the CBOT and the Merc underwent dramatic changes in response to the collapse of the Bretton Woods Agreement and the birth of a new world order.[48]

The CBOT was founded in 1848 as a grain exchange where buyers and sellers could come together in a reasonably orderly fashion. The impetus for the exchange was the wild fluctuations in prices due to the vagaries of weather, the ability of farmers to get their commodities to the markets, and the availability of storage facilities. When supplies were low, prices would skyrocket. A glut of grain could cause prices to plummet. CBOT, like similar exchanges in other places, formed because farmers, grain storage operators, and grain users like bakers and millers (known as hedgers) needed a way to guarantee a stable price. Others (speculators) were willing to take on the risks of the hedgers by speculating on future prices of grain. The hedgers accepted the possibility of receiving less for their grain by selling or buying it before it actually came to market. By buying these "futures," the speculators bet that the price at that future time would be more than they paid for it and that they could sell their grain futures at a higher price and make money. The CBOT continued to grow by trading commodity futures for more than a century. Their major competitor in Chicago was the Merc, which started in 1850 by trading butter, eggs, onions, and pork bellies (bacon).

But the expansion of debt beginning in the late 1970s and its trading also created a market for financial derivatives. All of this growing financial activity brought with it high risks. Bonds, notes, T-bills, and mortgages had become a way to hold on to capital until it was needed for some other venture. Trading these assets was also a way to make the money price value of that capital grow over time. But investors needed a way to limit the risk of not gaining a specified rate of return on these investments when they wanted or needed to sell them. Similarly, transnational corporations with operations around the world had to hold foreign currencies and they needed to know what those currencies would be worth when they purchased or sold things in foreign markets. In short, in the financial world of the late 1970s, there was a demand by financial hedgers for a degree of certainty in the returns they could expect on their holdings. And just as the speculators had stepped forward in the agricultural sector a century ago, financial speculators were available to meet the needs of the new world order.

The financial derivatives markets brought hedgers and speculators together. Exchanges like the CBOT and the Merc served as a clearinghouse to make sure the buyers and sellers met all their obligations. Initially, the derivatives traded at CBOT and the Merc were futures or options on different forms of debt. A speculator would be willing to sell a contract on a batch of a particular type of debt at a specific price to be delivered at a specified date in the future (a bunch of U.S. Treasury bonds, for example). The speculator did not have to own the bonds. He or she was only selling a contract—a promise to deliver the bonds at a particular price on a particular date. If the contract was not offset somehow, however, the speculator was still obligated to deliver the bonds. An oversimplified view of this process is one in which the buyers of the futures want to make sure that they know they can get the bonds at a known price on a particular date. In practice, few of these contracts are ever really delivered because the hedgers are using these markets for insurance purposes. As their physical commitments of bonds (or grains, or even Swiss francs) are satisfied, they lift their hedges in the futures market by taking an opposite position (if they were buying they sell or vice versa), which closes out the hedge. They have no need to take delivery of the product; they only want the price insurance that the hedge offers. The speculator, on the other hand, buys or sells futures contracts because she or he believes that the market is too high or too low for anticipated economic conditions. The speculator never expects to take delivery of anything, but plans on offsetting futures positions held prior to delivery even if it means losing money. Thus, the speculator takes risks in expectation of profit. Futures contracts are traded back and forth as the traders try to make (or lose) money out of thin air. In this world, the line between hedgers and speculators can get pretty fuzzy. If you are a really big-time player in this game, you can hedge some of your assets and speculate with the rest. In 1975, only 1.3 percent of CBOT contracts were in financial futures; the rest were agricultural commodities. By 1980, financial futures' percentage of CBOT contracts had risen to nearly 20 percent. The following year finance jumped to over a third of all CBOT business, and by 1985, the volume of trading was over two-thirds. Today finance constitutes over 80 percent of CBOT business.

The Merc had a similar metamorphosis. It had floundered as a butter and egg outfit and, by 1960, was in danger of extinction. Their recovery and meteoric rise came when President Nixon took the U.S. dollar off the gold standard in 1971. At this point international currency speculators began to purchase German marks and Japanese yen, driving the exchange rate of the dollar down. But the rules of the Bretton Woods Agreement called for exchange rates to remain fixed and pegged to the dollar. West Germany and Japan were thus forced to sell their own currencies for dollars. By the middle of 1971, Germany and Japan held over $24 billion.[49] The situation was chaotic. World trade and the emerging regime of mobile capital needed some certainty in exchange rates. Yet the economic crisis and the declining political and economic strength of U.S. capital meant that legislated fixed exchange rates were not sustainable. Conservative University of Chicago economist Milton Friedman, who had played a key role in the economy of Pinochet's Chile, also had an essential role in instituting a regime of floating exchange rates. Along with Merc directors he advised President Nixon to cancel the Bretton Woods, releasing a paper that made the case for floating exchange rates.[50] Days after President Nixon cancelled the Bretton Woods Agreement, the Merc launched its International Monetary Market in which the value of currencies could be determined through the relationship of hedgers and speculators.

Since these not so humble beginnings, the trading of financial instruments and derivatives has become an exploding industry.[51] The products being traded at the CBOT and the Merc and throughout the world have grown in numbers and in complexity. The relative compostion of different kinds of contracts has changed. Currency trading at the Merc, for example, has diminished in importance. The creation of the Euro made trading in European currencies less profitable. At the same time, the creation of these futures markets has give rise to big-time speculators whose selective purchase and sale of particular currencies in calculated time frames can and has altered their exchange rates as huge amounts of money enter and leave nations. In addition, both the Merc and CBOT have developed new "products." There are futures markets, for example, on stock indices like the S&P 500. Buyers of an S&P 500 future are likely to be also trading stocks but hedging their risk in the stock market by taking an opposite position in an index. The index is a number that shows the relative growth or decline of a bunch of stocks, and has no actual value in and of itself. But there are "index funds" that create a physical portfolio of stocks that mirrors the index. Such funds will perform identically to the index. For this reason a stock index future is a perfect hedge for stock investors who are nervous about the future of their stock portfolios. The value of the index is derived from the value of the fund. There are all sorts of derivatives like this. And there are always the speculators who make money buying and selling "products" like this that are not really products and that they don't really own.

Such activity has carried far beyond the exchange floors of the CBOT and the Merc. What we are talking about is the explosion of a very old but in some ways new industry in the buying and selling of fictitious capital. Its growth in the 1990s alone can be seen in terms of the amount of U.S. dollars exchanged through banks each day. In 1987, that amount was $600 billion. By 1998, the amount had risen to nearly $1.5 trillion.[52] Its huge growth was initially a by-product of the new world order, but it is rapidly becoming the means to sustain it. And we are talking about an industry that has moved from its impetus— bringing together hedgers and speculators—to the realm of pure speculation. In the terms of Minsky's model, we have moved, at a minimum, beyond a hedged credit structure to one based on speculation and perhaps to full Ponzi finance.

The expansion of credit, the trade of the resulting debt paper, and the subsequent expansion of derivative markets have fueled other types of speculation. Stock market activity is one of them. In the developed nations of the world, the value of stock assets is, on average, 81 percent of GDP.[53] In the United States the figure is 116 percent. In the LDCs, that percentage now stands at 37 percent, but it is growing very rapidly. And in some LDCs it is already huge. In Malaysia, South Africa, Taiwan, the Philippines, Chile, and Thailand, stock market capitalization as a percentage of GDP is 310 percent, 191 percent, 105 percent, 96 percent, 89 percent, and 54 percent, respectively. Even with the fall of stock prices in the early millennium years, these prices in the United States are far above their historical levels, and there is evidence to support the view that the present level is built on speculation and cannot be sustained.[54] The run-up in U.S. stock prices in the 1990s was unprecedented, far surpassing the price run-up prior to the Great Depression of 1929.[55] The U.S. stock market does not finance corporate capital expenditures. That was its original purpose. But that has not been the case for some time.[56] Payouts to stock and bond holders in the form of dividends and interest and gains from buybacks were in fact 5 percent greater than the firms' capital expenditures between 1985 and 1997. These payouts went mostly back into the stock market and have become a factor in stock price rises. Similar to the credit markets, most of the trading in the stock market involves people buying and selling old shares of stock rather than buying to become an owner of a particular corporation.

Obviously if so much trading is being done with old shares of stocks, people must be making money doing it. They are making money because the price of the shares keeps going up. In theory the prices should reflect what the non-financial corporations—those that make products, which people use—are doing. Price of stock should depend on what profits might be expected from these corporations. Yet that does not seem to be the case. The stock market is getting farther and farther away from the real economy. What seems to be driving the price of stocks is simply the expectation of investors that other investors will keep buying and driving up prices (or not). In addition, there is evidence that many major corporations are making a substantial portion of their profits not by selling their products and services but by purchasing the stock of other corporations. These profits made by speculating in the stock markets and credit markets make their own stocks look good to other speculators and drive their stock prices up. In January 2000, Intel Corporation made a gain of $327 million in stock trading that boosted earnings for the quarter above predicted levels. In response, its stock jumped 13 percent.[57] Similar stories were reported about Microsoft, Compaq, America On Line, Wells Fargo, Chase Manhattan Corporation, Coca-Cola, General Electric, and Delta Airlines. While some intercorporate buying is justifiable if a firm does so to gain a foothold in strategic sections of its industry, worried analysts claim that increasingly the motive is profits through trading. An analyst for a major securities firm was quoted in the *Wall Street Journal* in response to Intel's stock increase: "If the market deteriorates, Intel's earnings will as well. Intel's earnings are dependent on the continued strong performance of the stock market."[58] One analysis of the situation reported in the same article found that 124 firms in the Standard and Poor's 500 stock index had profit gains through stock trading. Without these gains the S&P 500 would have been 3 percent lower than the level reported in the fall of 1999. Stock prices boosting stock prices means that speculation is feeding on itself.

Feeding the New World Order: A Ponzi Scam?

It is clear that the new world order has an insatiable need for a system of continuously expanding credit and that speculation makes this possible. But has
the system as a whole become a global Ponzi scam? It is really hard to say. Let's
just take the case of mortgages. The question we would have to answer is this:
Is the value of and income from the real estate that is mortgaged sufficient to
pay off the money price value of the packaged mortgages and derivatives tied
to these mortgages that are floating around the nation and around the world? If
it isn't, then the mortgage credit structure could be classified as Ponzi using
Minsky's typology. But the question is hard to answer because it would be
difficult to fix a price on all the instruments tied to mortgages. The various
prices are in a state of constant flux. Now, consider the fact there are many
many different species of credit. In addition to mortgages, there are consumer
debt instruments like credit cards; stocks; government bonds, notes, and T-
bills; corporate bonds; and foreign currencies. All of these are being traded
and their money price value on the market varies from day to day, hour to
hour, minute to minute. Then there are the related derivative "products"—
futures, options, swaps, floors, collars, swaptions. And there is the ongoing
development of new credit and derivative "products" like junk bonds, options
on futures, tuition futures, zero-coupon convertible debt, commodity-linked
bonds, exchangeable remarketed preferred stock, foreign currency denomi-
nated bonds, interest rate futures, futures on notes and futures on swaps, and
on and on and on![59] Who knows how far this structure of credit has moved
from the functioning of that part of the economy that actually makes things
or even offers services to people?

Some have called all of this a huge speculative bubble. But to me it more
like a giant iceberg that remains largely hidden beneath a sea of frantic financial activity. From time to time little pieces of the giant chip off and float
to the surface and we get a peek at what may be going on. The U.S. savings and loan collapse in the 1980s was a piece of the iceberg. So was the
Asian financial crisis that began in 1997 when the Thai bhat (the national
currency) collapsed, sparking inflation, capital flight, decline of real wages,
rising interest rates, and unemployment not only in Thailand but throughout
Asia that threatened to spread to the entire global economy. Another piece
of the iceberg surfaced on September 18, 1998, at 7:30 A.M. At that moment
some of biggest financial players in the world gathered for an emergency meeting at the New York Federal Reserve Bank. In addition to representatives of
the Fed there were executives from such firms as Goldman-Sachs, Merrill-
Lynch, J.P. Morgan, Salomon, and Bear-Stearns. By the end of the day fourteen
major financial firms agreed to put up between $100 million and $350 million each—a staggering total of over $1.4 billion—to bail out a competitor
who had fallen on hard times. The failing firm was named Long Term Capital Management (LTCM), whose top consultants were University of Chicago

economists who had recently won Nobel prizes for their work in the investment field.[60]

LTCM was a "hedge fund." Such funds pool the capital of very rich people and use it as leverage to borrow money, which is used in turn to buy and sell the ever-growing range of financial products. In the United States today, there are roughly 1,000 hedge funds with combined capital assets of $100 billion, which are leveraged by a factor of anywhere between 5 and 20.[61] LTCM, however, was huge even by hedge fund standards. In 1995, they took their $4.8 billion in equity capital and leveraged it 27 times. With the proceeds they reportedly acquired an estimated $1.25 trillion in derivatives and another $120 billion in borrowed bonds. When the Asian crisis began to spread and Russia defaulted on its debt, LTCM lost over $550 million in a single day. At this point the investors made an assessment of LTCM's financial situation and concluded that even if they were suddenly to liquidate everything, there would probably not be enough money to pay everyone off. LTCM turned out to be a Ponzi game. Even worse, however, is that if they had to liquidate rapidly, the prices of various financial "products" would plunge to such an extent that it could have brought the new world order to an untimely end. The U.S. Federal Reserve Bank intervened, forcing the largest financial institutions to make good on LTCM's debts and forcing LTCM out of business.

So what does all of this add up to? Is the fuel of the new world order a big Ponzi scam or merely excessive speculation? Actually, it really doesn't matter. The S&L collapse, the Asian financial crisis, LTCM, and various debt default crises have all threatened to boomerang into the collapse of the entire new world order. That is why billions and billions of dollars are going to bail out the precipitating speculators. The contradictions of this system become more and more apparent every time a piece of the iceberg breaks off and there is some local collision. The local collisions of the new world order are generally reported in the media in terms of the misfortunes of one or more big players. A trader like a LTCM's Merriwhether does not, however, just bankrupt a few billionaires who get "ruined" to the extent that they are forced to live out their lives as mere millionaires. When big speculators buy and sell financial "products" and foreign currencies and there are bumps in the road, currencies are devalued, and prices for real products on which people depend on for survival collapse. Then millions of people starve or sink into unspeakable poverty. And the billions put up in the rescue package go to rescue the speculators and their system, not the victims.

Constructing a New World Order Infrastructure

Because the new world order has victims and because they are the vast majority of human beings on the planet, the continued existence of the new world order depends on the construction of an infrastructure to maintain it.

This infrastructure includes a military to keep the new world order orderly, the development of a network of economic interdependence, and both international and domestic public policies that are based on an ideology consistent with the aims of this new mode of accumulation. The construction of such an infrastructure presents the appearance of a system that is permanent. Military power, growing economic interdependence, and a dominant ideology expressed as public policy mediates what is "practical" and "reasonable" for those who are being victimized by its day-to-day operation as well as its excesses. Thus, this infrastructure serves not only to manage the operation of the new world order itself, but it also functions to place limits or boundaries on appropriate behavior on the part of those who organize to contest its terms.

It is important to note that the development of this infrastructure is not the outcome of an egalitarian political process. The new world order has produced some very powerful stakeholders who have shaped the debate over the direction of its evolution. Because the new world order must be fed a steady diet of speculation-generated credit, the interests of financiers are playing a huge role. And financiers are encompassing an ever- larger portion of world leaders. The division, for example, between financial and non-financial corporations is breaking down as so-called non-financial firms depend on the fruits of speculation for their own bottom line. And the expansion of the financial "products" and the players that use them means that even the number and scope of financial firms is growing relative to the "real" economy. Short of a long analysis of specific manifestations of this power, it is important to simply note that the need of the system for people to make money with money rather than through the direct exploitation of human labor power lends itself to a certain logic of infrastructure development. Making money with money means that capital must be mobile. And that means that it is necessary to begin to remove barriers to that mobility. Making money with money also means that inflation becomes a greater evil than unemployment. Making money with money means that returns on capital cannot be threatened by social welfare considerations like living wages, health care, and social safety nets. When organizers or even political leaders propose measures that threaten these needs, there are ominous predictions that "the markets will be unhappy and retaliate."

Of course, the markets boil down to people with a lot of political power. Some of that power is directed to domestic politics. The rise of so-called political action committees (PACs) in the United States is an example of this. It is interesting to note that as the Merc and the CBOT moved into financial futures, they began to actively work in the U.S. political arena. In 1973, a Merc membership letter threw down the gauntlet.

> We will oppose efforts to hamper free markets with all the legitimate tools at
> our disposal. . . . Until now, we have operated on the theory that discretion is the

better part of valor. We do have eyes and ears in Washington, and we do have friends whom we have used, in order to modify, remove and oppose restrictive measures.[62]

Three years later the Merc had assembled a fund of $137,000 for political contributions to dozens of Merc-friendly office seekers. In that same year the CBOT established their own Auction Markets Political Action Committee (AMPAC). While these actions were significant enough, the political presence of the exchanges would not be ignored. As one analyst points out, in Chicago alone, the exchanges rented in excess of one million square feet of space that paid over $2 million in taxes. And they handled over $500 million a day in margin funds that were deposited each night in Chicago banks. Multiply this by the multitude of financial players throughout the world and one can understand why political leaders do not want to "anger the markets."

The "markets," therefore, have had a lot to say about the shape of the new world order infrastructure. Since this infrastructure mediates the impact of new world order operations on people at a local level, it is important to examine some of its features. I have already looked at some of this when I described the nature of SAPs and "free trade" agreements. But in order to truly understand the nature of the local collisions that have resulted from the operation of the new world order, it is necessary to examine briefly a few additional features: militarism, economic interdependence, and public policy/ideology.

Militarism

The new world order requires order. Militarism serves that function. Yet the militarism serving the new world order is qualitatively different from that of previous eras. During the Fordist period, rapid growth and expansion in the developed capitalist world was based on mass production at home. Accumulation of capital was the product of domestic workers increasing their productivity and the exploitation of the natural resources of the developing world. It also required expanding markets for the products of a mass production society. During this era there was fierce competition for markets and raw materials among capitalist nations and between those nations and those in the orbit of the Soviet Union. Rising militarism in the capitalist world developed in that context. By the end of World War II, the United States had economic and military supremacy among developed capitalist nations. But that supremacy was threatened by the Soviet Union and later China. "Containing communism" was the basis of U.S. foreign policy and military policy; a similar stance was taken by the other capitalist powers. The North Atlantic Treaty Organization (NATO) was one result. Containing communism was not only ideological or even political. It was closely linked to capitalism's strategy for capital accumulation, which was threatened by the rise of Soviet influence.

But right on the heels of the collapse of the Bretton Woods Agreement, which officially put an end to the Fordist era, came the weakening and eventual collapse of the Soviet Union. The Berlin Wall fell in 1989 during the term of Ronald Reagan. In 1991, the Soviet Union collapsed during the term of George H. Bush. Yet military spending continued to climb, fueled by a series of "little wars" that has until now been the hallmark of the new world order. President Reagan had already increased military spending in the United States even after the Vietnam War. Between 1982 and 1986, military spending increased by 32 percent. Subsequent administrations did not really alter the dominant position of military spending in the U.S. federal budget. While the size of military expenditures declined to some extent beginning in 1990, human services spending also declined. And military spending still accounts for roughly half of U.S. federal government discretionary spending. Budget proposals and projections beginning with fiscal year 2000 would increase that percentage. The terrorist attack of September 11, 2001, has set off a new round of military spending. As I write this it is too early to tell exactly where the U.S. response will lead militarily.

But putting September 11 aside, and with the cold war officially at an end, why the persistence of military spending? Mobile capital needs a mobile military to make sure that local "instability" (or resistance) does not threaten the emerging markets of the new world order. Some of the "little wars" have been multilateral "peace keeping" actions while others have been unilateral invasions. Covert aid was given to the Taliban and other forces in Afghanistan during the Carter administration even before the Soviet invasion of 1979. President Reagan began a program of covert aid to topple an unfriendly regime in Nicaragua, a program that was continued by President Bush. Reagan also initiated invasions of Panama, Grenada, and Libya. President Bush sent troops into Somalia, the Balkans, and Iraq. President Clinton led an attack on Iraq once again and deployed troops in the Balkans, this time to Kosovo. He also sent "advisors" and military aid to Colombia. The so-called peace dividend for ending the cold war never materialized. And now as I write this there are military operations again in Afghanistan that will likely dominate U.S. budget priorities for some time to come. The new world order needs a military to keep markets open throughout the world and to protect interests in natural resources.

Global Economic Integration

Another part of the infrastructure of the new world order is the growing interdependence of nations. That is one of the impacts of capital mobility. Firms can now source raw materials, parts, and labor from many different geographical locations. The stronger interdependence becomes, the greater the changes in the notions of space, place, and time from the old system. What is significant about interdependence is that the old conceptions of space, place, and time had become the basis for strategies to contest the terms of the old order. Interdependence undermines these strategies. In the case of labor organizing, for example, firms can say that if you don't like the way things are here, we will simply close up your workplace and move elsewhere. Or if you push too hard for better wages and working conditions, you will be shooting yourself in the foot because we have to be competitive with Japan, Germany, and Korea. If you can't even get a job or are forced to work at low wages, the problem is not seen as having anything to do with class, race, or gender. The problem, many people will believe, is that you as an individual are not competitive with workers elsewhere.

One thing worth noting is that global economic interdependence is not uniform. Particular nations are more interdependent with some nations than others. The United States and Canada trade more heavily with each other than with a lot of other nations, for example. Similarly, certain industries are more international than others. The automobile industry, for example, is more international than processed food. A "U.S." car may consist of parts from many different nations. It may actually be assembled in several different nations. And the ownership of corporations that make "U.S." cars is increasingly international. This is not as true of food processing. Most of the chickens you buy in a U.S. supermarket were born, fed, and killed in the United States. And perpetrators of this cycle were most likely U.S. corporations and their workers. For this reason, it can be misleading to overgeneralize on the subject. You can't treat total global production as if everything looks like an automobile or a chicken.[63] But there are some measures that can give us an idea of the direction things are going.

One measure of interdependence is the relative importance of the trade of goods and services. There is no question that exporting goods and services to other countries and importing them from other countries is much more important than it was at the time of the collapse of the Bretton Woods Agreement. As we have seen, part of the post–Bretton Woods strategy has been to make nations depend more on trade. Structural adjustment programs were geared to forcing nations to shift their economies to emphasize exports and in turn open themselves up to goods and services from other nations. NAFTA and the WTO also are partly about increasing trade. Nations like Mexico, Bangladesh, Vietnam, El Salvador, and Honduras have become dependent on the "export platform" industry in which foreign firms use local labor to assemble all sorts of products and export them to other nations. Other poor nations depend on the export of a single product or a few products—often food or natural resources—for their survival. This means they are also dependent on wealthier nations and a handful of transnational corporations that have the power to influence the price of their export crops. The big "emerging market" nations like Korea, the Philippines, Mexico, and Brazil are building their economies on trade. And even highly developed nations like the United States are increasingly stressing trade as the motor of their economic development strategies. The numbers on trade reflect this reality. In 1973, trade in goods and services constituted about 12 percent of world output. By 1996, the percentage had increased to 24 percent.[64] Another change is that services have become a more important part of the trade mix. These include things such as tourism and travel, communications, advertising, legal services, financial services, and entertainment. In 1980, such services constituted about 18 percent of all the exports in the world. By 1996, the proportion had grown to over 20 percent.[65] This change has been particularly dramatic in the United States, where during the same time frame, services as a percentage of exports grew from 18 percent to nearly 30 percent.

A second indicator of economic integration is the flow of money from one place to another. Between 1977 and 1982, net capital flows from the United States to developing nations averaged $30.5 billion. The figure for the period between 1990 and 1995 was $129 billion.[66] It is a little harder to quantify total global capital flows because there are different kinds of flows that are measured and valued in different ways. And their application and impact is also uneven in different parts of the world. So the problem of generalizing is very great. But we can say that the flow of capital is increasingly important. Again, mobile capital is the keystone of the new world order strategy. SAPs and NAFTA have detailed rules that open up nations to capital flows. Between 1991 and 1996, there were close to 600 changes in national rules globally pertaining to foreign direct investment, and 95 percent of these changes made nations more open to this type of capital flow.[67] It has been estimated that foreign direct investment alone has been growing at about four times the rate of growth of the flow of goods or merchandise trade.[68] Because these flows involve money moving from one part of the world to another, these data are an indicator of increasing global economic integration.

One final indicator of global economic integration is the role being played by transnational corporations. Data in this area are not very good and so we are forced to rely on anecdotal evidence. The question is to what extent the world's economic activity has become dominated by the activities of a relatively few corporations who are truly global rather than national corporations. This question has to be examined from a number of different angles. One of these is simply the growth of transnational corporations. In 1970, there were 7,000 non-financial firms that were considered by the United Nations to be transnational. Today there are 60,000 such corporations with 800,000 affiliates all over the world.[69] The top 200 of these firms had sales that amounted to over a quarter of the value of world output. Transnational corporations manage about 75 percent of the trade in manufacturing goods.[70] Financial corporations also operate globally. The top 100 global banks have combined assets of over $21 trillion, which is equal to the value of about 75 percent of total world output. All of this suggests that corporations that operate outside their own national boundaries are doing a lot of the world's business and their ranks are growing.

Another way to assess the role played by transnational corporations in global economic integration is to look at evidence of global assembly lines, where corporations take pieces of their products from different parts of the world and bring them together for assembly in specific locations. There is a lot of anecdotal evidence that this is happening in some industries. I already mentioned the automobile industry. There really are "world cars." But it is unclear how many firms or even industries really operate this way. There is evidence that many transnational corporations cooperate with each other through a variety of licensing and joint venture agreements.[71] There is also evidence of the common use of different countries as "export platforms." This is where foreign firms make use of cheap labor to assemble final products. Sometimes the factories are footloose sweatshops. This is particularly prevalent in the apparel and electronics industries. But in other instances, firms like Ford, and Boeing establish state-of-the-art factories so that productivity is high and wages are low. There is no real measure of such "global assembly line" activity. And even it there were, a single measure would mask differences among industries.

One final angle on the role of the corporation in global economic integration is the extent to which trade among nations is actually trade within corporations. When corporations source parts and materials for their products from production facilities in different nations, that is a form of global economic integration. To the extent that corporations are engaged in this type of global production, it shows up as part of trade—the imports and exports of different nations. Some estimates have placed the intrafirm portion of global trade from one-quarter and one-third of all trade. Data on U.S. trade from the U.S. Department of Commerce traces this over time.[72] In 1982, the percentage of U.S. exports shipped to the foreign affiliates of U.S. firms was a little over 30 percent. By 1994, that portion had grown to over 40 percent. The same trend is evident for imports. The percentage of U.S. imports that were sourced from U.S. foreign affiliates in 1982 was about 35 percent, and by 1994 it had grown to nearly 50 percent.

Some people contend that global economic integration is a measure of "globalization." Much bickering in the literature has focused on whether these claims have been exaggerated.[73] My own view is that integration is part of the infrastructure of the strategic perspective of the global capitalist system on how to accumulate capital in this era. What is important is to see is that such an infrastructure is being built, which is what the data above demonstrate. Its significance is as much political as economic. The growth of global economic integration and interdependence does not mean that opposition to the new world order is futile, as some of the debate on globalization has contended. It does mean that the space-time context of social movements is changing and that these changes imply new tasks for these movements. Moreover, seeing economic interdependence as one part of the infrastructure needed to implement a broad strategy of capital accumulation also implies that it is futile to isolate integration in an effort to contest the broader strategy. I return to this discussion in the final chapter of this book.

Ideology and Public Policy

The developing infrastructure for the new world order requires public policies. These provide the building blocks and institutions that can cheapen production through capital mobility. Public policies are also needed to fuel the new mode of accumulation through ever-expanding credit that is built on the sand of speculation, while diminishing social claims on surplus value. Internationally these policies include SAPs and the "free trade" agreements. In many of the wealthier nations, immigration policies are increasingly more limiting. Cheapening production costs through capital mobility does not work well if labor is also mobile.

Chapters 4–7 develop the point that the new world order has caused a shift in urban policy in the United States. That has meant the elimination of social safety nets and affirmative action and replacing these with programs that improve national and individual "competitiveness." "Individual responsibility" has replaced the concept of social welfare. Housing for the poor is being replaced with housing for the rich as the public housing program is privatized. Public employment policy has eliminated a prior emphasis on using macro economic programs and affirmative action to expand job opportunities. Instead, the focus is on the behavior and personality characteristics as well as skills of individual workers—enhancing their competitiveness through job training that often emphasizes so-called job readiness skills. These policies represent a dramatic shift from the previous regime. In the U.S. context it is a shift from the social policy that was constructed from the "new deal" to the "great society," to policies that are now geared to individual responsibility. A crucial component of these policies is to remove the social dimension from everyday life. We have become a society where "every man for himself" is the preferred approach to life. It is a world without classes, races, or genders, where the maxim of "dog eat dog" becomes the ultimate politically correct form of behavior.

Race and class relations take a definite form in this context. The global drive to cheapen labor power leaves many worse off. That is deliberate. Policies and actions to cheapen the cost of labor power have their most devastating impact on those with the least political power. The new world order has created social polarization—rich getting richer and poor getting poorer. There are growing divisions between and among nations as well as among groups of individuals within nations. Some people in the developing world are literally starving to death or living in unthinkable poverty. In the wealthy nations like the United States, many people, if not most, are either living in a house of credit cards or are seeing their standard of living deteriorate. Some have fallen off the edge, joining the ranks of the homeless, engaging in petty crime or working at temp jobs and supplementing their poverty wages with dumpster diving. All of this is done in the name of "austerity," but also with the promise that better times are on the horizon if some of us will just "tighten our belts." While starvation and poverty have pointed to the limits of previous eras, they rear their ugly heads again, suggesting the pitfalls of the present age.

As more and more of the world's population gets impatient for the new world order to include their lives, the system itself is threatened. If the basis of hope for something better is social, then people will organize themselves on the basis of class, race, gender, or other group identities. That is what happened at the turn of the twentieth century and again in the 1930s. World War II created the conditions through which workers could substitute national identity for class identity and the disaffected and disillusioned were provided an outlet through world war. Workers were given license to kill one another. In the 1940s, the class dimension and the racial dimension of inequality surfaced again. Once again, national identity was able to submerge class identity, particularly in the United States. Fordism represented an accommodation through which a portion of the world's working class was offered a share of the growing capital accumulation in return for capitulation to the isolation and repression of those who were subjected to higher levels of exploitation. The appeal to all "civilized people" to unite to fight "terrorism," made in the aftermath of the September 11 attacks and the subsequent war appears to be a revisiting of the substitution of national and ethnic identity for class. But the new world order heightens contradictions in such substitution. In a regime based on high capital mobility, you can't easily move people's livelihood out of the country and then appeal to nationalism when they take exception. So a different kind of appeal had to be made.

That appeal is to individualism. At the root of the public policies that form part of the infrastructure for the new world order is the idea that success can come only through individual effort. That idea has been sold, in part, by blaming the need to tighten the belt on the excesses of social action. That includes the notion that labor unions became too strong under the old regime, which resulted in their members being overpaid. Overpaid workers, the argument goes, are not competitive workers when there are others in the world who can do an equally good job for less money. The attack on the social dimension of life extends to the welfare state. Those who partake of its largess, whether through affirmative action (if you are a person of color or a woman) or through various social safety net programs, lose the incentive to be competitive and become part of an underclass and a drag on society as a whole.

The attack on the social dimension of life is reinforced as the system forces workers to compete with one another rather than contest the terms of the sale of their labor power as a class. Under the guise of individual rights, different groups of workers band together to press their advantage over other workers. As the competition among workers moves to a world scale, the tendency to place group over class interests becomes ever more complex, and class interests themselves become hard to sort out. Divisions among workers take particular forms in different geographical, political, and cultural contexts. In many of the wealthier nations there is an increase in xenophobia that is aimed at immigrant workers. Racially based anti-immigrant rhetoric has given momentum to nationalist political parties in countries like France and Austria. Racist ideology directed at immigrants is strong in the United States as well. Immigration laws have been tightened; a wall and a militarized border with Mexico face those who dare to try to come into the country without papers. And in some states the rights of immigrants are seriously restricted both formally and informally. In addition, U.S. academics and political leaders have attempted to disguise the nation's historical racism directed at African Americans and Latinos as a manifestation of individual characteristics that make people in these groups unfit to compete in today's labor markets. The significance of race is said to be declining.[74]

In reality, though, race discrimination is becoming heightened in this period. The vehicle for discrimination against people of color in the United States is not solely overt forms of racism (although there is still plenty of that). Discrimination is facilitated and intensified by the day-to-day functioning of economic and governmental institutions that operate to encourage competition among workers toward the end of cheapening labor power. The reason for increased discrimination in this period is that the expanded basis for competition among workers leaves groups with a legacy of economic vulnerability more vulnerable. The fact that masses of African Americans in the United States are without living wage work and are living in poverty is a measure of their vulnerability. So is the fact that African Americans and Latinos are much more likely to end up in prison than white people in the United States. Prison growth rates in the United States are currently between 4 and 5 percent a year, while the growth of population stands at 1 percent and crime rates are declining.[75] Vulnerability based on class, race, and gender is built into the economic and political system itself. Oppressed groups face the limitations of capitalism in this and previous eras when they find again and again that human rights are nothing more than individual rights—the right to compete with other workers.

Forcing the most vulnerable groups to assume the burden of the new world order's need to cheapen production costs has taken the form of segmented and unequal societies both within and among nations. In the United States, public policies built on individual competitiveness have deepened segmentation and inequality. Some are in prison, where they are engaged in forced labor without compensation. Some are forced to work in jobs that pay less than a living wage as temporary or part-time workers. Some are relegated to "permanent" jobs that also lack the wages and benefits required for basic human development. Public policies in such areas as economic development, housing, and employment that reinforce individual competitiveness and undermine the social dimension of life contribute to this. They are the domestic counterpart to the SAPs and trade agreements like NAFTA. These policies and their local impact will be the subject of Chapters 4 to 7. But first I want to draw some conclusions about the evolving new world order.

Global Decisions and Local Collisions

The global decisions that are behind the evolution of a new world order have inevitably led to local collisions. Consider this. African nations pay about $13 billion a year in debt service alone. The United Nations International Children's Fund (UNICEF) has estimated that $9 billion would save the lives of 21 million children in Sub-Saharan Africa who are presently dying from hunger, disease, or malnutrition. Over the past seventeen years, the developing world as a whole has paid its creditors $1.5 trillion more in debt service than it received in loans and investments. The United Nations Development Program (UNDP) has estimated that $40 billion per year for ten years would be enough to achieve universal access to education, health care, nutrition, clean water, and sanitation for everyone. For another $40 billion a year we could raise incomes for the 1.3 billion people who subsist on less than $1 per day to a basic standard of living.[76]

But the new world order mode of accumulation is built on cheap labor and mobile capital and is fueled by expanding credit that is generated by speculation. So comparing debt burden to potentially decent living standards makes little sense. The efficiency criterion of the new world order simply does not consider starvation and poverty as costs of the system. They are only seen as possible threats to world security or at best as a few more bumps in the road to the expansion of the system. The apologists and advocates for the new world order argue that excesses of global capitalism can be contained and that the system has produced economic growth and rising incomes everywhere free markets have been allowed to operate.[77] What they fail to mention is that in the process, most people in the world are left out. A recent World Bank study of global income distribution makes this clear. Between 1988 and 1993, world income distribution has changed in favor of the rich and these changes are present in virtually all regions of the world.[78] In numerical terms, the average income of the world's richest 5 percent divided by that of the world's poorest 5 percent has increased from 78 to one to 114 to one. That means that today someone with an income of about $US25,000 a year is richer than 98 percent of the world's population.[79]

The continued justification for this state of affairs in terms of efficiency and economic growth demonstrates how bankrupt these concepts are in the context of the new world order. The notion of efficiency measured in terms of cost per unit of output is confined to very narrow boundaries that do not include the inefficiency of people living in poverty or soiled environments, let alone starving children. The cost side of the efficiency equation only includes the costs of those who own the businesses. It excludes the costs of people who lose their jobs or suffer from a debilitating work injury or who don't have enough to eat. And it excludes social costs to entire nations that are forced to live in debt bondage and the social costs of environmental degradation. On the output side, money price is the sole measure of value. Broader notions of the contribution of "output" to human self-development are likewise missing from the equation. Value is seen strictly in terms of money prices.

The consequences of this narrow and individualized view of efficiency and value are the local collisions that have historically intensified as a new regime gathers steam. The new world order is not creating value in terms of contributing to human development. Credit and speculation are no substitute for this. Think about this. The top 200 transnational corporations presently produce 26 percent of the world's output. But they employ only 0.74 percent of the world's labor force.[80] In a capitalist system, if production is not the vehicle for the populace to sustain itself, what is? It isn't simply that we are "overproducing." The people who are not part of the production system or who languish in jobs that are paying poverty wages still need the fruits of production. They need food, homes, clothing, and health care and they need education and cultural fulfillment to develop as human beings. A system that merely cheapens the costs of those who own the means of production is not creating value. The money lenders and the speculators that feed this system and enrich themselves in the process are also not creating value. The income and wealth polarization that has intensified under the new world order are one result. Poverty and starvation are others. The system is unsustainable. And at this point in history, people are once again joining to contest the terms of the system's mode of accumulation.

The appearance of a contradiction and the social struggle that ensues is always place-specific. The militancy of a social movement comes from the association of people with a particular place—a work place or a neighborhood. I pointed out in Chapter 2 that the evolution of a new mode of accumulation alters the place, space, and time dimensions of social movements, giving rise to the need to change the nature of the movement itself. In this era that means that place-based movements must link resistance to their local collisions together somehow. Yet, the movements to contest the terms of any mode of accumulation must begin and end in the place where people live and work. What is needed, therefore, is to try to understand local conditions very concretely in the context of the broader social and economic forces that shape them. Today that requires concretizing the new world order in specific places. I have chosen Chicago because that is where I have spent much of the past three decades. I have witnessed the collapse of Fordism while working in Chicago factories. I have worked doing research and popular education with community organizations and labor unions there that are trying to find ways to stop the loss of jobs, incomes, homes, and neighborhoods that have been generated by the new world order. Based on these experiences and research, I now turn to the task of concretizing the new world order as it comes to the United States, and particularly Chicago.

CHAPTER 4

Manufacturing Collapses in Chicago

When I go to bed I got the pressure. When I get up I got the pressure—the same thing. I don't know if it's really through or what. But I feel so little when other people work. I feel like they are saying: "You are nothing! You're a nobody!" And that's the way I feel myself. So I just keep to myself.
———Laid off Chicago steelworker, 1984

We're lean and mean. Today we have a future.
———Donald D. Lennox, Chair Navistar Corporation (which had a hand in laying off the above steelworker), 1986

There can be no doubt that part of the income and wealth polarization of the present period is rooted in the collapse of unionized manufacturing jobs in the United States during the 1980s. In Chapter 3, I attributed that collapse to the systemic strategy, which former President Bush called a new world order. But others have offered conflicting explanations. The mainstream view concerning deindustrialization is that it represents a natural and positive adjustment to a post-industrial or information age economy and new competitive conditions. Manufacturing job loss is potentially positive, in this view, because it can result in greater efficiency. Economic development strategies based on this outlook are geared to "capacity building" or being more "competitive."[1]

One influential proponent of these ideas is Harvard economist Michael Porter.[2] Porter does acknowledge that global capitalism is in a new period. But he sees this new period as one of opportunity for those nations, communities, and individuals who become competitive. His analysis of global competition posits a world of nations competing with one another through "their" respective corporations on the basis of new technologies and increasingly efficient operations. He argues that nations and inner-city communities can succeed by developing their "competitive advantage." The inner-city advantage is based on the location of communities, the existence of "clusters of competitive companies," the degree of unmet demand for inner-city goods and services, and the unemployed and underemployed people who live in these communities.

A contrasting view can be found in the work of Harrison and Bluestone. Their view is that deindustrialization was the result of a "profit squeeze" in the 1970s, which was caused by declining productivity growth and increased foreign competition. In response, American management embarked on a strategy of cost containment that led to a complete elimination of certain product lines or encouraged the transfer of production to lower-cost regions.[3] Unlike Porter, Harrison and Bluestone see the loss of manufacturing jobs as largely negative in terms of lost jobs and wages. Moreover, they argue, there could have been options other than the "low road" cost containment strategy for U.S. corporations if the public sector had a positive industrial policy.

Another explanation for the loss of manufacturing jobs during the 1980s and 1990s is that technology has made certain kinds of occupations obsolete.[4] Jeremy Rifkin, in his book *The End of Work*, argues that this can be beneficial because wealth created by technology can be used to pay people for less work and to compensate them for socially useful work.[5] This prescription to eliminate declining living standards and poverty assumes that technological development is a neutral phenomenon, which generates wealth that can be readily distributed. In other words, the prescription depends on technology's status as an independent force. Yet technology's treatment as an independent, wealth-producing variable, as formulated in *The End of Work*, is an analytical assumption never critically examined by the author or by others who adopt some version of the technology thesis.

One implication of Chapter 3 is that technology can be better understood as the outcome of a society's class relations. The recent development of technologies making capital more mobile, together with the use of such technologies to lower global living standards, is one chief way the owners of capital are lowering production costs at the expense of labor. It is important to consider that much technological investment has resulted in advanced forms of telecommunications and lower transportation costs. The most direct effect of this technology has not been to reduce labor but to make capital more mobile—enabling firms to move production geographically or to move investment into different industries. This mobility enables firms to lower their costs by moving to cheaper areas. In some instances, living wage jobs are eliminated in one region and replaced by jobs elsewhere that yield significantly lower living standards. In other instances, profits derived from lower-cost production are used to invest in technology or implement mergers and acquisitions that actually reduce jobs. In the United States, during the 1980s and early 1990s these mergers were accompanied by over 100,000 layoffs, a third of which have been directly attributed to the mergers themselves.[6]

Various proponents of a globalization thesis tend to focus on job losses and ignore broader aspects of the new world order. The new mode of accumulation described in Chapter 3 involves much more than jobs going "overseas." Some of the mobility of capital and jobs has resulted in movements within the nation as well. This chapter examines the experience of deindustrialization in the Chicago area during the 1980s. The point of the chapter is to examine the complexities of manufacturing job loss at a time when the new world order was being born. Case studies of plant closings further concretize the separation of value from values and the social construction of time, space, and place that were discussed in Chapter 2. I begin by revisiting the closing of Wisconsin Steel, which was first introduced in Chapter 2. Although plant closings are nothing new, the form this one took was clearly related to the emerging new world order and thus offers a preview of what was to come. Following this case, I broaden the discussion to include an analysis of all manufacturing job loss in Chicago during the 1980s. I conclude with a return to some of the philosophic questions raised in Chapter 2.

The Closing of Wisconsin Steel

The closing of Wisconsin Steel occurred during the dawning of the new world order.[7] It was a particularly brutal beginning. It wasn't simply a matter of management locking the plant gates and sending in an occupying army of New York security guards and the Chicago police. Nor does the brutality of bouncing paychecks and the need for a decade-long court fight to gain pension rights tell the whole story. All of these things were bad enough. But in addition there is the fact is that management planned all of this for six years! And when workers perceived that something was going very wrong, just days before the closing, the company called a meeting and lied about it. As one former worker recalls,

> We had this big meeting with the President and some of his associates. He says, "We are having this meeting to tell all you people who work for Wisconsin Steel not to worry about the mill shutting down. All this talk is just rumor. . . . This plant is going to be rolling right along. So don't have no fears about its shutting down." Two days later I call up to get my schedule. The guy tells me, "There is no more plant. We are shut down . . . Your job is over. You lost everything."

The lies, the suddenness of the closing, and the callous disregard for the workforce were in part a reflection of a particular corporate culture. But in addition, the emergence of a new mode of accumulation in the late 1970s provided an important context for the form that the closing took. International Harvester was in financial trouble and Wisconsin Steel, one of its subsidiaries, was part of the problem. IH profits declined 42 percent between 1966 and 1970. It is important to note that falling profit rates were not unique to IH, nor were they caused solely by internal management decisions. Profit rates were falling throughout the capitalist world as the era of Fordism was beginning to self-destruct. But the solution for IH, which I describe in detail below, was made possible by the emergence of a period characterized by high unregulated capital mobility, exotic credit expansion, and the anti-labor climate that went with these features.

New management took over IH in 1971 and began to look carefully at the profitability of each division. In 1973, IH did a study of Wisconsin Steel's potential to produce cheap steel as a way to shore up the other divisions. The idea was to return the mill to its historic role as primarily a supplier to the parent company. But the study indicated that it would cost an additional $250 million to complete the needed modernization program. IH management decided they couldn't afford it. And because the mill was in the midst of a renovation program, Wisconsin Steel suddenly became a liability. The other thing that the study showed was that it would cost more to close the mill than to keep it open. Closing meant that IH would have to write off more than $200 million in assets. Furthermore, there were $62 million in unfunded pension liabilities and another $25 million in contractual severance pay and pension supplements that would have to be paid off. So the decision was to sell Wisconsin Steel.

The problem with the decision was that it was made as a crisis in global capitalism was emerging and at a time of dissolution of the U.S. economic/political hegemonic position in the world. In the United States that crisis took the form of the very deep 1974 recession. One aspect of the recession was that steel shipments in the United States declined by 22 percent. Thus, no one wanted to buy a steel mill; particularly a mill with such liabilities. A member of top management, James Doyle, was told to come up with a solution. His solution was nasty, but it was in keeping with the growing anti-labor climate and the evolving use of credit expansion and speculation that are central to the new world order.

In 1977, Doyle was having lunch with George Sealey, an old friend who was president of Envirodyne Industries. Envirodyne was founded by an engineer named Ronald Linde. Linde's idea when he started the firm was to buy up other companies that had promising technological processes and use his company's engineering prowess to develop and commercialize them. At the time Doyle met with Sealey, Envirodyne had purchased eighteen different firms financed by stock swaps. Each of the firms Linde brought under the Envirodyne umbrella had patents on unique technological processes. None of them had anything to do with steel.

Sealey was looking for a major acquisition that would enable Envirodyne to jump into larger-scale operations. Indeed, the firm's profits the previous year had been a meager $264,400 on revenues of $24.4 million.[8] Sealey asked Doyle if he knew of any major industrial facilities. Doyle had found what he was looking for. But how could such a small company with no background in steel making afford to buy Wisconsin Steel? It was the sort of question that was a perfect fit in an era built on expanded credit. Legend has it that Doyle and Sealey worked out the answer then and there on the back of a paper napkin.

Envirodyne would buy the mill, including its mines and ore freighters, for $65 million. The purchaser of the mill would actually be a limited liability subsidiary of Envirodyne called EDC Holding Company. EDC would borrow $50 million of the purchase price from Harvester with 8.5 percent notes that did not require any payments for ten years. The iron and coal mines were put up by EDC as collateral on the loan. EDC would pay the remaining $15 million in cash. The cash didn't come from Envirodyne, but from a $35 million loan from Chase Manhattan Bank. The collateral for that loan was Wisconsin Steel's inventory, including its large supply of coal, iron, and coke. In the deal, EDC assumed all of Harvester's Wisconsin Steel-related liabilities, including the unfunded pension obligations.

There were executives inside IH, including Wisconsin Steel's general manager, who expressed reservations about the capacity of Envirodyne to run a steel mill. But they were brushed aside and accused of "negative thinking."[9] Another executive recalled the time Envirodyne Chairman Ronald Lynde and his wife toured the mill shortly after the deal had been put together:

> They seemed surprised that all 3,000 workers were not present. I said, when you work at a steel plant, you work 21 turns in primary operations, so you have four crews—three working in the day and one off. That's where a lot of people are. Home sleeping. And they asked, does that mean you work Saturdays and Sundays? And I told them it never stops. They didn't know that, a fundamental of the business, and I thought, Uh-Oh, we're in big trouble.[10]

While Envirodyne may have wanted to make a go of Wisconsin Steel, it was clear the IH knew that the venture would likely fail. Before the sale, a federal agency, the Pension Benefit Guarantee Corporation, required IH to make a study of the viability of the deal. The firm of Lehman Brothers made the assessment and concluded that the deal was not viable. So a second consultant was hired who concluded just the opposite. The problem was that the second consultant was in on the deal. He had a contract with the creditors to buy the inventory in case of failure, which could then be sold at a profit.[11]

The workers could see that the deal was not going to work as well. IH had let things deteriorate badly even before the deal was made. As one longtime production worker put it: "They didn't ever fix things properly. If there was a breakdown, they would just patch things up." Another worker added:

> There was a lot of pride in making high-quality steel until the company came in and really made us put stuff out. When I started, you didn't order steel on a weekly basis. It was monthly because that's how long it took. When Brooks came in you could order steel and he would supply it in a week. His plan was production on demand and not on a schedule where you could get the thing right. Around 1976

there was this whole relaxing of quality control. It was a matter of getting the stuff out. Rushing! Rushing!

These changes were even more apparent to the foremen. One man who was a supervisor during the McCormick years recalls:

In the 70s you could see the change from quality to quantity. They'd call a supervisor's meeting. They'd say we're going to talk about production. And they'd just say "we want 25 ton a man and anyone who thinks he can't do it just leave your white hat on the rack." It wasn't a meeting where you'd discuss the possibilities of what you thought could be done or how you thought it could best be done. No such thing. What bothers you so much is you got the guys who condition the steel and they almost cried. "Look! This ain't right. Why do I have to let it go out this way?"

After Envirodyne took over, things went from bad to worse. The faster pace of work that had resulted in lower-quality steel over the past few years was intensified under the new regime. To many workers these changes were the beginning of the shutdown. Here is how one worker saw it:

We had good foremen but they were getting old and the company wanted to kick them out and they got all these kids from school. A lot of the old ones had thirty to thirty-seven years but the company didn't want them. When they kicked those guys out that had the knowledge, they found out different. That's when they started to close.

In part, the changes perceived by the workers were due to a lack of knowledge on the part of management about steel making. In part, they represented an increasingly desperate effort by Envirodyne to halt operating losses in order to give the company time to raise badly needed cash so that the mill could run efficiently. Just prior to the sale in 1977, workers attempting to repair faulty equipment were injured in an explosion. Later, gas fumes killed four men as they attempted to get an old blast furnace to work again. One coke battery had to be permanently closed to meet Environmental Protection Agency requirements. In 1979, a key blast furnace was seriously damaged when hot iron got through its wall of brick. The three-week shutdown forced the cancellation of millions of dollars' worth of orders.[12]

In September 1978, EDC Holding Company completed a business plan that called for a $74 million capital improvement program. EDC put together a complex financing package that rested on government-guaranteed loans. The key guarantor was to be the U.S. government's Economic Development Administration (EDA). Additional working capital was to come from a special Urban Development Action Grant from the Department of Housing and Urban Development (HUD). But it took nearly two years for the government to agree to the arrangement because of questions about the ability of the EDC Holding Company to proceed. Also, EDC was in violation of the Clean Air and Waters Act for pollution violations and the Civil Rights Acts for discrimination against women. The environmental compliance problem was solved politically through negotiations involving the local congressperson, Environmental Protection Agency officials, and Envirodyne. The civil rights violations were resolved by the hiring of the first women production workers at Wisconsin Steel. EDA finally agreed to guarantee a $30 million loan over a twenty-year period.

But as these problems were being cleared away, production costs were skyrocketing. This caused EDC Holding Company to revise its loan application twelve times and to increase the amount sought to $90 million. The fact that the loan application went through at all seems incredible. During the two years that it took to secure the loans for a badly needed capital injection, the mill practically fell apart. By the summer of 1978, two blast furnaces were down, making it impossible to fill orders. The company bought raw steel from area mills in order not to lose customers, but the hole they were digging got deeper and deeper. Workers were borrowing parts from one section of the mill to use in another section. They were fabricating some parts out of whatever was available and hosing the walls of the blast furnaces with cold water to keep them from burning up.

Once the loan came through, the needed investments began. The construction of a new blast furnace was started and a continuous caster (a new technology at the time) was put into operation. But events at International Harvester at this point delivered the final blow to Wisconsin Steel. In 1977, the year of the sale of Wisconsin Steel, new IH CEO Archie McCardell, launched an aggressive campaign of cost cutting matched by increased capital spending as well as increases in research and development. Between 1977 and 1979, capital spending increased by 70 percent from $168 million to $285 million. Research and development spending in 1979 totaled over $240 million, representing a 33 percent increase. To finance the increases in capital spending and research and development, McCardell's number one priority was cost cutting. And a major part of that cutting was to be labor. According to *Crain's Chicago Business,*

> McCardell saw Harvester's contract with the UAW as a perfect target for his cost-cutting campaign. In fact, he identified the contract—a product of compromises that had ended the labor turmoil of the 1950's—as the culprit most responsible for the competitive gap between Harvester and rivals Deere and Caterpillar.[13]

From the beginning of his tenure as chairman at Harvester, McCardell began to confront the unions and their members. A wildcat strike in East Moline, Illinois, resulted in serious disciplinary action against the workers involved. McCardell also broke a five-week strike in Louisville. Now, as he planned to make the UAW contract a key part of his cost-cutting campaign, there is evidence that McCardell was anticipating a strike. Months before negotiations, McCardell hinted at a strike in an interview with *Crain's.*[14] Furthermore, six months before the strike began Harvester started an unprecedented inventory build-up. From April to November 1979, a subsidiary, which finances equipment sales to domestic dealers, experienced a 30 percent increase in wholesale receivables. The comparable figure for the previous year was only 5 percent.[15]

The *Crain's* analysis of the strike claimed that Harvester and McCardell underestimated the resolve of the UAW workers and leadership, discounting the legacy of the old Farm Equipment Workers Union radicals who still held sway at the local level in 1979. In any event, Harvester negotiators put forth a series of demands that they claimed they would never relinquish. They focused on the ability of workers at the local level to control the pace and place of work, including an increase in the number of weekly shifts, some mandatory overtime, and the right to limit transfers within the plant. When these demands were laid on the table, the chief union negotiator stated that he knew there was going to be a strike. Inside the company, a number of long-term executives were alarmed over the extreme hard line being taken. They even went to Brooks McCormick and asked him to intervene on the ground that this would be the ruination of the company. McCormick refused and the strike lasted six months. The union won and Harvester ended up in deep trouble.

But the strike was the final blow to Wisconsin Steel, which at this point depended on Harvester for 40 percent of its orders. The strike began at the very point that money for the modernization program was coming through. Despite the fact that McCardell had been clearly planning the strike for six months, he never informed the EDC Holding Company management of his plans. He knew, given the condition of the mill, that the strike would seriously threaten Wisconsin Steel's survival. As the strike was settled, the mill was shut down and it was Harvester that administered the coup de grâce by foreclosing on the iron and coal mines. Chase Manhattan Bank, another major creditor, then flew a security force to Chicago to secure its assets. 3,200 jobs were gone, just like that. Two days earlier, EDC management had told the workers they had nothing to worry about. It was an obvious lie.

The closing of Wisconsin Steel came, as I have noted, at the very beginning of the emerging new world order. It was a "pioneer" closing in this sense. Prior plant closings were isolated and occurred in an era where U.S. manufacturing was flourishing and there had been a social compact between labor and management to share the growth of post–World War II prosperity. But that pact had begun to deteriorate and the U.S. economy was vulnerable after the 1974–75 recession. Also, the United States had been weakened politically after losing the Vietnam War. IH's problems, while independent of these events, occurred within a context created by them. The IH management thus responded to their own crisis, drawing both from their own corporate history and from the new conditions that were evolving. There are three aspects of the Wisconsin Steel story that make this plant closing something new, thus offering a preview of what was to come.

First, the IH strategy of cost cutting at the expense of labor fit well with the growing anti-labor climate that President Reagan officially launched at the very time Wisconsin Steel was being closed. IH had no second thoughts about getting rid of its workforce by whatever means, including workers at Wisconsin Steel, to regain its position in the various industries in which it operated. The mill and its workers were immediately expendable once it was determined that they could not produce steel cheaply enough to enable IH to compete with John Deere and Caterpillar. Thus IH forced a strike with the UAW in order to achieve cost-cutting objectives. They undoubtedly knew that the strike would mean the end of Wisconsin Steel.

Second, IH's financial and competitive problems were resolved by a complex financial deal, that is commonplace today but at the time was quite rare. Rather than absorb the loss that a more conventional sale or plant closing would involve, IH and Envirodyne created a new company (EDC Holding Company), which had neither assets nor any knowledge of steel making. As the new world order was being created with expanded credit, EDC "bought" Wisconsin Steel without any money, making it a pioneer of the leveraged buyout. Essentially IH gave the mill to EDC in return for the collateral of its mines and other assets. They also helped EDC secure a loan from Chase Manhattan Bank to meet immediate financial needs in return for liens on its inventory. IH helped to arrange the loan through a consultant who played two ends of the deal. On the one hand, he agreed to purchase the inventory from Chase Manhattan Bank in the event of a shutdown. He also did a study for the government and declared that the deal was solid and there would be no shutdown.

Third, the competitive strategy of both IH and Envirodyne involved using capital mobility to move easily in and out of a variety of ventures. IH was moving its capital among farm equipment, construction equipment, motor vehicles, steel, research and development, and marketing outlets. They were also moving capital to different locations, closing some operations and opening others. Envirodyne was doing something similar by purchasing facilities for the purpose of developing and marketing product and process technologies. The deals were financed with stock swaps and loans. Because these deals were secured with the assets of the mill, there was little risk involved to the investors. When these deals went bad, it was the workers who felt the pain.

Chicago Plant Closings in the 1980s

As noted earlier, Wisconsin Steel was the beginning of a major national trend, which had a particularly devastating impact on Chicago and its workforce. Between 1979 and 1989, net manufacturing job loss in the city of Chicago (jobs lost minus jobs gained) was 128,986, representing a decline of 36 percent.[16] Virtually every manufacturing industry in the city suffered a net loss of jobs during this period. The greatest absolute losses were in primary metals (which includes steel), non-electrical machinery, electronics and electrical machinery, fabricated metals, printing and publishing, and paper products. This loss was not simply a matter of firms moving their factories to the suburbs as happened during a previous period. The Chicago metropolitan area, which includes a region defined by five counties, suffered a net loss during the same period of 151,744 manufacturing jobs. Furthermore, case studies of the individual establishments that were shut down reveals that 60 percent of the Chicago job loss could be directly attributed to corporate parents with significant overseas operations. And in the majority of these cases the corporate parents were expanding overseas while closing down Chicago operations.

I also estimated the indirect job loss in Chicago from the actions of corporate parents with international operations. Many firms that were locally based were attached economically to factories that were closed by transnational corporate parents. For example, in South Chicago there were many steel fabrication shops that were located close to the mills. They were able to be competitive because they could use locally produced steel without incurring transportation costs. There were numerous small "job shops" in the vicinity of most major factories in Chicago that rebuilt wornout machines, rewound burned out electric motors, and made specialized parts on demand. And there were a variety of manufacturers and distributors of things like tools, shoes, welding equipment, and nuts and bolts. And there were food services, restaurants, and bars whose market was entirely dependent on nearby factories. Adding in such indirect job loss, I estimate that a total of 106,200 jobs were eliminated during the decade of the 1980s that could be attributed, directly or indirectly, to the capital mobility that is a key part of the new world order. Brief vignettes of a few key closings demonstrate this contention.[17]

- A major plant closing in the electrical machinery and electronics industry was Western Electric. In 1980, Western Electric was a wholly owned subsidiary of AT&T. Its Chicago plants employed 8,000 workers who produced telephone switches, electrical switches, cable, copper rod, and wire. In the mid-1980s, it began a program of restructuring to reposition itself to dominate markets for long-distance, local service, cable television, cellular service, and the internet. It entered into many joint ventures and pushed to expand into Canada, Mexico, and Latin America. One of its early efforts in this direction was to eliminate its manufacturing operations. In Chicago this meant that 8,000 workers lost their jobs. Over the next decade they eliminated over 100,000 jobs in the United States as they led the lobbying effort to pass NAFTA and other new world order policies. The Western Electric plant was torn down, although a tower that had been a key visual feature of the factory was preserved and became a symbol for the shopping mall that was built on the factory site.
- In 1980, Sunbeam was the largest producer of small appliances in the world. Its Chicago plant employed 2,700 workers who produced thirty-five different appliances. In 1981, a specialty steel company, Allegheny Steel, purchased Sunbeam. A year later, Chicago's production activities were moved

to both non-union lower-cost U.S. regions and to other countries—principally Mexico. The Chicago plant was then closed. The huge Chicago facility was eventually turned into a manufacturing "incubator," where small start-up businesses could share fixed costs. The new firms employed few people and did not begin to match the wages and benefits of Sunbeam.

- Stewart-Warner, another electronics firm, was a privately held corporation in 1980 that employed nearly 3,000 workers. They mainly produced electronic components for the automobile industry. In the mid-1980s, a British firm, BTR, which had operations all over the world, acquired Stewart-Warner. Eventually the Chicago operations were moved to some of the other BTR locations and the plant was torn down. Today the site includes condominium developments in a gentrifying neighborhood.

- Job losses in primary metals were dominated by the steel industry. Only a fraction of these losses were due to the closing of Wisconsin Steel. A major loss came from USX, who eliminated nearly 9,000 jobs at its Chicago Southworks Division during the 1980s. It eventually closed the South Chicago mill in 1992. The elimination of jobs began in 1982, when United States Steel Corporation (USS), the largest steel producer in the world, decided to move capital into energy and bought Marathon Oil. Marathon had extensive overseas subsidiary operations that included Liberia, Tunisia, Norway, and Australia, among others. In 1986, USS changed its name to USX and its CEO stated, "Our business is not to make steel, but to make money." USX also invested in real estate but chose not to invest in the huge Southworks facility in Chicago. The site of Southworks, which runs for approximately a mile along South Chicago's lakeshore, has been vacant for nearly a decade. There are currently plans for a "mixed use" development that will include "light industry," condominiums, and some open space. As I write this USX is negotiating with four other large steel companies to create a mega merger that would eliminate more jobs.

- In Chicago's food processing industry, thirty-one plants either closed or drastically downsized in the 1980s. The industrywide downsizing represented a range of products—candy, dairy products, meat and fish, cereals, cookies, and crackers. Most of the closings involved job losses in the range of 200 to 500 people each. Many of the corporations were familiar household names—Beatrice, Borden, Campbell Soup, General Mills, Libby, Nabisco, Swift. The largest job losses came from Campbell Soup and Libby. Campbell closed its Chicago facility in the mid-1980s and eliminated 1,200 jobs. The Chicago shutdown was part of a program of closing older facilities and replacing them with more modern ones. The company claimed that the Chicago plant operations were moved to a new plant in Ohio, a so-called right to work state that outlawed fully union shops. Savings from the plant closings (which in part were derived from lower wage costs) were used to expand worldwide operations in a variety of product lines which, in addition to soup, included pet food, fitness equipment, snacks, frozen foods, salads, and restaurants. The other major food processing closing was the Chicago plant of the Libby McNiell and Libby Corporation. The Chicago closing eliminated 1,100 jobs. In the 1980s, Libby, which was making fruit juices, was bought out by Nestlé. Nestlé, a Swiss-based transnational corporation, is one of the largest corporations in the world. Their strategy was to treat the entire world as their market and to simply move capital to locations where they could make the most money. The demise of the Chicago-based Libby plant was part of such a move.

This study of the collapse of manufacturing in Chicago in the 1980s focused on those cases instigated by transnational corporate parents—corporations with major operations in at least four nations, including the United States. Such closings directly accounted for 60 percent of the net loss of manufacturing jobs in Chicago during the decade. And that percentage would be even higher if we took into consideration the considerable indirect job loss. The detailed case of Wisconsin Steel and the vignettes of other closings provide a flavor of the complex reasons for the collapse of an entire industrial sector. Being more efficient in order to be competitive does not appear to be a major factor. Huge corporations that dominated global markets were responsible for most of the large closings. The actions of these large parent corporations were often geared to reducing competition by eliminating competitors, rather than becoming more efficient. AT&T was using capital gained by closing out its manufacturing operations to dominate service markets in Latin America. LTV Corporation bought three steel corporations to dominate that industry and when the steel market dropped it simply downsized some of its many operations. Nestlés, Allegheny, Campbell Soups, and BTR closed plants so that they could move operations to lower-cost areas. International Harvester/Navistar, USS/USX, and Rockwell International were enhancing their profits by moving capital from one industry to another—steel and farm equipment to trucks; steel to oil and real estate; forgings to military and space equipment. Nor do these scenarios support a simplistic view that "technology" is eliminating jobs or that deindustrialization is mainly about moving production in Chicago to a particular developing country.

What is common to each case is a corporate strategy that enhances profitability through capital mobility. What is also common to each case is that they represent a major attack on the living standards and lives of those who were displaced. Cheapening or devaluing the labor power of workers in the developed nations achieved greater profitability, which was gained in the 1990s by these corporations. Chicago was a part of this.

Local Collisions: Efficiency, Value, and Values

What did the collapse of manufacturing mean for Chicago workers? I made estimates of some measurable costs of the new world order job loss. Direct and indirect job loss represented a loss of $3.2 billion in personal income and $5.4 billion in the value of lost production (gross regional product) in the Chicago area.[18] But these monetary values do not begin to tell the whole story of the costs of the collapse of manufacturing in Chicago.

For one thing, even this quantitative loss was not equally distributed. We made a further analysis of the job loss by race and gender.[19] We estimated that of the 79,744 jobs that were directly lost to transnational corporate parents, 34 percent of those losing jobs were women, 27 percent were African American, and 23 percent were Latino, percentages that were higher than their participation in the workforce. Furthermore, the occupations of these groups of workers were concentrated in clerical, assembly, and machine operator work. While the demand for clerical workers was growing in the early 1990s, the number of people seeking these jobs was growing even faster. In the case of assembly and semiskilled machine operators, the demand was down while the supply of workers was high. These jobs, for the most part, had paid a living wage that could keep workers out of poverty. The massive deindustrialization of the 1980s in Chicago caused the supply of workers for these jobs to exceed the demand. Thus, many women and minority workers had a particularly difficult time finding replacement jobs.

These findings are reinforced by local and national surveys concerning the experience of dislocated workers during this period. A survey of more than 600 workers who were laid off from U.S. Steel Southworks (Chicago) in 1981 found that by 1984, only 32 percent of the workers were working full-time and 47 percent were unemployed.[20] Furthermore, unemployment rates differed among workers of different races and genders. While 32 percent of white workers were unemployed, unemployment rates for African Americans and Latinos were 62 percent and 46 percent, respectively. While 45 percent of all men were unemployed, the rate for women was 61 percent. Those who were employed found their economic status greatly diminished. Median family income was cut in half, and only 56 percent of workers had health insurance at their new jobs. Also, the wage and income differentials between whites on the one hand, and African Americans and Latinos on the other, widened significantly. Although Chicago's displaced steelworkers were hurt worse than workers for the United States as a whole, the results of this Chicago survey are supported by a study conducted by the U.S. Bureau of Labor Statistics (BLS).[21] Of all manufacturing workers in the United States who lost their jobs in 1979, 26 percent were still unemployed in 1984, while 39 percent of workers in primary metals industries were unemployed. Like Chicago, race was an important factor in employment status. While 23 percent of white displaced manufacturing workers were unemployed in 1984, the comparable figures for African Americans and Latinos were 41 percent and 34 percent, respectively. The average decline in wages for all U.S. manufacturing workers who lost their jobs in 1979 but who had regained employment by 1984 was 11 percent. For primary metals workers, the wage loss was 40 percent.

Earlier, I used the term "devalue labor power" to describe the social dimension of the lost jobs and wages. The experience of workers in Chicago during the 1980s makes this abstract term very concrete. In the Chicago metropolitan region today, some industries, including steel, are producing more than they did before the plant shutdowns. But they are doing this with far fewer workers and often at lower pay rates with fewer benefits. Many jobs that were once done by union workers at living wages and with good benefits are now in the temporary help industry. Pay rates are often below what it takes to support a family, and health benefits are often nonexistent. Also, union jobs in the service sector that pay living wages are currently being cheapened through privatization and outsourcing. These more recent developments will be the subject of Chapter 7. Here I wish to make the point that many of the workers who were victimized by the collapse of manufacturing in the 1980s have never really recovered. And their children have never found a place for themselves in the workforce that is comparable to what their parents had prior to the collapse. They are the homeless, the residents of public housing, the welfare recipients who are currently dealing with welfare "reform." And they are demonized as an "underclass" who are sternly told to get to work. The roots of the so-called "underclass" phenomenon are in the stories told above.

To many economists, public policy analysts, and politicians, this is all to the good. They consider the wages of the old jobs to have been too high and lacking in competitiveness. And these "distorted" wages kept workers from going on to school and doing better. My story about the debate with the Citicorp economist described in Chapter 2 is applicable here. She considered the decent wages paid to her autoworker family members in Detroit to be a tragedy because they sent the wrong "signals" and prevented them from getting the kind of education that would allow them to become a bank vice president like her. Similarly, at the beginning of this chapter, I quoted the CEO of Navistar Corporation. He said: "We're lean and mean. Today we have a future." In the aftermath of the Wisconsin Steel debacle, International Harvester shed a number of its operations. Disinvestment and layoffs were not confined to steel. Subsequently, International Harvester changed its name to Navistar. Such activities represent the individual corporate adaptation to the new world order. Navistar is a transnational corporation that moved its capital not only to different geographical locations, but also into and out of a number of production activities.

Those who argue that such moves have made companies like Navistar more efficient and competitive are correct, but only in a limited sense. These corporations have survived to become players in a new global system of capital accumulation. But also note the other quotation at the beginning of this chapter by a displaced Wisconsin steelworker who now felt he was "nothing." In 1984, I visited the offices of an organization called the Wisconsin Steelworkers Save Our Jobs Committee. This was four years after the closing of Wisconsin Steel. The organization was engaged in a lawsuit to gain their pension benefits and back pay. At the time I was helping these workers produce a newsletter. There were twelve workers sitting in the office, passing the time. The worker who felt he was "nothing" was one of them. We began to talk about their efforts to find work, their families, and their feelings about what had happened to them. I asked if I could record the conversation and they agreed. They wanted their stories told.

Many of these workers had been in the mill a long time. Their average tenure was twenty-nine years. Six were African American, four Latino, and two white, which is similar to the composition of the workforce in the mill before it closed. Eight of the twelve were still unemployed. Of the four who were working, three had worked at more than one job since Wisconsin Steel went down. Two had worked three jobs in four years. These were all fairly skilled workers. But their new jobs represented a decline in both pay and benefits and did not utilize skills acquired through years of work in the mill. An electrician was working as a forklift operator; a boilermaker was packing cookies; a coke sorter (inspector) was parking cars; a steel loader/crane operator was managing TV concessions at a local hospital.

There is a general perception of hardship when a layoff occurs. But the pain of the collapse of manufacturing in Chicago ran deep. It ruined the lives of the workers and their families. Listen to the voices of the workers as they talked about their own situation.

It's hard for me to stay home because all my life I wanted to move up and do something. I can't do nothing now. Even at home I can't do nothing because whatever I try to do, it costs money and I don't have it.

I can't afford to give my kids anything. They need shoes. I tell my wife that I don't have the money.

My girls, they see me when I finish (at the mill). Everything just ended right there. That's when they started working. That's when they dropped out of school.

I'm scared to death that I may get sick and without health insurance get wiped out. If me or my wife got sick, I would have no alternative but to just die.

There ain't enough money. I stay angry all the time.

And they also commented on what had happened to their friends.

I know fifteen guys who got divorced on account of this. I know quite a few guys who turned out to be drunks. I know four guys that committed suicide. The situation is bleak and getting bleaker.

A lot of them committed suicide since the mill closed. A lot just died. Three hundred people are dead already with worry—lots of worries. I don't blame them.

Some lost their homes and lost their wives. When the husband loses the job, he loses his wife. She wants someone else who has some money.

I know a number of people with health problems because of this. Also a number had divorces, beat up their kids, etc., because they just couldn't cope.

Some turned themselves into alcoholics. I think it's because of their nervous system. Some fight too much with their wives. Some divorce and separate. My friend went back to Mexico and tried to start up there. But business is so bad there he didn't make it. So he comes back and is still looking for a job.

There was also the situation with the children and their ability to find work. Before manufacturing collapsed in Chicago, the union was a point of entry into the mills. The mills offered young people a place to learn marketable job skills or the opportunity to save money and go to college. It was an informal system of entry into the workforce. It was totally destroyed. The man who talked about his daughters dropping out of school added, shaking his head, "They are walking around the streets every day looking for a job. And they can't find anything. They are in the same position I am."

This very personal impact was also social. We are not talking about a handful of workers in a rundown office in South Chicago. In Chicago alone, over 100,000 workers went through this sort of thing during the 1980s decade. That can be multiplied in cities and towns across the United States, Canada, the United Kingdom, Germany, France, and Italy, to name a few. And when the collapse of manufacturing occurred in Chicago, there was nothing in place to help the people who were its victims.

The social service apparatus was woefully inadequate, and harried case workers took out their frustrations on the workers who, many for the first time in their lives, came seeking relief. Two of the Wisconsin Steel workers talked about this and others added their own stories of inadequate service and humiliation.

You go in line and they give you a number and you get to see this one. Then you see that one and then you got to go in the other line. When I get through over here, they send me over there. I go to the window there and nobody's there. I ask the other girl and she said she's on coffee break. So I'm there forty-five minutes. Then she comes back from her break. She started giving me a hard time, so that pissed me off. Hey, you had a long coffee break. You got nobody to take care of people. She got kind of smart so I get pissed off. So they got the security guard to come over.

Yeah, you think the people don't care about you. I feel they are frustrated with all the people putting pressure on them. I saw a guy crying in front of everyone. He asked for help because he had no money and the kids had nothing to eat. I got my check but the hardest part was that it was $177 a week when I was making $400.

Chapter 2 presented the view that capitalism, as a system, separates value as money price from other sorts of values. Furthermore, in this separation, money price rules. This division appears in bold relief during a period of change in the mode of accumulation. Writers like Charles Dickens in England and Upton Sinclair in the United States portrayed this separation in the earliest periods of capitalist development in the starkest terms. The collapse of manufacturing in Chicago portrays this separation in modern terms. The greater efficiency and competitiveness achieved by corporations like Navistar, USX, Nestlé, and BTR in the 1980s is seen only in terms of money price. The efficiency equation does not include the cost to workers. And the kinds of costs so articulately presented by the Wisconsin Steel workers is not even part of the conversation. Yet the contradiction remains. The displaced workers, whose standard of living was destroyed and who today have adapted to a more "efficient" lower-wage economy, have the same needs as they did before their lives were changed forever. And the next generation also has these needs. They are pretty basic—a home, decent food, clothing, health care, and the fulfillment that comes from self-development through labor. The system isn't providing these things today as well as it was twenty-five years ago. For many people, it isn't providing them at all.

Local Collisions: The Destruction of Place

There are some economists who argue that we should not be so concerned about the blossoming of sweatshops in the developing world because they are actually a positive step in the process of development.[22] The relatively safe and clean conditions many workers in the United States enjoy today, they argue, were the result of a natural process of development that began with sweatshop labor. What this view leaves out is that improved conditions came not through sweatshop labor but through the organized struggle against it. The horrible conditions in the U.S. meat-packing industry as we entered the twentieth century that were chronicled by Upton Sinclair in *The Jungle* in 1906 did not lead to improved health and safety conditions for the workers. It was the organization of the Packinghouse Workers Union and the bloody strikes that followed that did that. But resistance to the excesses of a relatively new mode of accumulation that produced sweatshops and horrible factory conditions in the United States did not happen automatically or immediately. While the onset of a new mode of accumulation exposes the contradiction between money price and other forms of value, the place basis for organizing is often destroyed or seriously disrupted. At the turn of the twentieth century, many of the laborers were immigrants—Europeans from both Western and Eastern Europe and African Americans who were migrating from the South. Workers in the sweatshops and the more organized factories came from different cultures. They spoke different languages. Some ethnic groups had a history of antagonistic relations with other ethnic groups. And they had recently been uprooted from their homes and had come to a new place. Neighborhoods were just forming, and the owners of capital ruled the workplaces. Organizing to halt the abuses of the new order was difficult under these conditions. The path forward was murky.

In the immediate aftermath of the shutdowns and layoffs of the 1980s and into the 1990s, the path to making demands on the system has likewise been obscured. And it remains obscured today. One of the biggest factors obscuring a direction forward has been the destruction of places that had historically been the base from which organized resistance to abuses of the old order were launched.

I frequently meet with workers as part of a project to enhance their understanding of the economic forces that they are facing. Often I begin our dialogue by asking, "How many have lost a factory job or have a close friend or relative who did?" Invariably, nearly everyone in the room raises a hand. We then begin to compile a list of these factories. Depending on the neighborhood, names like Wisconsin Steel, Western Electric, Sunbeam, Stewart-Warner, USX South Works, Republic, Campbell, Libby, and Harvester will inevitably go on the list. But there are also names I never heard of, names that didn't show up in my study. They are the small plants that were scattered throughout the metropolitan region and were tied economically to the plants that did show up in my study. When we expand the list to include layoffs generally, it is also striking how many people were dependent on these factories for service jobs. In my study, I called these "indirect job losses." But to the people who held them they are often referred to as simply "the job." And their loss was no less painful than those at Wisconsin Steel.

The job and home had historically been the focal points around which these workers organized and conducted their lives. The home included not only place of residence but the community of which that place was a part. Schools, shops, parks, and other facilities had been a part of the place that was home. The home and the job were integrally connected. South Chicago and South Deering were two neighborhoods where many of the steelworkers were living when the mills went down. The living wage jobs in the mills and the related factories and businesses enabled the residents of these neighborhoods to buy homes, take their families to nearby restaurants, shop at the local grocery, clothing, hardware, and drug stores, socialize in local taverns, and pay taxes that supported schools and contributed to the maintenance of streets and parks. These communities were tightly organized not only through a well-connected alderman but also through community- and church-based organizations that were often independent of the Democratic Party political machine. The United Steelworkers Union was a force not only at USX South Works and LTV Republic but in the community as well. Two union halls also served as community centers where local groups could meet and the people of the community could gather for wedding receptions, anniversary parties, and other social occasions. The workplaces were also a focal point for labor actions focused on both workplace conditions and electoral politics. But with the collapse of manufacturing in Chicago, all of this began to unravel. Here is what the Wisconsin Steel workers observed:

> Most of the people in my neighborhood are dependent or employed in steel industries. Lots of people are unemployed. Stores and gas stations have closed. I know of seven or eight families who have lost their homes. There are lots of houses boarded up in the neighborhood. Banks have taken over the houses and have sold them on a broker basis.

> You just come here in South Chicago. Clothing stores, they closed. A lot of places are going out of business. The laundromat went; the drugstore, that's gone. It's all over the Southside. Pretty soon it's going to be a ghost town.

> Everything is deteriorating, falling apart. There's no money. People can't afford to pay their gas; they are shutting off the gas. They are shutting off the lights. They are taking telephones out. People are behind in their mortgage payments, car payments.

This sort of deterioration is not confined to South Chicago and South Deering. Many neighborhoods, like these, became peppered with boarded-up homes, abandoned warehouses, and rusting factory buildings. Small job shops of every kind were simply abandoned and left to rot. Stores and taverns closed. One of two things has happened to such neighborhoods. Either they have continued to deteriorate, or they have become gentrified. Gentrification will be discussed in more detail in Chapter 6. But it is important to situate today's gentrification in the destruction of manufacturing and living wage jobs in Chicago. The new world order has polarized society into rich and poor. Many of those who have profited by the rise in finance capital and high technology are attracted to the convenience and rising land values of many inner-city locations and are willing to pay a premium to live there. Those who have been displaced by the destruction of manufacturing jobs if they don't lose their homes by mortgage default are quickly priced out of their neighborhoods by skyrocketing property taxes. Thus, some neighborhoods actually experienced resurgence, as the former factory workers are forced to leave the area and wealthy residents take their place in new or rehabilitated buildings. Sometimes these rehabilitated buildings are the homes or former workplaces of the displaced workers. Then upscale shops move in with names like Whole Foods, Starbucks, and Crate and Barrel.

But these places are no longer a focal point for the workers to contest what is happening to them. Where are these workers? No one really knows for sure. But they are now scattered about. Some move into public housing. Some receive vouchers from the federal government and use these subsidies to try to find housing in the private market. Others move in with relatives or move to substandard housing in the areas that did not gentrify. Some are homeless. But the places—both the job and the home—that had been the focal points around which these workers organized and conducted their lives are gone. The sense of militancy from which struggles to improve the conditions of life and contest the division between money price and value had been based on the conditions and resources offered by the old places. And at the dawning of the new world order, not only are these places destroyed, there are no new places from which a new militancy and organization can proceed. Moreover, the individualism that is the bedrock of the new world order ideology is reinforced by the geographical dispersion of workers from their places of work and their homes. The social dimension of life is obscured by this dispersion. And thus the proposition that the way forward can be found only through individual effort and becoming personally competitive appears to be the only alternative.

But just as the sweatshops and the horrible conditions of Upton Sinclair's "jungle" did not lead to a better life for those who worked there, the "efficiency" and lean and mean competitiveness of the this new period has not ushered in new prosperity for the next generation of workers. As we will see in the chapters that follow, individual effort in the current social-political-economic context will do little to relieve the contradictions that the new period maintains. Nor can public policy correct these conditions. Public policy only reflects the state of development of social movements. So the destruction of manufacturing in Chicago and the collapse of homes, communities, and living standards require finding the basis for a new militancy. As we will see in the chapters to follow, however, this will require a major effort to contest the terms of the new world order itself.

CHAPTER 5

The New World Order and Local Government: Chicago Politics and Economic Development

One response to deindustrialization and the destruction of jobs and communities in Chicago was to call upon local government to defend Chicago's workers and communities. The workplaces, which had been the center of efforts to improve the lives of those who toiled there, could no longer serve this function. They were rapidly being dismantled. Similarly, community-based organizing was faltering because of the lack of jobs and incomes of neighborhood residents. Third, the attack on the living standards of Chicago's workers was exacerbating racial tensions. As an era of highly mobile capital gained steam, competition among workers was heightened. Under these circumstances groups with a legacy of economic vulnerability become more vulnerable. In Chicago this was the situation with the African American and Latino population. The loss of jobs and the decline of communities hit them the hardest. But the white population was also threatened. And thus racial antagonism intensified.

This was the context of the 1983 and 1987 elections of Chicago's first African American mayor, Harold Washington. His campaign called for unity, economic development, and "a fair share" for all of Chicago's residents. Economic development would give priority to Chicago's inner-city neighborhoods rather than an exclusive focus on the central business district, which had been the preoccupation of previous mayors. An unprecedented coalition of African Americans, Latinos, and progressive whites brushed aside traditional ward politics to put Harold Washington in office. But once in office he was

thwarted at every turn. Locally he was in constant combat with the aldermen of Chicago's white working-class wards whose constituency had been hit
with deindustrialization and felt threatened by a city hall that was suddenly
calling for a "fair share." He was thwarted by a business establishment that
felt threatened by the dissolution of a political machine with which they had
developed a comfortable relationship over more than two decades. A federal
government led by President Ronald Reagan, who was cutting funds for cities
at a time when they were sorely needed, also thwarted him. Yet, the Harold
Washington movement that put him in office and the Harold Washington
administration represented an effort to shift the nature of local politics and
government.

The present chapter focuses generally on Chicago politics and specifically
on the economic development program of the Harold Washington administration. But it raises the larger issue of the role of local politics and government
in the new world order. Can local government led by a people-oriented reform
mayor offset the negative impacts of the new world order on workers and their
communities? Cities must be understood in relation to the dominant mode
of accumulation in which they play a vital role. City government not only
provides public services. It helps to organize production and distribution at a
local level, and thus it must deal with contradictions and conflicts that the
broader system generates. These roles shape local politics and place limits on
what local government can accomplish for city residents. Harold Washington
was trying to change the fundamental nature of Chicago government and politics. In doing so he attempted to both address historic inequities that evolved
out of the political machine that had governed Chicago for more than two
decades and promote an economic strategy, which he hoped would benefit all
citizens.

The system that he was trying to replace was well entrenched. It had evolved over a period of more than twenty-five years during the Fordist era. As
that era began to disintegrate, the old system of local politics became vulnerable. The Harold Washington movement and later the Harold Washington
administration attempted to fill the void. However, as we will see, the limits
on local government and politics during the Washington years included both
remnants of the old era and the imperatives of the new world order. Thus,
the story of the Washington administration begins nearly thirty years before
Harold Washington became mayor. It begins with the building of Chicago's
political machine to meet the rigors of the post–World War II Fordist period.

The Fordist Era and Chicago Politics

As I discussed in Chapter 2, the basic purpose of government at any level is to
preserve the prevailing political-economic system. In that capacity, the state is
also a key forum through which individuals, groups, and classes of people can

contest the way the system affects them. Each era of capitalist development presents the state with new tasks and with new sets of demands from citizens. This construction of the role of the state is a way to view the role of all levels of government, including city government and its politics.

Chapter 3 demonstrated that in the United States, the Fordist era was marked by rapidly expanding industrial production stimulated by the post–World War II reconstruction. Corporations, government, and labor unions agreed to cooperate. Corporations agreed to share the vast profits that rising incomes, a global market, and cheap raw materials from the developing world would bring. Organized labor agreed to guarantee labor peace and production continuity and to support U.S. foreign policy in return for a share of these profits. Government mediated the conflicts that arose in the course of implementing the bargain. The local governments of large industrial cities like Chicago played a key role in this process.

Chicago was well positioned at the end of the war to be a major player in the development of the new era. It had an infrastructure of railroads, highways, and waterways that could serve industrial production. It had an economic base that was strong in producers' goods—steel, fabricated metals, industrial machinery, transportation equipment—which were needed for all other forms of industrial production. It was also a center for producing, processing, and marketing agricultural products. Chicago produced agricultural machinery, processed food products, and played a major role in the marketing of agricultural commodities through CBOT and the Merc. It was also a center of finance in the Midwest, which was geared to making the funds available for the period of industrial expansion that was under way. Chicago was also the home of the corporate headquarters of many of these activities. And it had a skilled, experienced, and highly organized workforce.

But from the very beginning of the era, Chicago and similar industrial cities manifested many of the contradictions of the era itself. And local government had to deal with these contradictions. The higher wages enjoyed by some workers in this era stimulated a demand for better housing and better schools. The federal government responded with finance programs for housing and by building transportation facilities that enabled white workers to live in new homes outside the city. Retail trade followed this population to the suburbs. The search for room to build modern manufacturing establishments needed for industrial expansion caused the dispersal of Chicago's factories. Fordist production technology required horizontal space that was not always available in the central city. Thus, some manufacturing establishments left the city for the suburbs or for other regions of the country where land was plentiful and relatively cheap.

At the same time, the jobs and wages available in industrial centers like Chicago also attracted new migrants. At the end of World War II, Chicago experienced a third major wave of African American migrants from the South. There was also a smaller yet significant wave of Puerto Rican and Mexican immigrants. These groups did not receive the same level of benefits of the post–World War II deal as whites. The jobs they received had lower pay and benefits, and they were confined to segregated and inferior housing and schools. As whites left the city, the numbers of African Americans grew both absolutely and relative to the white population remaining.

This dynamic created a strain on the city of Chicago's tax base and hence its ability to provide basic services. This is a critical point in understanding city politics. Chicago, like other major cities in the United States, depends heavily on a tax on real estate to provide services. This tax is levied on the assessed valuation of the property within the boundaries of the city. In Chicago, seven separate political jurisdictions, including the city of Chicago, the Board of Education, Cook County, and the Park District, levy taxes on this value. Twenty percent of municipal revenues for the city of Chicago come from real estate taxes. About half of Board of Education revenues come from this source. Property owners generally pass this tax on to tenants so the tax affects rent levels. There are two political ramifications. The taxes are substantial so that increased property tax burden is often a lightning rod at election time. Second, the quality of local government services—especially education—is directly affected by the property tax.

The mayor of Chicago is the key figure managing local politics. A Democratic Party political machine built on patronage, personal services, and favors has prevailed in Chicago since the mid-1930s. The city is divided into fifty wards represented by aldermen. The aldermen dispense the patronage—jobs, special city services, personal favors—which is the lifeblood of the machine. Their job is to turn out support for the mayor and other machine-backed politicians at election time. The mayor, in turn, uses zoning powers, construction, and urban improvement projects to benefit the wards of his loyal aldermen. He also gives these aldermen city jobs and neighborhood services to use as a source of patronage.

The migration of manufacturing, commercial establishments, and white residents to the suburbs during the 1950s represented a tremendous loss of revenue to the political jurisdictions that depended on the tax revenues from the property there. As whites left the city, they abandoned neighborhoods that were in turn occupied by the growing African American and Latino population. Realtors took advantage of the situation by encouraging panic selling by whites remaining in these neighborhoods. They did this by playing on racism, raising the fear that the value of property would decline. They then offered to buy the homes of white residents at low prices. Absentee landlords then divided some properties into apartments, which were allowed to deteriorate, causing property values to fall and promoting further panic selling. Whites who remained in the city treated their neighborhoods as white fortresses and used their political power in local government (and violence when politics failed) to keep others out.

The central city, however, remained a center for the management of the Fordist era and continued to be a very important location for industrial production and corporate headquarters. Thus, something needed to be done to soften these contradictions and stem the fiscal, social, and political crisis that emerged. The solution, for most major industrial cities, was found in what was termed the "pro growth alliance." The basic idea was to build the tax base of the city through investment in the central business district and by "smokestack chasing"—offering tax incentives and land cost write-downs to corporations who would locate their factories and corporate headquarters within the city limits. The alliance was an alliance among city government, a variety of business interests, and some elements of organized labor.

The mayor of Chicago during most of the Fordist era was Richard J. Daley. He served more than five four-year terms that lasted twenty-one years—1955–76. He died in office while serving an unprecedented sixth term. When Mayor Daley assumed power, the legacy of the early years of the Fordist era was a city plagued by deteriorating infrastructure, the ongoing departure of people and economic activity, and the in-migration of people of color. These dynamics, in turn, exacerbated racial conflict that on occasion boiled over into racially motivated violence. Daley's approach to a pro growth alliance was defined by the particular forms that the contradictions of the era took in Chicago and by the chaos caused when the era ended and began its evolution toward a new world order. During the twenty-one-year reign of Mayor Daley, the city of Chicago enjoyed an image of the "city that works." That image was built on Chicago's version of the pro growth strategy. It had four key features. One was to promote building in the city's central area known as the Loop. Second, federal government funds and borrowing were used to clear slums and create upscale neighborhoods to stem or reverse white flight to the suburbs. Third, the fiscal crisis created by demographic and economic decentralization was softened and obscured by the creation of separate taxing authorities under the control of Daley's Democratic Party machine combined with the full use of the city and related taxing districts' borrowing power. Finally, racial conflict was managed both by the creation of a separate yet subservient African American political machine and by forcing the city's growing African American population into segregated neighborhoods and schools.

These four pillars of the Daley years were implemented through the use of patronage to buy political loyalty from aldermen and other Democratic Party regulars and through the assembly of a coalition of key business and labor leaders. These included the banks (Continental Bank, First National Bank); Marshall Fields and other major department stores; the major utilities (Consolidated Edison and People's Gas); the *Chicago Tribune* and other newspapers; major real estate developers; major architectural firms; major corporations with downtown headquarters; and members of the Chicago Federation of Labor—especially the building trades and public employees unions.[1] The coalition was formally constituted in a number of civic organizations, including The Commercial Club, Chicago United, and the Central Area Committee.

These organizations joined the mayor in the implementation of a major downtown building boom that changed the city skyline. It included corporate headquarters buildings for Sears Roebuck, Prudential Insurance, Inland Steel, and Amoco. The mayor and the *Chicago Tribune* backed a project to use government bonds to build a major exposition center, which was named after the *Tribune's* founder, Colonial McCormick. There was also a boom in office construction in the Loop. Between 1958 and 1963, over a million square feet of office space were added to the area. The Loop was made even more accessible by the construction of over 500 miles of freeways during his reign. Daley also built O'Hare Airport, using his political clout to annex suburban territory to do it.[2]

The effort to clear slums and upgrade areas of the city to halt the flight of middle- and upper-income people to the suburbs was likewise extensive and backed by the pro growth coalition. Funds from the federal Urban Renewal program were used to subsidize developers to clear land and build upscale housing and one university. Three major urban renewal projects displaced thousands of people—mostly poor African Americans. Expressways that connected population centers to the downtown also involved extensive displacement. Land was condemned, cleared, and redeveloped in a remarkably short time.[3] Some residents tried to organize, objecting to the lack of relocation plans and affordable housing for the displaced. But these objections were swept aside and the projects went forward.

The third feature of Mayor Daley's pro growth strategy was his approach to the fiscal crisis. Subsidies to developers, the loss of manufacturing and retail establishments, and a general expansion of the city workforce contributed to the crisis. Between 1955 and 1963, the number of city employees increased by 33 percent. Mayor Daley, in order to enhance the value of his patronage, which enabled him to control the aldermen and also to hold organized labor within the pro growth coalition, paid the growing number of workers well. But the property tax rate doubled between 1958 and 1962. The mayor avoided financial meltdown through the creation of multiple tax and borrowing jurisdictions, which enabled him to tax and borrow far beyond the limits imposed by state law on a single political entity. The extensive use of government bonds, however, merely put off some of the negative effects of the fiscal burden to the future. But to the outside world, Daley had avoided a crisis that had afflicted other cities in similar straits. Thus Chicago became known as "the city that works" and the mayor was considered a highly skilled administrator.

These policies, however, intensified racial conflict. The displacement of people of color to build upscale neighborhoods and highways created pressures on other white ethnic neighborhoods. And residents of these communities were prepared to fiercely resist the integration of their neighborhoods and schools. The mayor attempted to manage this racial conflict, using machine-based favors for political control of African American wards and racial segregation to appease white working-class constituents.

Mayor Daley had inherited a dual machine structure based on race from his predecessors that was crucial to his ability to control African American wards. But between 1967 and 1971, the number of African Americans on the city council grew from six to nineteen. This major increase was in part the result of the civil rights movement, which precipitated a historic initiative on the part of African American citizens of Chicago to organize outside the machine. Mayor Daley and his African American machine fought this movement and continued to dominate the city council and local politics. This domination included a successful effort to force Dr. Martin Luther King Jr., who had come to Chicago to push for open housing in 1966, to end his campaign and leave town.[4] The rebuff of Dr. King and the violence he was met with did not sit well with many Chicago African Americans and began to heighten the dissatisfaction with plantation politics. But this was just the beginning of a series of events that would challenge machine politics in Chicago.

While the Fordist period had brought considerable gains to many U.S. workers, many others—particularly workers of color—had been excluded from these benefits. These disparities nationally gave rise to a movement on the part of African Americans initially and later Latinos and women for civil rights and equal treatment at the workplace. Chicago was very much a part of this movement. Mayor Daley, his city council, and his African American politicians were equally a part of the resistance to the civil rights demands, which added fuel to the fire of an already divided city and began to threaten machine control. Opposition to Dr. King was part of that resistance. Containing African Americans in segregated housing and schools and within certain occupational categories was an important element of what made "Chicago work."

As noted earlier, the residents of white wards were feeling pressure from two sources. Massive slum clearance projects resulted in upscale neighborhoods, which they could not afford. Second, displaced African American residents were looking for housing. This situation exacerbated racist feelings that carried over into a strong reaction against open housing and for "neighborhood schools." Moreover, the labor union federation that stood with Mayor Daley and the machine was dominated by white building trade unions that had historically practiced racial exclusion. But the larger movement for civil rights and equal treatment began to turn Chicago's racial containment policies into a major contradiction for Mayor Daley.

In 1962, the U.S. Civil Rights Commission censured the Chicago Board of Education and the superintendent of Schools, Benjamin Willis, for policies that resisted meaningful school integration.[5] Mayor Daley, who controlled the school board and had the power to remove Willis, supported the superintendent, who had taken an uncompromising stance in favor of neighborhood schools. In response, a series of school boycotts included more than 200,000 students—half of Chicago's entire student enrollment. Throughout all of the controversy Mayor Daley remained silent on the school situation and allowed his superintendent and his school board to take the heat. In 1963, Mayor Daley was booed when he attempted to address a meeting of the NAACP.

In the area of housing, the mayor and the city council not only cleared African American and Latino neighborhoods, they built thousands of public housing units and relocated many of the African American displaced families into them. Between 1955 and 1966, fifty-one public housing developments were constructed, nearly all in African American neighborhoods. By 1959, 85 percent of the residents of Chicago public housing were African American.[6] That same year the U.S. Commission on Civil Rights released a report citing Chicago as the most residentially segregated city in the nation.

This was the context of Dr. King's rebuff by the mayor and his hand-picked African American politicians when King and his organization attempted to march on a white community demanding open housing. In 1966, the American Civil Liberties Union (ACLU), based on the U.S. Civil Rights Act of 1964, filed suit against the Chicago Housing Authority. The suit, *Gatreaux v. Chicago Housing Authority,* charged that the CHA was in violation of the act by being "an active and willing partner of a segregationist City Council in a vast expansion of housing segregation in Chicago."[7] The courts ruled in favor of the ACLU. The judgment included a detailed plan for complying with the decision, which demanded that future public housing not be built in areas with a non-white population of more than 30 percent until a specified number of units had been built in other areas. Mayor Daley and the CHA refused to cooperate and essentially placed a moratorium on the building of more housing.

Racial conflict boiled to the surface on Thursday, April 4, 1968, in the aftermath of the assassination of Dr. King. On Friday, thousands of school children and other residents of Chicago's West Side gathered in a park and began to attack the businesses in an adjacent neighborhood. Fires were set that burned most of the night. By Saturday the mayor had set a curfew and called in the National Guard. The mayor's initial reaction was: "Why did they do this to me?"[8] But in a later statement the mayor was sharply critical of the police, indicating that they should have had instructions to "shoot arsonists and looters—arsonists to kill and looters to maim." For many the last straw in the heightening controversy over the city's racial containment policy came in May 1969. In the middle of the night a contingent of police under the command of a machine-connected state's attorney, Edward Hanrahan, attacked the headquarters of Chicago's Black Panther Party where many party members also slept. The Party's chairman, Fred Hampton was shot to death in his sleep as was another party member, Mark Clark. Hanrahan was a political insider and close associate of the mayor's. Initially, a quick coroner's inquest ruled the deaths of Hampton and Clark justifiable homicide. But an investigation by a grand jury resulted in an indictment against Hanrahan. The mayor decided not to back Hanrahan for reelection, but never contradicted his contention that the raid was justified and that the officers "acted with restraint."

Despite the fact that the momentum of the civil rights movement and Chicago's reaction to it were undermining a key to machine power in Chicago—the use of African American politicians and urban development policies to contain the African American population—Mayor Daley continued to prevail. In 1971, Daley ran for an unprecedented fifth term. When issues connected with segregated schools and housing were raised, Daley stood firmly behind his record. He won 70 percent of the vote and carried forty-eight of the fifty wards. But the voting turnout was the lowest ever—and it was particularly low in the African American wards. During the next four years, the Daley administration was beset by one scandal after another. Yet he was still able to prevail at election time. In 1975, he ran for a sixth term. For the first time he had to face a serious challenge in the primaries. A white liberal and an African American state senator opposed him. He won the election easily, but failed to gain the majority of votes in seventeen predominately African American wards.[9] In the general election, he won by a huge plurality, amassing 78 percent of the vote and winning all fifty wards, most by more than 60 percent. But the voter turnout set another record as the lowest in Chicago history.[10]

Chicago Politics and the Emergence of the New World Order

When Mayor Daley first came to power in 1955, he inherited a political machine that had been constructed in an earlier era. But he very skillfully adapted that machine to play the needed role of managing the imperatives of the Fordist period at a local level. But as the Fordist period began to unravel, he was not so quick to adapt to new imperatives. In the United States, race was a contradiction of the Fordist period from the beginning. But as that period picked up steam, the contradiction began to heighten as the civil rights movement demanded a fair share of the proceeds of the Fordist deal with white workers. The contradiction heightened even more as the period began to come apart and the largesse of the postwar reconstruction dried up. Now whites and people of color were placing demands for a share of a shrinking pie. As we have seen, managing racial conflict was key to Mayor Daley's success. But heightened racial conflict threatened it. His response was to dig in his heels and use the iron fist when racial rebellion surfaced. In many ways, the Democratic Party Convention of 1968 was to be a showcase for the mayor to prove to the world and the National Democratic Party that he could still deliver. But that convention was disrupted by another sign of the ending of the Fordist period: the conflict over the Vietnam War. The mayor's overreaction was an indication that he and his machine were losing their grip.

Mayor Daley thus entered his sixth term of office in a weakened position. The pro growth strategies adopted by Chicago and other major cities were dependent on continuously expanding production and rising productivity, and these conditions were no longer being met. As the global crisis deepened and President Nixon cancelled the Bretton Woods Agreement, economic stagnation set in. In the United States, workers were beginning to lose their jobs and income due to both economic stagnation and the beginnings of a new round of deindustrialization, which encompassed the entire metropolitan area, both city and suburbs. In addition, many federal government programs, vital to urban centers like Chicago, were cut back. Economic stagnation meant less government revenues at a national level, yet the government continued to pursue its cold war foreign policy, which required military spending. Public housing, job training, and social welfare programs were all under attack as resources began to shrink. Locally, fiscal resources were also shrinking. This was due not only to the diminished intergovernmental revenues but also the loss of business enterprises and the slowdown in the downtown building boom, which ate at the property tax base.

U.S. cities facing a fiscal crisis at the birth of the new world order used the general expansion of credit as a way to soften the crisis. The nature of municipal borrowing strategies underwent an important shift at the time.[11] One aspect of that shift was that commercial banks and insurance companies withdrew from the municipal bond market. The slack tended to be taken up by wealthy individuals who liked the bonds' tax-exempt status but also looked carefully at the quality of the bonds of different municipalities in selecting candidates for their hefty investment portfolios. As cities became increasingly dependent on selling municipal bonds to keep afloat, big city mayors had to become more sensitive to the reaction of "the markets" to their policies. And "the markets" were increasingly wealthy businesspeople who were looking for safe, tax-exempt havens to store and expand the profits they had derived during the era of Fordism.

As these events unfolded, Mayor Daley continued to pursue the strategy that had kept him in office for nearly two decades. As school teachers and city workers demanded higher pay, the mayor continued to win the support of organized labor by granting large settlements. He adeptly made use of multiple taxing and borrowing jurisdictions under his control to avoid limits placed on any one jurisdiction. Such practices kept bond ratings (which were essential to his ability to borrow money) high and kept the city from fiscal collapse. But they also caused the tax burden to continue to grow. One year into his sixth term in office, Mayor Daley suffered a sudden heart attack and died before these problems could come to a head.

Michael Bilandic, Daley's floor leader on the city council, was appointed as interim mayor after a brief but intense struggle for power among machine aldermen. There was then a primary for a special election in April 1977. Several factions both inside and outside the machine challenged Bilandic. One challenger was African American state senator, Harold Washington, who had broken with the machine. He campaigned exclusively in his district, stating that "there is a sleeping giant" in Chicago.[12] Bilandic narrowly won the primary and easily won the general election, which enabled him to fill out Mayor Daley's term. Jane Byrne, another machine regular who had been appointed by Daley as commissioner of consumer sales, weights and measures in 1968, challenged Bilandic in the 1979 election. She had remained a commissioner and a loyal machine regular until fired by Bilandic in 1977. In her campaign against Bilandic she publicly broke with the machine, labeling them as "an evil cabal of men who ran city hall." Byrne narrowly defeated Bilandic in the primary election with strong support in the African American wards. She went on to win 82 percent of the vote in the general election. Bilandic had simply carried on the policies of his predecessor. Byrne had promised reform. But months after her election, she dropped all pretense as a reformer and turned to the "evil cabal" for help. The city was in financial trouble and the global economic crisis was deepening. It was the time of the second OPEC oil shock, when there was double-digit inflation and double-digit unemployment. So she turned to the machine regulars and the pro growth alliance for help and support. That required that she continue policies that were displacing poor people of color, stonewalling the public housing and schools controversies, and focusing on improving the Loop. Her racial stance was identical to that of her predecessors. African American voters felt betrayed. Reverend Jesse Jackson led a boycott of a major music festival that Mayor Byrne had initiated. The boycott was highly successful and it ended the festival. It also demonstrated not only Mayor Byrne's political vulnerability but also the flagging strength of the pro growth alliance and their strategy. Their solution to Chicago's ills depended on both a strong economy and a passive African American electorate. As the new world order began to establish itself, Chicago had neither.

Harold Washington and Economic Development

As Mayor Byrne's term came to an end, it was clear that she would face a serious challenge in the primaries. Machine regulars favored a return of the Daley family and backed the late mayor's son, Richard M. Daley. All major newspapers endorsed him. Byrne maintained some machine support and appeared to be leading in the polls. But it was state Senator Harold Washington who posed an unexpected challenge—and it was a challenge to the machine itself. Washington had served as a state representative and two terms as a state senator, and was a U.S. congressperson when he challenged Mayor Byrne. He had also run against Bilandic in the special election primary in 1977. While originally a part of the regular Democratic Party organization, he had broken with the machine as racial contradictions heightened. Mayor Daley and African American machine regulars had refused to support him in his bid for a second term as senator. He ran anyway as an "independent Democrat" and won, and later won a seat in the U.S. Congress. As it became clear that Washington was a threat, Alderman Edward Vrdolyak, who had become party chairman under Byrne, said what was on many people's minds as he announced his support for Byrne. He appealed directly to white voters not to split their vote. "A vote for Daley is a vote for Washington. . . . It's a racial thing; don't kid yourself."[13]

But Washington had put together a formidable coalition of African Americans, Latinos, and white liberals who were not only tired of the machine's racial policies but were also fed up with political corruption and the pro growth alliance's entire strategy that was now in disarray. Before the campaign even got under way, Washington supporters launched a massive voter registration drive that resulted in over 180,000 new African American voters. While Byrne and Daley split the white vote, Washington won the primary election with only 36 percent of the total vote.[14] In the general election, machine Democrats, including the local party chairman, Edward Vrdolyak, turned and supported Republican candidate Bernard Epton. Epton's campaign drew the lines clearly on the issue of race. His appeal was to white voters who feared an African American mayor. His slogan was: "Epton, Before It's Too Late!" Despite the centrality of race in the campaign, two additional prominent themes emerged in Washington's speeches that would ultimately come to characterize his Administration: "fair share" and "unity." After a campaign marked by racist attacks, Washington won the election by less than 50,000 votes out of a total 1.3 million.

Harold Washington was Chicago's first African American mayor. But that was not a first for the nation as a whole. Before Harold Washington, a number of U.S. cities with large minority populations had elected African American mayors. They included Cleveland, Gary, Oakland, Newark, Atlanta, and Detroit. This development that began in the late 1970s continued throughout the 1980s. By the mid-1980s, there were nineteen African American mayors in cities with populations over 100,000.[15] There have been several interpretations of the meaning and significance of this.[16] One particular school of thought refers to these local governments as "black urban regimes."[17] Using this conception, Adolph Reed Jr. argues that black urban regimes came out of the demographic and economic forces that left concentrations of low-income African Americans in the city and caused many jobs to leave the city. However, the same forces that brought in black urban regimes had embedded in them serious contradictions. While demographic dominance and economic decentralization brought African American political officials into power and offered many African American citizens employment in the urban bureaucracies, they also marginalized a significant number of citizens, causing social and economic polarization within the African American populace. Second, Reed argued, many black urban regimes found it necessary to buy into the pro growth strategies in order to attain office, but these strategies made progressive redistribution of city resources impossible. According to Reed, the central contradiction facing black regimes was that they are

> caught between the expectations of (their) principally black electoral constituency, which imply downward redistribution, and those of the governing coalition, which converge on the use of public policy as a mechanism for upward redistribution.[18]

The need for these regimes to adopt the pro growth strategy, in this view, had to do with similar problems that had beset Richard J. Daley when he assumed office in the late 1950s in Chicago. There was a need for resources that business had. And Reed argues that the logic of the pro growth strategies now had ideological dominance. That logic required a perception that public policy would be subordinate to business interests. So in the case of black regimes, black political representation was substituted for any challenge to the politics of prior regimes. That resulted in a division between African American leaders and their constituency. While there were some employment benefits to the black regimes, the dominance of pro growth policies left most African American citizens no better off than before.

In the case of the Washington administration, there were some differences from other black regimes. For one thing, Washington was elected as the policies of the pro growth alliance were under significant attack and becoming increasingly ineffective. Furthermore, Washington's election was contested on the terrain of race itself. And Washington responded with the message of "fair share" but also with a detailed program that seemed to negate key features of the pro growth alliance strategy. A set of policy papers was released during the campaign that detailed a program aimed at redistributing resources and moving the political control of resources away from the Loop to the neighborhoods and to neighborhood groups who had actively opposed the pro growth alliance policies. It also proposed to mobilize previously inactive citizens and to redistribute benefits specifically to those at the lower end of the continuum.[19] In 1984, the Washington administration released *Chicago Works Together*, which laid out a detailed development program that reflected these priorities. Job development programs that stressed retaining living wage manufacturing jobs, local buying and hiring, targeted job training, and infrastructure development had strong possibilities for redistribution. There were specific programs to promote balanced growth between the Loop and the neighborhoods. There were proposed programs aimed at neighborhood planning and development and increased public participation. Neighborhood activists were placed in key positions in city hall. All of this seemed very hopeful.

But the Washington administration faced two significant kinds of problems. First, the program was a direct threat to the power base of the machine politicians who still controlled the city council and they opposed the mayor on everything he tried to do. Similarly, city hall was full of machine bureaucrats whom Washington could not get rid of. Just as Mayor Byrne was leaving office, a court case that had been initiated by opponents of the machine to limit Mayor Daley's power by prohibiting hiring and firing based on political considerations was finally concluded. Ironically, the decision made it impossible for Washington to get rid of Daley supporters. Far more serious, however, was the fact that Washington came into power at the birth of the new world order. That initially showed up in Chicago in the form of massive deindustrialization and a decline of federal government resources, causing a greater reliance on credit in order for the city to survive. Thus, many of the proposed programs relied on what Reed referred to as "counter-Keynesian" policies in which public policy followed from business practices instead of the other way around.[20] In Washington's case, he tried to link these with a stipulation that jobs resulting from business development should benefit his African American constituency. But policies included such things as using industrial revenue bonds for business development, micro loan programs to stimulate small business, small business "incubators," and task forces to come up with policies to save industries in decline. The direct objective was still business growth, while employment and income objectives were to be met through business development.

Furthermore, with local tax resources strained and with the cutback of federal funds under devolution schemes, such an approach was highly dependent on credit. Unlike the federal government, cities can't simply print money and their borrowing is extremely limited by law. As I mentioned earlier, the birth of the new world order during the reign of Mayor Richard J. Daley had resulted in increased borrowing from wealthy individuals who were looking for safe, tax-exempt havens for their investment portfolios. Mayor Daley had already stretched both taxing and borrowing by utilizing special administrative and taxing districts. This had important political ramifications for Mayor Washington. The safety of municipal bonds to investors was determined by the credit rating, which in turn was determined by private investor services like Moody. A critical aspect of the rating of the bond issue was the nebulous notion of "business climate."[21] Any mayor, therefore, including Mayor Washington, now had to court "the markets" through the investor services by convincing them that the business climate in their city couldn't be better.

The birth of the new world order increased the importance of the municipal business climate and partially defined what that term meant. In the post–World War II period, municipal debt finance had been used primarily for public facilities. Between 1966 and 1979, 93 percent of municipal debt was used for this purpose.[22] But beginning in the mid-1970s, city governments began borrowing to promote private-sector activity in areas like business development, housing, hospitals, utilities, and recreation facilities. By 1985, up to 80 percent of borrowing by some municipalities went for such purposes. Harold Washington's business-oriented programs were no exception to this.

"The markets" thus became a very important factor in municipal economic development policy since their purchase of municipal bonds was crucial to the implementation of these policies. For this reason the growth coalition partners were still needed to shore up the "business climate." Jayne Byrne learned this very quickly after she became mayor. Harold Washington knew it even before he ever took office. His economic development proposals, on which his call for a fair share were based, were full of business development projects that would require the use of debt finance.

The fact that the city of Chicago had to be governed within the context of the broader new world order initially influenced Harold Washington's choice of partners in the process of forming his government. After his victory in the February 1983 primary election, he formed a transition team that advised him during his campaign in the general election and helped establish the programs that would mark his entire administration.[23] The co-chairs of the new Transition Committee were Bill Berry, former head of the Chicago Urban League, and Bill O'Connor, who was chairman of Commonwealth Edison, the area's utility monopoly. Commonwealth Edison had been a major player in the growth coalition from the beginning of the Daley Administration in the 1950s. There was also an Oversight Committee that was part of the transition team. It included representatives of neighborhood groups, which was very new. But it was also, in the words of a top Washington government official, "*dominated* by chief executive officers of Chicago corporations."[24]

Also, the realities of municipal governance in a new world order seriously limited the notion of fair share, which had been a central theme in Washington's campaign. During his initial campaign, Mayor Washington implied that unity and fair share meant redistribution from whites to people of color.

> The people of Chicago who have been neglected by the political bosses have announced their willingness to become involved, to unify and to act. If I am to be mayor, it would be as the spokesperson of this new movement . . . We devoutly search for unity . . . Fairness will be our standard.[25]

In concrete terms—those determined by the political and economic powers of the city of Chicago—the reality of fair share was quite limited. While the African American and Latino communities could find in the humane practice and rhetoric of the Washington administration some improvement in their treatment by city government, their overall condition changed very little. Nevertheless, the anti-Washington forces, that had been allies of the late Mayor Daley, were infuriated and threatened by even the possibility that a fair share for African Americans and Latinos could become a reality. Their fears and fury took the form of various labels and charges that reflected more what they were afraid of than reality. A case in point is the fact that the Washington administration was labeled "anti-development" in the midst of a major downtown building boom and the destruction of a black neighborhood, which was replaced by a highly subsidized baseball stadium! Increasingly, the response of the Washington administration to the persistence of white racism combined with the realities of life in a new world order was to turn to political compromise, professional administration, and a preoccupation with its own preservation.

As one who worked closely with many of the "middle management" people in the Washington administration, I was struck by the fact that nearly everyone at this level and higher worked exceptionally long hours. When asked what they did each day for so many hours, one of these industrious colleagues replied, "Crisis management." This not only meant many meetings in which there were long discussions about how to appease this or that person who was irritated by this or that decision, but it entailed the practice of placating one group relative to another. The overall principle of all this "crisis management" meant balancing of the interests of the pro growth alliance against the interests of the largely African American and Latino Washington constituency. Because this was the process that evolved out of the practice of building unity for a fair share, I examine this crisis management in the context of two case studies in which I played a personal role: the practice of the mayor's Task Force on Steel and Southeast Chicago and the location of the Chicago White Sox baseball stadium. Both involve the implementation of Mayor Washington's economic development programs that were aimed at concretizing the meaning of fair share.

Economic Development Planning: Two Cases

Economic development and planning activity in a city like Chicago involves a multiplicity of concerns, initiatives, and goals. Among them are the encouragement of different types of development using federal, state, and local subsidies and, increasingly, credit; establishing priorities among different types of development—factories, office buildings, sports stadiums, high-cost housing, low-cost housing; efforts to attract jobs to the area and retain those already there; setting priorities among different types of jobs for retention efforts; and the establishment of job training programs. The Washington administration attempted to implement such activities through a process of "strategic planning" that involved "reform, industrial policy, and progressive planning."[26] "Reform" meant a balance between efficiency (eliminating waste, patronage, and controlled access to government) and equity ("a better deal for those who have been shut off from society"). Industrial policy involved establishing priorities in line with the reform objectives. Progressive planning meant addressing "the claims of constituencies heretofore ignored."[27] Overall, Washington administration officials defined strategic planning as

> a process wherein *key* actors agree on a *limited* number of goals based on a careful analysis of the wide range of strengths and weaknesses in the *organization's* internal and external environment. Then they develop strategies to achieve these goals and deploy resources to support the strategies.[28]

Although abstract, this definition describes quite accurately what the Washington administration attempted to do. Jobs, housing, and development priorities directly affected the lives of the people who made up the Washington movement. In addition, there was a linkage between the institutionalized racism of Chicago's political life prior to the Washington administration and the city's economic development policy. Because of this historical linkage, an end to overt forms of discrimination through contract awards and developmental priorities was the "bottom line" of all this strategic planning.

To that extent, the campaign battle cry of fair share was engaged and a real effort was made to implement it. However, the limitation of the concept of fair share as expressed in economic development and planning practice was also evident. The concept of "key actors" illuminates the nature of the limitation. The practice of strategic planning included the formation of a series of task forces, which were composed of "experts" and others who represented important political interests. In the context of these task forces, unity for a fair share meant an effort to balance interest groups. The constituencies "heretofore ignored" were represented and "citizen input" encouraged. But the choice of "key actors" and the careful analysis was indeed based on the "strengths and weaknesses of the organization's internal and external environment." The organization, however, was the Washington *administration* and not the *movement*. The external environment was the balance of the pro growth alliance in relation to the movement.

Steel Workers Get a Task Force

As part of the economic development planning process, Mayor Washington formed citizen task forces to establish policy for different industries. The mayor's Task Force on Steel and Southeast Chicago was charged by Mayor Washington to "prepare a redevelopment plan that would ease the plight of displaced (steel) workers and stimulate growth in southeast Chicago."[29] The Department of Economic Development staff (presumably in close communication with the mayor and his advisors) spent months developing the structure for the task force and selecting its participants. The task force included four "working groups" concerned with business development, real estate, technology, and the role of steel in the economy. (I served as a member of the Business Development Working Group.) Each group defined issues, conducted research, and made policy recommendations to a policy committee, which in turn made the final recommendations to the mayor. The task force recommendations were presented in their draft form to various groups of steel workers and community organizations for their comments and "citizen input" and then, so informed by the people, the task force made its recommendations final.

The task force was aided by a consultant who conducted major research mostly related to the role and prospects for steel in the Chicago area. Six staff people and the commissioner of the department of economic development were involved in task force activity, mainly doing research and coordinating meetings. The working groups included forty-five people. There were nine members on the policy committee, some of whom also participated in the working groups.

The composition of working groups and policy committee was a study of what I referred to earlier as balancing the interests of the pro growth alliance against the interests of the Washington movement. African Americans, Latinos, women, and white males all had membership on each working group and the policy committee. Some idea of class and other orientations can be gleaned from table 1. "Experts" is a broad category including academics, technical assistance professionals, and scientists affiliated with labs and universities. The extent to which they were inclined toward pro growth versus Washington constituency interests isn't completely clear. The same may be said of a number of other categories. The consultant was clearly oriented toward the mayor's core constituency, as were a number of Department of Economic Development staff people.

What is more important than the exact balance of the task force is the fact that it was assumed that through strategic planning, these key actors could find a common ground between the unemployed steelworker who had lost her or his home and was eating out of garbage cans and millionaire developer Philip Klutznick, who served on the policy committee of the task force. That example may sound extreme, but such class divisions were real. Bankers, lawyers, developers, and university professors discussed the fate of thousands of displaced steelworkers and the future of a declining steel industry. The assumption that there was a common ground that could address the problems the task force was supposed to deal with was at the heart of Washington's theory of fair share through unity. Despite the fact that the task force sought "citizen input," the nine-member committee of key actors defined the issues for discussion and made the policy recommendations. The selection of those individuals was based on a careful analysis of "the organization's [Washington administration] internal and external environment."

Despite the best efforts of Washington's people to bring pro-displaced-worker and community interests into the agenda-setting and decision-making process, it proved difficult to find common ground. It took months of debate and many drafts to find a report the committee could agree upon. The report by the consultant, which was eventually published separately by Northwestern University, was clearly disassociated from the task force itself.[30] The report agreed to by the policy committee included recommendations to encourage retention of what remained of Chicago's steel industry, to aid the development of basic industry technology, and to "facilitate labor adaptation and human resource development." The latter recommendation was the least defined and was to await further development until after the policy committee had disbanded.

TABLE I. Composition of the Mayor's Task Force
on Steel and Southeast Chicago

Background	Policy Committee	Working Groups
Experts	4	17
Lawyers	1	3
Real Estate	2	5
Banking/Finance	2	5
Steel Management	1	4
Union Management	1	0
Workers/Local Union Officers	0	4
Other Business	0	2
TOTAL	9	45

While the decision to attempt to retain steel and other basic industry should not be passed off as insignificant, the recommendations after so lengthy a process were not particularly penetrating. As the task force met, the steel industry continued to decline and it took a major effort to get the committee to agree to intervene when a large steel-making facility was threatened with closure. There was no lack of opinions and ideas among the Harold Washington movement rank-and-filers in Southeast Chicago. But these could not prevail or even achieve full expression given the process and composition of the mayor's task force.

At one point during the task force's deliberations, a group of former Wisconsin Steel workers met and came up with a proposal, which they asked me to submit to the task force. The workers were organized as the Wisconsin Steelworkers Save Our Jobs Committee. They had been strong supporters of Mayor Washington during the election and were a microcosm of what I have termed the Harold Washington movement. At the time, I was working for a university-based economic development research and technical assistance center that focused on low-income communities. In that capacity, I was assisting this group by doing research on issues that concerned them. They met with me at a time when some of the buildings on the Wisconsin Steel site were being demolished. They wanted to try to save the mill and regain their jobs. We invited an engineer to tour the remaining buildings and look at the equipment. Based on our discussions, the workers proposed that the steel task force conduct a feasibility study for a city of Chicago purchase of the Wisconsin Steel facility. Their idea was that the city could then take measures to preserve the buildings and machinery until the demand for steel picked up. They could then sell it to a steel maker, who could rehire the workers. It was also proposed that the city place a moratorium on further demolition of the mill until the feasibility of the idea could be determined.

The meetings of the nine-member task force policy committee were closed. Even though I was on a working group, I had no automatic standing to attend meetings and speak. So I called the commissioner of economic development and asked if I could bring a communication to the task force on behalf of former Wisconsin Steel workers. He agreed. When I stated briefly what the workers had proposed, several members of the task force rolled their eyes. One member literally shouted that the idea was absurd and that Wisconsin Steel was "a bucket of rusty bolts." Most of those around the table chuckled and the chairman, millionaire developer Philip Klutznik, pounded his gavel and asked for the next item of business. I was still standing to one side of the conference table (I never was asked to sit down at the table) and I raised my hand to be recognized. I was ignored by the chair so I interrupted, saying that the proposal was for them to do a serious study of the situation before determining the mill was a "bucket of bolts." The chair pounded his gavel (there were only a dozen people in the room) and stated that I was "out of order." I persisted, saying that people's livelihood and lives were at stake and I had hoped that the mayor's task force on steel would have some concern about this. All the while the commissioner of economic development sat silently glaring at me. The task force members also sat and glared. Then the chair informed me that if I continued to disrupt their meeting he would call in security and have me forcibly removed. I decided to leave on my own power.

The next day the commissioner called the director of my center and said he wanted to see both of us right away. We went to city hall for the meeting. He complained bitterly about my disruptive behavior. I explained to him that our center (which he used to head) was assisting former workers at Wisconsin Steel. I told him that I thought the request for a feasibility study and temporary moratorium on demolition was reasonable. He replied that the reaction of the task force members to the idea said it all. I argued that not only was the reaction not informed by facts, but that the members of the commission did not represent Wisconsin Steel workers' interests and many had conflicting interests. He began to lecture me on interest group politics and how nothing would get done without a committee so constituted. We continued to argue and finally he said, "The trouble with you, Dave, is you just don't know how to behave when we are in power." At that point the meeting ended. When I reported back to the Wisconsin Steel workers, they were enraged. Their leader, Frank Lumpkin, shook his head and said, "We have to talk to Harold." He picked up the phone and called the mayor. He had his direct number. In a half hour we were on our way downtown. Frank, myself, and a lawyer, Tom Geoghegan, who represented the workers, walked into the mayor's office and had a thirty-minute private meeting. The mayor asked to hear the story. He listened carefully, taking notes. He then asked a series of questions about how we came up with our idea and our estimate of the possibilities for a renewal of the steel industry. He then said he thought that the request seemed reasonable, but to please understand that as mayor he did not have the power to act unilaterally. He said he would see what he could do but could offer no promises.

To me the exchange with the steel task force, the commissioner of economic development, and the mayor demonstrated how the concept of fair share was limited not only by "local politics" but by the larger system within which local politics operates. In this case it was the new world order. The fact that there would be such a negative reaction to a proposal for a feasibility study was stunning to me. The task force had been hiring all sorts of consultants to make studies. But this one struck a nerve. A feasibility study to determine if the mill had longer-term viability once the steel demand slump picked up was clearly in the interest of the steelworkers who had lost their jobs. The mayor respected this but also had to contend with the political forces represented on the task force. The commissioner had skillfully brought these forces together to create a broader base of support for the mayor. He was thus upset when the Wisconsin Steel workers through my agency threatened to create a division. Broadening the base of support for the mayor meant accommodating those interests—land developers, lawyers, big organized labor, and others—that in an earlier period had formed the backbone of the pro growth alliance. At this point this alliance was trying to come up with strategies in line with the "realities" of the new world order. Those realities included rapid deindustrialization and shrinking resources. In this light, the very idea that the steel industry in Chicago might recover appeared absurd. And in a developing ideological climate that preached the virtues of free markets, the idea that the city might buy and hold a private enterprise that sat on prime industrial real estate was unthinkable. Thus, the limits of fair share could not even include a feasibility study of the idea.

The work of the task force resulted in two reports, one by the consultant (which the task force refused to publish) and one by the task force. But nothing was done that resulted in either the easing of "the plight of displaced workers" or the stimulation of "growth in southeast Chicago," which was the task force's charge. Steel demand, of course, eventually picked up. Even in the present era of high capital mobility and increasing steel imports, there is still much steel produced in the United States. But now U.S. steelworkers earning far lower wages and benefits than in the past largely produce it in smaller mills. During the deliberation of the task force another major mill was closed, displacing more than 10,000 workers. The parent company, USX, had received subsidies from the state of Illinois to construct a rail mill, which they never did. The task force was unable to act decisively by forcing the company to live up to its end of the bargain. The Wisconsin Steel buildings continued to deteriorate and were eventually demolished. Now, nearly twenty years later, the land sits idle.

The Chicago White Sox Get a New Stadium

The relocation of a baseball stadium in Chicago's South Armour Square neighborhood is another example of the limits of Mayor Washington's application of fair share and unity. South Armour Square is a small African American community located 2 miles south of Chicago's Loop.[31] It was destroyed by the relocation of an adjacent professional baseball stadium. The neighborhood is isolated from the surrounding residential communities by railroad tracks to the west, a major expressway to the east, an industrial area to the south, and the Chicago White Sox, Comiskey Park to the north. South Armour Square has historically been a working-class district. Its first settlers were Irish, German, and Swedish laborers. African American workers looking for city jobs after World War I brought them to the area to live. By 1930, 44 percent of South Armour's population was African American. The availability of cheap land in close proximity to the rapidly developing industrial areas nearby and the overcrowded conditions of other African American residential areas attracted the descendants of South Armour's current residents.

South Armour has a history of mixed land uses, which have included residential, industrial, commercial, and baseball parks. Since the turn of the century, professional baseball stadiums have played an important role in South Armour development. In 1900, the Chicago White Sox played in an open-field park that was later taken over by the Negro League team, the American Giants. The White Sox built their first baseball stadium, Comiskey Park, in 1910 nearby. In 1946, Wentworth Gardens, a 422-unit Chicago Housing Authority (CHA) public housing development occupying 16 acres, was built on the site of the former American Giants baseball field. This development was built to house African American veterans returning from World War II. Later, in the 1970s, the Progressive Baptist Church, which is located adjacent to Wentworth Gardens, built the T. E. Brown Apartments, which is a 12-story building that houses 117 African American residents who are mostly senior citizens or people with disabilities. This development was funded with federal government monies and its rents are thus subsidized. There is also a public grammar school in the area to the south of T. E. Brown Apartments. Prior to the summer of 1986, the South Armour Community had 89 private residential buildings that contained 179 housing units occupied by African American families. The area also contained 11 businesses, including a grocery store, restaurant, gas station, and tavern. South Armour had been a unified and cohesive mixed-income community. Many of the residents who live in T. E. Brown and Wentworth Gardens had friends and relatives with whom they frequently visited in the private residences. They patronized the local businesses and attended the church in the area.

Despite the strong bonds within the community and its stability and cohesion, South Armour became the target for redevelopment and displacement for relocation of the old White Sox stadium. The new Comiskey Park bisects the community and has created a barrier, which further isolates its residents from the white and Chinese communities in the surrounding area. The construction of a new Comiskey Park in 1989 meant all of the private residences and commercial establishments were destroyed, leaving only the T. E. Brown

Apartments, Abbott Grammar School, the Progressive Baptist Church, and the public housing development of Wentworth Gardens. These institutions abut each other and form an island, surrounded for the most part by parking lots for the stadium. The stadium wall now forms the northern boundary of the remaining community. It is next to T. E. Brown Apartments. On top of this wall there is an exploding scoreboard, which in good White Sox tradition shoots off fireworks whenever a Chicago player hits a home run. The scoreboard explodes less than 200 feet from the homes of the mostly African American senior citizen residents. The 12 displaced businesses resulted in a loss of over 300 jobs. One company, which had been in the area for 60 years and employed 70 persons, moved to Indiana. Seventy percent of the employees in the displaced businesses had lived in the neighborhood.[32] This development is a case where the residents of the neighborhood, who were part of the Harold Washington core constituency, came up against the interests of the old pro growth alliance as they were seeking to accommodate the growing realities of the new world order.

The displacement and destruction of the community did not occur without a fight. In 1987, the residents of South Armour formed an organization to contest the relocation of Comiskey Park. The organizing began as Harold Washington faced a tough election fight for a second term. The mayor was also seeking to gain a majority in the city council, which would prevent his opponents from blocking his programs. The Chicago White Sox had been agitating for a new stadium and were looking at sites in the suburbs as well as in Florida and Colorado. There was strong sentiment among Chicago baseball fans to keep the Sox in the city. Sports franchises are part of a city's image, contributing to its "business climate." Modern sports stadiums enhance this image through the creation of corporate "sky boxes," fancy restaurants overlooking the field, and high ticket prices. The new Comiskey stadium incorporates all of these features. The image aspect of the sports franchise was not lost on Mayor Washington. He told one of his top aides that if Chicago lost a major sports franchise neither he nor any African American candidate could win the next election.[33]

This was the context in which Republican Governor Jim Thompson of Illinois and the mayor supported a law that formed the Illinois Sports Facility Authority (ISFA). This authority was specifically set up to build a new stadium for the Chicago White Sox professional baseball team. The ISFA is a unique government entity. It is governed by a board of directors that is appointed by the governor of Illinois and the mayor of Chicago. Even before the legislation was signed, the politicians had decided to build the stadium adjacent to the existing Comiskey Park in the South Armour Square neighborhood. The planned relocation would destroy nearly one-third of the community. When asked about this displacement, Mayor Washington said, "Any displacement is unfortunate, but one must resort to it. A fair offer will be made for their properties."[34] Mayor Washington responded to the threatened loss of the White

Sox by firmly supporting the stadium project. His concern about the political ramifications of losing the Sox led him to downplay the stadium's impact on the residents of South Armour, even though such downplaying contradicted his position as an advocate for the interests of low-income minority communities. The South Armour community was politically weak because it was within the political jurisdiction of a white-controlled ward whose political leaders' interests led them to make sure that white families were not displaced by the relocation of the White Sox stadium.

The owners of the White Sox and other professional sports franchises occupy a unique position within the civic and economic structures of Chicago and similar U.S. cities. They control a scarce commodity, the supply of which is determined by the expansion policies of the sports leagues.[35]

There are a limited number of professional baseball franchises, which allows the owners of these franchises to use the threat of leaving as a wedge to get what they want. Most public officials feel a sense of "peril over the prospect of losing professional sports entertainment."[36] In Chicago, this power was used by the owners of the White Sox to pressure Mayor Washington to go against the interests of members of his constituency who were living in the South Armour community. And they were also able to gain support and major concessions from the city of Chicago and the state of Illinois for the financing of the stadium.

The formation of the ISFA and its financing power was a modern development representing the shift in public borrowing for the benefit of private enterprise described earlier. The ISFA was critical to the development of the stadium because its financing and eminent domain authority gave it political power outside the sphere of city politics. The ISFA was not accountable to elected officials, and that further diminished the power of the South Armour residents to resist and counteract its authority. Eminent domain is the right of government to take private property for public use. The state legislation gave the authority this power and also the ability to sell bonds to finance the stadium development. The city also committed a 2 percent hotel/motel tax to pay back the bonds and provided an additional $150 million in tax-exempt bonds for the project. The ISFA's eminent domain authority was known as "quick take" eminent domain. This meant that the ISFA could take control of private land by a certain date and negotiate later with the owners for price and relocation costs. The "quick take" powers became an important tool in threatening the South Armour Square residents and breaking some away from their coalition.

The residents of South Armour first learned that their neighborhood would be the site for the new stadium from the newspapers. According to the manager of T. E. Brown Apartments, the fact that the residents were not part of the planning process at the very height of the Washington years was a very sore point of contention.[37] In response, the residents formed the South Armour Square Neighborhood Coalition (SASNC) to organize themselves to respond to the threat of the stadium. The SASNC included people from private homes within the site of the proposed stadium, as well as residents of Wentworth Gardens, T. E. Brown Apartments, and adjoining communities. At first, SASNC organized to preserve their neighborhood by fighting for an alternative site that would minimize displacement. SASNC argued that the stadium could be developed a few blocks to the north of the existing stadium on the large expanses of parking lots there. A Chicago architect drew up plans for this alternative site as part of a project for the Society for American Baseball Research. Neither the White Sox owners nor ISFA ever seriously considered this option.

SASNC then developed a number of position papers in their organizing campaign to negotiate with ISFA. They continued to press for the alternative site. They also prepared a list of demands that included the following: (1) if residents were to be displaced, they should receive more than fair market price for their property and be given the option to remain in a reconfigured South Armour neighborhood; (2) SASNC wanted to be the main negotiator for the community; (3) SASNC wanted economic development opportunities as part of the stadium project, which meant job set-asides for neighborhood residents and the creation of a dedicated revenue stream from stadium profits for neighborhood industrial and commercial development; and (4) SASNC proposed that a trust fund be established to rehabilitate and improve the housing stock in the remaining neighborhood.

After a series of protests, ISFA agreed to meet with representatives from SASNC. Three representatives were chosen to represent SASNC in the negotiations with ISFA. All three of the negotiators were homeowners. ISFA appealed directly to the interests of the homeowners and offered them a very generous relocation package. The SASNC president, one of the negotiators, along with the help of an attorney who had offered her services to the SASNC, cut a deal for the homeowners without consulting the other members of the coalition. This created a split between homeowners and the seniors and public housing residents. One of the public housing residents commented that "the homeowners were told you had more to lose . . . and if you don't go along with us we will take your property and you get zapped. So, therefore, the homeowners were scared."[38] The homeowners thus formed a separate group, which ratified an agreement with ISFA that was generous to them but left public housing residents and seniors with nothing.

ISFA's "quick take" authority enabled them to put a gun to the head of the residents. The homeowners and renters had to enter into a contractual agreement with ISFA by September 15, 1988, to receive their relocation assistance. If agreements were not reached by October 15, 1988, ISFA had the authority to take title to the properties and negotiate later for compensation. Most of the homeowners and renters settled before September 15. A number of the businesses went to court to fight for more compensation for their properties. All the properties were vacated in March 1988 to make way for the bulldozers.

The remaining members of the original SASNC, who were now residents from the T. E. Brown Apartments and the Wentworth Gardens Public Housing development, continued to fight the stadium location. After two years of organizing and attempting to negotiate with ISFA to modify the site plan and respond to the other demands of the remaining residents, the SASNC filed a federal lawsuit on February 9, 1989, which charged the development was racially biased. The lawsuit had forty-nine plaintiffs from the neighborhood. The suit made several key allegations. First of all, the location of the new Comiskey Park south of the old Comiskey Park displaced more people than if it had been located to the north. All of the residents of South Armour were (and are) African American. If the stadium were located to the north, the displaced people would have been white. Moreover, the suit contended that in mid-1986, the mayor's office directed the city's Department of Planning staff to assess the best location for a stadium in the general area of the existing Comiskey Park. The city planning staff person who undertook this study was aware of the racial tension and politics of the neighborhood. After substantial analysis, the city staff person recommended that both sites in the area should be considered. The city staff person also contended that the advantages of both sites were about equal, although the northern site had some distinct advantages such as less housing and commercial displacement and the likelihood of a more expeditious and economic construction.[39] Yet, the site to the north was never considered because the more powerful white voters in the area would not allow it. The southern site was politically more viable only because the residents were politically weak. A memo written by a Chicago Department of Planning and Development staff member to the commissioner of development stated that the South Armour community was "isolated" and that the "black residents" in South Armour had no political support in the 11th ward.[40]

Another key point of the lawsuit was that there never was a public hearing on the relocation site of Comiskey Park. In the initial legislation, which created the ISFA, there was a stipulation that the ISFA must conduct a study and hold public hearings to determine the site of the stadium. No study or hearing was ever conducted. This is in stark contrast to an earlier attempt by the White Sox to build the new stadium in a white suburban area outside Chicago. In this case, an advisory referendum was taken in which the white citizens had an opportunity to voice their opinion on whether the White Sox could relocate into their community. Local politicians hoped that the referendum would show a strong preference one way or the other for or against the stadium. But, the final vote was close: 50.3 percent against and 49.7 percent in favor. Without a strong mandate to go ahead, the politicians killed the possibility of the stadium being relocated into their suburban area. The residents of South Armour never had this opportunity to voice their opinion. In fact, the Illinois Sports Facility Authority deliberately refused to follow the 1986 legislative mandate that it seek public input and conduct public hearings on site selection. And after the site selection for the new stadium was made, the ISFA sought to repeal the notice and hearing requirements of the 1986 legislation. In June 1988, ISFA, along with the White Sox and the city of Chicago, requested that the original legislation be amended to eliminate the need for notice and hearings on site selection. The legislature approved these changes without debate.

After eight years, a federal judge ruled in the spring of 1996 that the case did not have sufficient merit to go to court and questioned the legal standing of the South Armour residents in bringing the suit. The judge also told the residents that if they agreed to a settlement and waived their right to appeal they would not be liable for more than $30,000 in legal costs claimed by the ISFA and the Chicago White Sox. Under the threat of liability for these costs, residents signed the agreement. In September, however, a number of residents who did not care about their liability (they had no assets) attempted to appeal the agreement. Again, the judge refused and after nine years all legal options were exhausted.

Nonetheless, SASNC was able to use the case to leverage government funds to pursue a planning project to replace the commercial development that was lost when the stadium was relocated. They proposed a $1.5 million convenience shopping center with residents as owners and operators. As one member of the SASNC said, "We need the community to be built by us. [The White Sox, ISFA, and City of Chicago] are responsible for building back some of the things we had."[41] Citizens were seeking reparations. The attitude of the ISFA was neatly summed up by a spokesperson for the Illinois Sports Finance Authority: "There was a story in *Cranes* [a business newspaper] two years ago. . . . They questioned why the new Comisky Park didn't deliver on the promise of economic development around Comisky Park. To be honest, it irritated us."[42] Eventually, the residents' efforts faltered. They were rejected for federal funding to construct the shopping center. Some residents became discouraged or left the community. While the actual building of the stadium and the court case occurred after Mayor Washington's untimely death in 1987, the Washington administration actually set up the conditions under which the stadium interests were able to implement their plan.

The above two statements—one by a SASNC member and one by a spokesperson from the ISFA—illustrate the conflict between the core constituency of the Washington administration and those of pro growth interests that Mayor Washington needed to accommodate. The main argument of this chapter has been that local government plays a key role in administering the prevailing strategy for the accumulation of surplus value. The Washington administration was attempting to implement a fair share approach to local politics at a time when the old order had dissolved and a new world order was emerging. This context placed limits on what fair share could mean. In the case of the White Sox stadium, the relocation plan and its implementation involved overt discrimination against Harold Washington's African American constituency.

Yet he was forced to go along. There were a number of things at stake. At a time of shrinking fiscal resources and a need for jobs that were generated by the dissolution of the old order, the loss of a major league ball team would have been a serious blow. Moreover, there were financial interests and business interests—led by the Republican governor of the state of Illinois—which stood to profit from the venture. They, in a sense, represented "the markets" in this case. To oppose them and lose the White Sox to boot would have meant, as the mayor pointed out so clearly, the end of not only his political life but that of any African American successor. His stance was thus the only decision he could make to preserve the notion of fair share local government. The fact that his stance destroyed an African American neighborhood in the process demonstrated the limits of such a notion in the new world order.

Local Government and the New World Order

Mayor Washington's sudden death in 1987 resulted in an African American alderman, Eugene Sawyer, being selected by the city council as acting mayor. Sawyer was one of those who had been supported by the late Richard J. Daley when he sought to weaken the power of more independent-minded African American leaders in the 1960s. At this point he was supported by some of the most notorious white anti-Washington aldermen. Sawyer's rival, alderman Timothy Evans, claimed the people supported him. Evans went on to form a "Harold Washington Party," leaving Sawyer to run against the late Mayor Richard J. Daley's son, Richard M. Daley, in the Democratic Party primary in 1989. Sawyer lost the primary and Evans lost big in the subsequent general election. Significant numbers of African Americans and Latinos who had voted for Washington in previous elections didn't vote at all and a number of white liberals who had voted for Washington turned and supported Daley. As I write this, Richard M. Daley has been mayor of Chicago for over eleven years. His political strength is the equal of his father's. He has adapted Chicago politics well to the new world order. I examine this theme with respect to housing policies in the following chapter. But first, it is important to draw some conclusions about local politics during the Harold Washington era.

Mayor Washington made an honest effort to address the inequities of machine politics in Chicago and to cope with the attack on the living standards of many Chicago residents in the wake of the onslaught of the new world order. The cases of the steel task force and the stadium relocation do not suggest that the notion of fair share and unity were a sham, but highlight the limits of local electoral politics generally. I began this chapter making the general point that the role of the state is to preserve the basic system of capital accumulation. At the same time, government is also the forum through which individuals, groups, and classes of people can contest the way this system affects them. But this forum has limits imposed by the need to preserve the system.

Each era of capitalist development presents the state with new tasks and new sets of citizen demands to deal with. The strategies of the pro growth alliance developed in U.S. cities in the 1950s and 1960s were a response to the urban contradictions that were inherent in the Fordist period. Rising incomes of white workers from industrial expansion in the postwar years gave rise to the demand for better housing and schools. The federal government responded with programs that led to suburbanization and racial segregation.[43] The imperatives of industrial expansion also generated a search for horizontal space for new manufacturing facilities, which also led to the decentralization of economic activity outside the central city. Meanwhile, African Americans came to the cities in search of higher-wage jobs. These forces combined left the core city in dire straits. The general solution of the pro growth alliances in cities across the nation was investment in downtown development. Mayor Richard J. Daley adapted this strategy to Chicago's conditions. A particular need in Chicago, however, was for racial containment.

Chicago's racial containment policies presented Mayor Daley and any mayor who was to follow him with an enormous contradiction, which only intensified as the system that generated the pro growth strategies began to unravel. Mayor Washington attempted to soften that contradiction through programs based on his notions of fair share and unity. He attempted to channel resources to the neighborhoods, reignite manufacturing development, and unite warring factions in the city around gaining a fair share of federal government funding. While Chicago's white aldermen attempted to thwart him at every turn, the mayor was also limited by the remnants of the old order, the severe problems that accompanied its dissolution, and the emerging contradictions of the new world order itself.

The racist opposition in Mayor Washington's city council was a manifestation of the death-throes of the old order. The deal with labor—especially white labor—which offered prosperity to Chicago's white working class was now off. The residents of the white wards were losing ground. African Americans were suffering even more, so they continued their struggle for civil rights. This offered a new context for Chicago's historic racism. And it goes a long way toward explaining the extreme racist attacks on the Washington campaign and the administration.

Furthermore, the dissolution of the Fordist era was accompanied by a period of economic instability. Beginning in the mid-1970s and into the 1980s, there was a series of deep recessions accompanied by high inflation. These crises caused many of Chicago's workers to be laid off from their jobs, even as double-digit inflation ate away at their standard of living. The crises were followed by the period of deindustrialization described in the previous chapter. The economic crisis gave rise to the need for more resources to improve the living conditions of Chicago's residents, particularly poor people of color. But the aim of the new world order development strategy was to reduce the claims being made on the value the system was producing. In cities like Chicago, that took the form of both deindustrialization and the reduction of federal government programs to help the urban poor. Mayor Harold Washington responded by attacking President Ronald Reagan's "war on cities" and calling on all Chicago citizens to demand their fair share. But the Washington administration's efforts to hold living wage manufacturing jobs in Chicago and to gain more federal government resources ran counter to the thrust of the new world order itself.

Meanwhile, the old pro growth alliance was attempting to force the Washington administration to return to the pro growth agenda. The evolving fiscal crisis and the subsequent need for credit strengthened their hand. The shift in municipal credit sources to wealthy individuals in order to stimulate private business increased the importance of "business climate," which the pro growth alliance could use politically. The pro growth alliance's power was also enhanced by the fact that corporations were gaining mobility and were no longer tied to the Chicago area, let alone the city as a place to do business. Thus the Harold Washington administration was forced to compromise. It attempted to do this by placing pro growth interests in key policy development roles. While there were new citizen faces in city hall and on the various task forces and boards that Mayor Washington created to develop his initiatives, they were limited by the dominance of those who could enhance the "business climate." The mayor's priority on neighborhood development versus the Loop, therefore, could not entirely relinquish political control to the neighborhoods. Ultimate control was always in the hands of pro growth forces. This is why a Washington administration perspective that neighborhood planning districts should administer planning and development in their area never was realized.[44]

Moreover, those African Americans and Latinos whose own interests were closely aligned with the imperatives of the "business climate" increasingly "represented" people of color on appointed task forces. What evolved was a widening division within the core constituency based on class interests. This division was illustrated by the two cases in this chapter. The mayor's Task Force on Steel and Southeast Chicago was multiracial, but it ultimately did not represent the interests of steelworkers, as the Wisconsin Steel episode illustrated. Similarly, the White Sox stadium revealed such divisions on two levels. The Illinois Sports Facility Authority was a multiracial entity that had interests that were contradictory to those of the residents of South Armour Square. In addition, the ISFA was able to exploit and widen the division within the neighborhood between homeowners and the residents of publicly assisted housing.

Thus, new alliances that included professional and affluent African Americans and Latinos as well as traditional pro growth alliance members were built to meet the imperatives of the new world order and preexisting divisions based on both race and class. It was the Washington administration that initially formed these alliances. The new alliances were an unintended by-product of efforts to change the political thrust of machine politics built by Richard J. Daley. Since Mayor Washington was genuinely attempting to offer an alternative to what Mayor Daley had built, these alliances represent the limits placed on local government and politics by the broader system of capital accumulation. Interestingly enough, the new alliances' ability to adapt to the strategic thrust of the new world order made them attractive to subsequent administrations, and they were honed to perfection once Mayor Richard M. Daley took office. The following chapter examines this development in relation to the issue of housing.

CHAPTER 6

Where Will Poor People Live?

David C. Ranney and Patricia A. Wright

America the beautiful, but beautiful for whom? Is it just beautiful for the politicians, the rich and the famous? Do poor people really have a place in America?

> ——Barbara Moore,
> Robert Taylor Homes (Public Housing) Resident,
> Chicago Coalition to Protect Public Housing,
> November 1999

As we got into this fight I began to see what they were proposing for my people. They were proposing for my people to be evicted and become homeless. . . . That is why I am in this fight; because I have been at the homeless shelters and I have seen people waiting to get in.

> ——Carol Steele,
> Cabrini Green Homes (Public Housing) Resident,
> Chicago Coalition to Protect Public Housing,
> November 1999

Shortages of affordable housing are nothing new. But the nature of the housing problem (and hence potential solutions) takes different forms in different eras. The previous chapter touched on this. The first Mayor Daley implemented housing policy in the Fordist era. The post–World War II deal with U.S. labor, which was a key aspect of that era, included housing. Simply stated, the U.S. government agreed to make sure that the nation had an adequate housing stock. However, this agreement fell short of making housing an entitlement. At the end of World War II, the United Nations Declaration on Human Rights included housing as one of those rights. But the United States never accepted that. Rather, U.S. housing policy softened the risks associated with housing. These risks include the risk of not being able to find decent housing and the risk of losing the housing you already have. U.S. housing programs assumed some of this risk by guaranteeing loans, subsidizing interest rates and building government-owned housing.[1] As we saw in Chapters 3 and 5, however, these policies generated contradictions. Their inequitable application stimulated the flight of white-working class families from the central city to the suburbs, opening the city to racially based panic selling, speculative buying, and absentee landlords who allowed the central city housing stock to deteriorate.[2] A growing African American and Latino population occupied the aging residential areas in Chicago. Lower-income and working-class whites who remained in the city made white-only fortresses of their neighborhoods. Overall, the city was in a state of decay because both people and jobs were departing for the suburbs, undermining the city's economic base.

On the housing front, the U.S. government responded by adding to their housing policy arsenal subsidies to developers. A program known as Urban Renewal used public tax revenues to clear land that had been declared "blighted" and sell it to developers at a price well below its market value. The public housing program was utilized to contain the people displaced by this program. The result was a process of gentrification, in which lower-income people, mostly African Americans and Latinos, were replaced by more affluent whites. Many of the displaced African Americans ended up in public housing. There was thus a decided racial and class contradiction built into government housing policy during the Fordist era.[3] Housing policies at the federal level and the contradictions they generated played a major role in shaping local politics in cities like Chicago.

These policies not only led to unequal distribution of housing resources and increased racial tensions; they were not sustainable once the Fordist period began to disintegrate. The entire post–World War II deal with American workers depended on an expanding industrial economy, incomes, and consumer purchases. In the absence of these features, the new world order housing policies were necessarily different. Chapter 3 argued that both international and domestic aspects of new world order policy emphasize private market deregulation, privatization of many government services, and an enhanced mobility of goods, services, and capital. In part, these goals have been implemented by combining market liberalization (elimination of capital controls, tariffs, and so-called non-tariff barriers to trade) with the undermining of public-sector activity. The latter includes the privatization of public services, including housing, and the balancing of government budgets through massive slashes in social program spending. The system is fueled by the expansion of credit and speculation.

Under this regime, housing policy has shifted in three important ways.

- Government has severely cut back on publicly owned housing. Government programs now emphasize privatization.
- There has been a shift away from viewing housing as a social good. Main-

taining an adequate housing stock, which was the goal of housing policy during the Fordist era, was a goal for American society as a whole. The shift that has become a part of the evolution of the new world order stresses individual competitiveness in housing markets and encourages individual home ownership. This emphasis on individuals has also effectively shifted the risks—both financial risks and the risks of losing adequate housing— from financial intermediaries and government to households. And the burden of this shift falls disproportionately on the poor.[4]

- The provision of housing is driven by the expansion of credit and speculation. The new world order credit mechanisms benefit developers and wealthy households and some moderate-income families, but they tend to leave out the poor.

These three shifts in public policy and private-sector practice have had a profound social impact relative to the question of where poor people can live. Housing in a capitalist society has always had a dual character. On the one hand, it is a commodity that is useful because it provides needed shelter (a use value). At the same time, it is a commodity that can be bought and sold (an exchange value). The combination of the retreat from public housing, the shift away from housing as a social priority, and the central role of expanded credit and speculation, has nearly turned housing into a pure exchange value. Housing as a useful commodity that offers needed shelter is being neglected in favor of housing's value as an investment. Because of this, the question of where poor people will live is not addressed by the new world order.

Moreover, the dominance of housing's exchange value over its use value has led to the destruction of affordable housing for the poor and the acceleration of the process of replacing affordable housing with housing for the rich (gentrification). According to Neil Smith, "the dismantling of public services and privatization of public functions since the mid-1980s has given gentrification an altogether more ominous social meaning."[5] It is producing cities of haves and have-nots, and Chicago is one of them.

The remainder of this chapter develops the above assertions. First, we explain some of the new world order housing policies and finance mechanisms in the United States. Second, we present two case studies that show how these policies have worked in Chicago. One involves the gentrification of an area just to the south of the Loop. This development spans the administrations of Richard J. Daley, Harold Washington, and Richard M. Daley. It was conceived under the programs and assumptions of the Fordist regime, but was largely implemented in the 1980s and 1990s as the new world order evolved. The second case involves the destruction of a public housing development in Chicago. The particular redevelopment in this case, Cabrini-Green Homes, is part of a larger plan to replace public housing with "mixed-income development" that affects nearly all public housing in the city. The plan has been conceived and implemented during Mayor Richard M. Daley's administration in the 1990s

and on into the next millennium. It is a new world order project. The final part of the chapter draws conclusions relating to the question of where poor people can live in this new world order.

Housing Policy and Finance in the New World Order: The Retreat from Public Housing

Background

The United States has had a program of publicly owned and managed housi for the poor since 1937. The original purpose of the program was to be a par the social safety net for persons who could not afford a decent and safe hor Its impetus was the Depression of the 1930s and the potential uncontrolle rebellion on the part of the homeless, unemployed, and impoverished.[6] ' original federal legislation established a goal that individuals should not k to spend more than 20 percent of their income for housing. That thres goal has been bumped up a number of times and now stands at 30 per Other eligibility definitions have been made to allow higher-income ter in public housing because they can pay rents that offset public costs.

Local public housing authorities are established to administer the p housing program. The CHA administers public housing in the Chicago It was established in 1937. The board consists of nine persons; the ma Chicago appoints all of them. Three of the members must be public h residents. When the public housing program was first established, ther relatively few units built in Chicago. But as we saw in the previous cha major slum clearance program in the 1950s began to displace mostly American families, who were excluded from much of the available h At this point the public housing building program boomed. Between 1 1966, the CHA built on average 1,000 units per year.[7] While the pace ing slowed abruptly after this period, by 1983 there were 40,781 unit

The previous chapter demonstrated that the slowing of public hou struction in Chicago after 1966 had everything to do with race. Publi in Chicago is thoroughly segregated. African Americans comprise 8 of the residents of public housing in Chicago. The remaining 15 p white (10%) and Latino (4.9%).[8] African American households m percent of the family housing units. As noted in Chapter 5, the _Gautreaux v. Chicago Housing Authority_, resulted in a federal c banning further construction of public housing in segregated areas and Mayor Richard J. Daley responded by nearly halting construci

Housing segregation, however, was already widespread, and fede ment programs had contributed greatly to the practice.[10] In the 19 the 1940s, realtors openly practiced housing discrimination wit restrictive covenants that conditioned future sales of property c

ethnic exclusion. The Federal Housing Act of 1934 provided mortgage guarantees and low to zero down payments, which were used almost exclusively for suburban development that excluded African Americans. Language in the Federal Housing Administration's (FHA) manual to banks that were using these subsidies reinforced the discriminatory practices of the real estate industry: "If a neighborhood is to retain stability, it is necessary that properties shall continue to be occupied by the same social and racial classes."[11] A 1948 U.S. Supreme Court case ruled that the courts could not enforce practices that maintained racial exclusion. But realtors simply refused to show housing to African Americans in white areas and the federal government did nothing to interfere.

The pattern of housing segregation throughout U.S. cities like Chicago and the predominance of African Americans in public housing specifically was reinforced by more federal legislation in the late 1940s and 1950s. The Housing Acts of 1949 and 1954 offered subsidies to developers to clear slums and to redevelop or rehabilitate housing in so-called blighted areas. In Chicago, the areas targeted for what the government called Urban Renewal were predominantly African American and Latino. This was true nationally as well, prompting civil rights leaders to dub the urban renewal program "Negro Removal." Urban Renewal generated a process of gentrification in which new and rehabilitated housing was beyond what former residents of redeveloped neighborhoods could afford. So they migrated to other segregated neighborhoods or, if they could qualify, moved into public housing. Gentrification throughout most of the Fordist era was thus predominantly government-driven.

The U.S. civil rights movement of the 1960s and 1970s began to change federal practices. In 1968, the Housing and Civil Rights Act banned housing discrimination. But enforcement provisions were weak. In the 1970s, activists were able to force the government to make changes in the racially biased policies and practices of the real estate and banking industries. The Community Reinvestment Act of 1977, for example, outlawed the practice of banks refusing to lend money for housing in mixed or minority areas and required them to help meet credit needs in low-income communities. Nevertheless, the pattern of housing discrimination persists to this day. As one analyst concludes, "Considered as a whole, the federal housing policies of the last three decades have surely contributed more to housing segregation than to its reduction."[12]

Housing Policy in the 1970s and 1980s

The retreat from publicly owned housing began in the 1970s. The president of the United States, Richard Nixon, placed a moratorium on public housing construction. At the same time, the administration introduced and passed the Housing and Community Development Act of 1974. This legislation included the Section 8 housing program. Section 8, renamed the Housing Choice

Voucher program in 1998, has become the federal government's chief mechanism for assisting low-income families, the elderly, and the disabled to rent housing in the private market. This program was first introduced to shift responsibility for affordable rental housing units from publicly owned and managed housing to the private market. Section 8 also replaced other programs that involved the direct finance of rental housing. When first established in 1974, the Section 8 housing program had two components: the project-based subsidy and the tenant-based voucher. The project-based program established dedicated affordable housing units. Anyone wishing to participate in this program could apply to the federal government for Section 8 status. The owner of the units so designated was obligated to house low-income households who would pay rent to the owner that amounted to 30 percent of their income. Landlords would have a Section 8 contract for units within the building for a designated period of time. To date, the Section 8 project-based program has produced 1.5 million units nationally.[13]

The tenant-based program gives tenants a voucher that is worth the difference between 30 percent of their income and the average market rent. In this case it is up to the tenant to find housing in the private market that will accept the terms of the voucher. Thus, under program-based Section 8, designated housing was available for occupancy by low-income tenants. In the tenant-based program the availability of housing is determined by the ability of the tenant to find landlords who want to participate in the program. In this program it is much more difficult to tell how much affordable housing is actually available. In 1983, President Reagan eliminated the project-based program. While the program has been ended, there are still units under the old system that have contracts that will soon expire. Nationwide, nearly two-thirds of the units made affordable by Section 8 contracts have subsidies that will expire by 2004. The loss of these affordable units will exacerbate the already tight affordable housing situation, particularly combined with the loss of public housing units and the increased reliance on the tenant-based Section 8 program.

In the Chicago region, the Section 8 program presently provides housing for approximately 41,000 households, compared to 31,000 households who are living in public housing in the metropolitan region.[14] More than 60,000 households in the Chicago region are on waiting lists for Section 8 vouchers. On average, 3,500 vouchers become available each year based on turnover and the number of new vouchers issued to housing authorities. The Chicago Housing Authority controls the majority of these vouchers. The CHA Section 8 program is subcontracted and administered by a private company.

In the 1980s, President Ronald Reagan began a process of privatizing public housing in three ways. First, he began pushing the use of tenant-based Section 8 vouchers as an alternative to public housing and eliminated the project-based Section 8. Second, he implemented massive spending cutbacks in community and economic development, federal housing programs generally, and public housing specifically. Between 1982 and 1986, federal funds for community development declined by 20 percent and those allocated to employment and training were cut by 52 percent. Federal housing funds were slashed by 82 percent during this period, which hit the public housing program hard. The lack of resources resulting from these cuts began a process of public housing decay that continues to this day. Public housing units have had almost no maintenance for the past fifteen years. Heating systems, plumbing, elevators, and electrical systems have deteriorated, making many of the buildings uninhabitable. Third, Reagan substituted a program of tax credits for direct housing subsidies. This program, which is highly profitable to developers and large corporations, was never designed to meet the needs of very-low-income people.

The tax credit program was initiated in the 1986 Tax Reform Act. It is not a program of the Department of Housing and Urban Development; it is administered by the Department of Treasury through the Internal Revenue Service. Each state receives a pot of tax credits that are currently worth $1.75 per person residing in the state. These are allocated to cities and counties based on their population. A developer—either private or not-for-profit—can apply for tax credits by submitting a plan that demonstrates how the sale of tax credits and other sources of funds will allow them to build units at particular rent levels. Federal guidelines require that 40 percent of units must be affordable (defined as 30 percent of income) to households earning less than 60 percent of the average median income (AMI), or that 20 percent must be below 50 percent AMI. If the plan is accepted, the applicant must then find (usually through a broker) a corporation that is willing to purchase the credits. Various transaction costs like broker fees mean that the average value of tax credits to the developer run between 50 and 75 percent of the amount allotted. In practice, the tax credit program has not produced much housing for very-low-income people. In Chicago, for example, the most pressing affordable needs are for households earning less than 30 percent AMI (about $22,500). These are the people who are being displaced from public housing, living in substandard units, or homeless. In the past two years only 17 percent of Chicago's tax credit units were affordable to this population.[15] In one of Chicago's African American communities it was reported that, in 2001, of 800 families applying for tax credit units, 700 were turned away for lack of sufficient income. Another problem with the program as it was originally designed is that the affordability restrictions only last for fifteen years. Units built in the early years of the program are reaching this limit and will likely revert to market rents unless measures are taken to prevent this. Yet the program is immensely popular politically. One reason for this is the extensive profits made by both brokers and the corporations who enjoy the tax reductions. In 2001, Illinois built 3,500 housing units with tax credits worth over $18 million. On average, the United States as a whole builds about 80,000 units a year with tax credits worth $4 billion a year. The production of these units is further subsidized by other funds, such as the federal Community Development Block Grant program. In this manner this aspect of the privatization process takes resources away from very low-income development.

Meanwhile, the privatization of public housing has drastically reduced the amount of resources available to house poor people. Moreover, the need to cobble together loans and work through a complex tax credit process in the face of declining resources for Section 8 subsidies acts as a disincentive to produce housing for the poor. The complexity of the process and lack of resources combined with a comparable problem with employment policy meant that oppositional citizen groups and new citizen groups began to form not-for-profit community development corporations (CDCs). In a sense they have become a "third sector," sitting somewhere in between the public and private sectors. The lack of funding for affordable housing and commercial and industrial development meant that these organizations had to learn to put together complex financial deals with different banks and governmental program sources. They combine these with complicated legal arrangements with corporate "partners" who maintain ownership rights over projects while enjoying the benefits of tax breaks. A new breed of urban professional skilled in "loan packaging" and "deal making" tried to take up some of the slack caused by government withdrawal. But they also began to displace the traditional grassroots organizers among the ranks of community activists.[16] Nationally these groups are producing 30,000 to 40,000 housing units a year.[17] But only a fraction of these are meeting the needs of very poor people.

In many ways, CDCs have unwittingly become part of the process of privatizing government housing programs, which was the intention of Presidents Reagan and Bush. Meanwhile, the problem of a lack of affordable housing has become worse. It is estimated that in the Chicago region there are 153,300 households earning less than $20,000 who lack housing that is affordable to them.[18] One consequence of this situation is that 37.5 percent of Chicago area renters are paying more than 30 percent of their income for housing.[19] A worse consequence is that approximately 41,000 different people in the Chicago region stay in homeless shelters each year.[20]

Housing Policy in the 1990s: Housing as a Personal Responsibility

The 1990s policies of the Clinton administration intensified those of Presidents Reagan and Bush in the 1980s. The retreat from publicly owned housing has continued. In addition, political support for viewing housing as a social responsibility has been nearly eliminated. Rather, the dominant political theme is that housing is the personal responsibility of "competitive" individuals. These policy and political shifts have been particularly evident in Chicago. The Chicago Housing Authority actually rewrote its mission statement. In

1937, their mission was "to build and operate public housing . . . for persons whose incomes are insufficient to enable them to obtain decent, safe and sanitary dwellings in the private market." In 1999, the CHA draft plan defined its purpose as follows: "The role of the CHA is to invest in or facilitate housing opportunities. Particularly, with the new freedoms made possible by recent legislation, the agency should no longer view itself as primarily an owner or manager of public housing."[21]

While the Clinton administration's changes began being formulated in 1996, they took legislative form in the Quality Housing and Work Responsibility Act in 1998. This legislation passed with overwhelming support of President Clinton and both the Republicans and Democrats in the House of Representatives. The vote was 409 to 14 for passage.

When Congressman Rick Lazio first introduced this bill into Congress, he stated that this was "a bill to bring hope and opportunity to millions of Americans now living in public housing across the country."[22] When the bill finally passed, Representative Lazio made the following statement.

> I am thrilled that after a three year effort, we are changing troubled public housing into clean, safe and dynamic environments. We are giving folks in public housing the tools they need to fill their lives with feelings of hope, independence and optimism. Finally, we have a bill that can truly get things done for both the public housing residents and taxpayers.[23]

In reality, instead of public housing residents being filled with hope and optimism about their future, this new legislation is demolishing their homes and replacing them with housing they can't begin to afford.

Provisions: Income Targeting. One of the main purposes of the Quality Housing and Work Responsibility Act is to facilitate mixed-income communities and decrease concentrations of poverty in public housing.[24] To fulfill this purpose, the legislation sets out guidelines for future admissions to public housing units and for the redevelopment of public housing developments. The guidelines now make it possible and even likely that families most in need of housing are passed over so that families with higher incomes can move into public housing. While there is obviously nothing wrong with mixing income groups in an area, the mixed-income concept becomes problematic when there is insufficient housing for poor people. Moreover, as we will see, there is no empirical support for the contention that concentrations of poor are inherently harmful. The legislation states that no less than 40 percent of new families moving into public housing must have incomes at or below 30 percent of the area median income. Most families presently living in Chicago's public housing units make less than $10,000 a year. This is less than 20 percent of the median income for the Chicago area. For future admissions, it means that most of the families on the CHA waiting list will be passed over for higher-income families. Moreover, housing authorities can now rent up to

60 percent of newly available or redeveloped units to households making 80 percent of median income, which is as high as $36,000 nationally.[25]

Provisions: The Loss of the Replacement Requirement. Until 1996, the law prohibited public housing authorities from demolishing any public housing units unless they could be replaced. In 1996, Congress suspended this "one-for-one replacement" rule; in 1998, the public housing legislation ended the requirement. In order to demolish public housing units the local public housing authority must only demonstrate to HUD that the units are obsolete and not cost-effective to operate. Residents who are in "good standing" with the housing authority and whose homes are slated for demolition receive other housing options. This usually means a Section 8 voucher to find a unit in the private market. There is considerable doubt that there are sufficient housing units in the private market to accommodate all who are forced to use these vouchers.[26] As we report in greater detail later, this is certainly the case in Chicago.

Provisions: Rights of Public Housing Residents. There are many other elements in the legislation that reduce or eliminate the rights of public housing residents. For example, public housing tenants' rights under the Uniform Relocation Act were reduced and the number of reasons for terminating a lease were expanded. In Chicago, the CHA has been using these changes to displace families due to what they are calling situations where the health and safety of persons residing in the buildings are threatened. This provision in the legislation has enabled CHA to close buildings with very short notice, making resistance to demolition difficult and causing great hardship for those forced to move. In Chicago, tenants have been given as little as two weeks. This has been particularly disruptive to families with children in school.

These provisions suggest a distinct shift in housing policy. Programs that make housing a part of a social safety net have been eliminated in favor of those that emphasize housing as an "individual responsibility." In the process, households rather than government bear the risk of not having housing or losing housing and not being able to find another decent place to live in the private market. The Section 8 program forces households to assume these risks.

Housing Finance and the New World Order

In the course of this shift, government continues to be involved in housing finance, but in a very different way. The analysis in Chapter 3 demonstrated that expanded credit and speculation that feed the new world order has had a profound impact on housing. We contend that the global system of finance has had an impact on government's role in housing finance and on its political stance that housing is the responsibility of competitive individuals. We develop this position through three points.

- Mortgages used to finance housing have become more and more integrated with other financial markets, which are international. This means that money to buy housing is dependent on the returns to lenders who estimate potential financial gain relative to a growing array of other investment opportunities all over the world.
- Money to finance large-scale urban redevelopment has shifted from federal to local government. Local government must borrow these funds by competing in the same integrated financial markets for investors.
- These developments politically generate the policy shifts described above and also skew the distribution of housing resources from the poor to the wealthy.

The Integration of Financial Markets

The integration of financial markets is a major factor driving the changes in the housing market and the gentrification of many cities. Chapter 5 noted that during the Fordist era municipal bonds shifted in terms of both use and who was buying them. They were increasingly being used to subsidize private enterprise. The holders were no longer large institutional investors but wealthy individuals. Furthermore, federal funds for the redevelopment of cities were used to subsidize the creation of higher-income developments, thus driving gentrification. In the era of the new world order, however, there has been another important shift. New financial mechanisms have drawn large institutional investors into financing private residential development. As a result, the gentrification of cities is now largely being driven by the private sector. A key to understanding these new financial mechanisms is the integration of real estate into global capital markets. For this reason we will spend some time explaining what we mean by the concept of financial market integration.

Financial products (stocks, government and corporate bonds, foreign currencies, etc.) are bought and sold in financial markets. Broadly speaking, there are two kinds of markets: those where the life of the product is less than a year (money markets) and those that are longer-term (capital markets). People and institutions (like pension funds or mutual funds) wishing to invest in either of these markets consider the range of products available to them toward the end of maximizing potential returns relative to the risk involved. Chapter 3 demonstrated that this kind of activity has become essential to the functioning of the new world order. When investors weigh different financial products relative to others in this manner, the individual markets for the products are integrated. When the investors are from different nations, the integrated markets are internationalized as well.

Real estate markets are relative newcomers to these integrated financial markets. Their entry is part of the process of credit expansion and speculation that feeds the new world order. A popular real estate textbook discusses the meaning of this recent integration from the perspective of potential investors. It states very clearly the relationship between international capital markets and local property values:

> In recent years [since the late 1980s], real estate markets have become much more integrated with the general capital markets. Investors compare the risk and return available from real estate investment with the risk and return of alternative real estate and non real estate investments (common stocks, corporate bonds, Treasury securities, etc.) resulting in a decision process that considers a portfolio of investment alternatives. . . . Although tenants and landlords interact in decidedly local markets to determine rental rates, *property values are increasingly being determined by the risks and returns available in national and international capital markets.*[27]

The remainder of this section explains exactly how international capital markets determine local property values and thus become the driving force of the housing market, creating a new form of gentrification.

When an individual or a corporation wishes to buy residential property to live in or to rent to others, they obtain a special type of loan called a mortgage, which is secured by the property. The lender, in a process known as underwriting, assesses the value of the property and the potential ability of the borrower to pay and makes a decision about whether to give the mortgage financing. Up to the late 1970s, most mortgages to potential homeowners were provided by savings and loan associations or commercial banks. Interest rates on mortgages were set at a level that was competitive with other lenders. They depended in part on the length of time (amortization period) the lender needed to pay it off. Mortgages generally ran from ten to thirty years. Extra fees known as points were charged to offset potential risks perceived by the underwriter. The savings and loan association (S&L) or the commercial bank held the mortgage until the borrower paid it off. Their profit came from the interest and points generated by their mortgages. Money could also be made in real estate by buying properties and selling them at a profit. That process, too, was mediated by the need to gain mortgages for the properties involved. After World War II, as the Fordist period got under way and there was a demand for single-family homes, the federal government used a depression era program, Federal Housing Administration (FHA) and a new program for returning military personnel, Veterans Administration (VA) to stimulate mortgage lending by providing lenders with a guarantee that the mortgage would be paid. As these programs grew, the government was increasingly involved in the underwriting process and mortgage guarantees.

Only banking institutions and the government were allowed by law to be involved in real estate finance. Because of this and the fact that each indi-

vidual mortgage application had to be evaluated separately and the resulting mortgages had different characteristics, mortgage markets were separate
from other capital markets. But several things happened to change this. As
the Fordist era began to crumble in the mid-1970s, savings and loans and
some commercial banks that were holding too many bad mortgages began
to weaken. The federal government stepped in with three new banking acts
that significantly changed the nature of banking regulation.[28] The first two essentially deregulated the industry and allowed savings and loan associations
to engage in other types of lending. They were no longer dependent on mortgages. In addition, non-banking institutions were now allowed to invest in
real estate to give the savings and loans competition. The S&L crisis beginning in 1982 caused the government to put more restrictions on the S&Ls in
1989.

While the 1980s banking acts opened real estate to different types of institutions, the fact that each individual mortgage had to be evaluated by potential
investors separately limited the kinds of investors who might have an interest
in real estate. With the demand for mortgages high relative to the supply of
mortgage funds, the government again stepped in and helped facilitate the
development of what are known as secondary mortgage markets. A process
was established through which lenders could sell their mortgages to investors,
freeing up funds that could be lent to other mortgage seekers. The effect was
to greatly expand the amount of credit available for real estate and at the same
time integrate real estate with a growing number of other financial products
that constituted the capital markets.

Here is how it works. Special firms were created, initially government institutions, known as "conduits," whose business it was to facilitate the movement of mortgages from the lender to the portfolios of investors such as pension funds and mutual funds. The conduit did this by pooling a group of mortgages with similar characteristics (interest rates, amortization period, type
of property, financial capacity of the borrower) and using this pool to back a
security, which could be bought and sold in securities markets like stock exchanges. The actual legal documents for each individual property were placed
in a trust until the mortgages were paid off to the investors holding the securities. These mortgage-based securities (MBSs), as they are called, could be
bought and sold like any stock or bond. Once this innovation was developed,
the growth of MBSs was phenomenal. By 1995, the value of outstanding MBSs
in the United States was $1.8 trillion, which is an amount 30 percent greater
than the value of all corporate bonds.[29] Real estate has become a big player in
the capital markets.

Secondary mortgage markets are not new. But their size, the range of players in these markets, and their dominant role in local housing markets didn't
begin until the early 1980s. There are three key U.S. institutions that are the
conduits for these markets. One is the Federal National Mortgage Association,
known as Fannie Mae. Established in 1935 as part of the New Deal, its sec-

ondary market activity was limited to remote rural areas that were strapped for capital in local housing markets. Later, it was used to supplement the FHA and VA programs.

In 1968, the Housing and Urban Development Act included provisions that constituted a major breakthrough in integrating FHA and VA mortgages with broader capital markets. Fannie Mae was privatized into a public corporation that could issue stock and included participation of many of the players in the financial markets. The 1968 act also created a second corporation, the General National Mortgage Association, known as Ginnie Mae. Ginnie Mae does not actually buy mortgages. Rather, it guarantees the mortgage pools created by Fannie Mae. Although the FHA and VA mortgages that underlie these pools are already guaranteed by the federal government, a default could mean a long delay for the holders of the MBSs generated by the pool of mortgages of which the defaulting one is a part. The cash flow problems that resulted made these MBSs relatively unattractive to a lot of investors. Ginnie Mae served to remove this risk and caused a virtual explosion in the FHA/VA secondary market.[30] In 1970, a third private corporation organized by the federal government expanded the potential of the secondary market even farther. In that year, the Federal Home Loan Mortgage Corporation (Freddie Mac) was established to do what Fannie Mae had been doing with FHA and VA mortgages in the conventional mortgage market. Since nearly 80 percent of all mortgages are conventional rather than FHA or VA, this development greatly expanded the scope of secondary market activity.

The creation of a secondary mortgage market through the establishment of Fannie Mae, Ginnie Mae, and Freddie Mac, although created prior to the evolution of the new world order, provided the necessary precondition for the full integration of local real estate mortgages into the growing global capital markets of the new world order. Initially, the deregulation of the banking industry in the 1980s greatly expanded the number of players in the mortgage markets, as did the rise of credit and speculation. As reported in Chapter 3, by the mid-1990s, Fannie Mae and Freddie Mac held over $1 trillion in outstanding mortgages. In 1995, Fannie Mae made a profit of $2.1 billion on its secondary market operations.

At this scale, profit potential and risk aversion on the part of big investors becomes a key consideration for local housing development. The full integration of housing into global capital markets brings the market power of these big investors to bear on local housing markets. The deployment of this market power causes the balance between the need for housing and the need for credit to shift in favor of the latter. Thus, it is the supply and demand for housing development funds rather than the supply and demand for housing itself that determines the value of local properties. With the government's withdrawal from the direct provision of housing, the very idea of housing as a human need, let alone a human right, is subsumed by the drive of international finance for profits with minimal risk. But this is not the entire story.

The full picture must include the local developer. Developers and their local political allies have adapted well to the new system. And this fact further substantiates our claim that housing markets and gentrification under the regime of the new world order are different from the past.

Large-Scale Urban Development Finance

While urban redevelopment continues to involve many small players using local finance mechanisms, they are operating within a larger context. That context involves large-scale development that depends on integrated global capital markets. A large-scale urban development project technically includes two stages. The first stage is land development, where land is purchased and improved to make it suitable for project development. The second state, project development, is the building of new structures on the improved land. A land developer will borrow money to make the needed improvements and then sell the improved land at a profit to one or more project developers. In a residential project, the project developers borrow money to build homes on the land and sell them to private individuals. In an urban redevelopment project, these two stages are often combined with the active participation of local government. Land development involves clearing the land of old structures, building or improving needed streets and utility hookups, and sometimes providing parks, open space, or even schools.

Under the old federal Urban Renewal program, a local redevelopment agency, which was part of local government, usually acted as land developer. The agency purchased the land, using powers of eminent domain to force owners to sell at a fair market price. The agency relocated the residents, cleared off the old structures, and made needed site improvements. It then sold the land to a project developer. But instead of making a profit, the land was sold at a price that was below its market value. This land write-down made the land attractive to local project developers. The federal government paid much of the cost, which the local municipality supplemented with funds secured from municipal bonds. Thus, the land write-down amounted to a tax-supported subsidy to the developer. This is the way the Urban Renewal programs in Chicago under Mayor Richard J. Daley were developed in the 1950s and 1960s.

Today's urban redevelopment works differently. Federal legislation in 1968 and 1974 eliminated multiple-year commitments of funds for land clearance and improvements. This meant that in order to attract private developers for large-scale projects another funding mechanism was needed since projects required a flow of public funds over a period of many years. The new mechanism, which has been adopted by most states, including Illinois, was pioneered in Minnesota in 1947 and California in 1952. It is called "tax increment financing" (TIF). Its use was minimal until 1975. Since that time, forty-seven states have adopted TIF legislation. Illinois' TIF law was enacted in 1977. TIFs allow a municipality to designate districts for redevelopment and sell bonds to raise the capital needed to clear and improve land to be redeveloped. The bonds are repaid with the added property tax and sometimes sales and utility tax revenues that are generated by the increased values of redeveloped land and by the more intense use of that land. Because the debt is to be repaid by the tax revenues generated by the project, these bonds do not count as part of the municipality's debt limit. Since the funds are used to redevelop "blighted" land, most TIF bonds are exempt from federal income taxes, which makes them attractive to investors. Those that do not qualify for tax exemption must pay much higher interest rates to attract investors. A feature common to all TIF bonds that differs from the bonds used under the old Urban Renewal program is that the municipality does not have to go to the voters to issue the TIF bonds. The only requirement is an advisory TIF public hearing.

Large-scale urban redevelopment using TIF funding combines land development and project development through public-private partnerships. While projects work differently, a common model is for a developer to borrow money to purchase large parcels of "blighted" urban land. The developer then submits a redevelopment plan to the local government, and requests that their redevelopment area be declared a TIF district. Sometimes it is necessary for the city to purchase some of the land, using its eminent domain powers. Once the district is established, the city sells TIF bonds and uses the proceeds to make the improvements needed for the developer to implement the plan. In theory, TIFs could and have been used to develop low-cost housing or to develop job-producing commercial and industrial areas. Municipalities can initiate TIF-funded projects according to a city plan. In practice, however, developers often generate TIFs; public planning is piecemeal at best. Because of the greater profit potential of higher-income development, such projects thus fuel gentrification. This has definitely been the case in Chicago. The reason for this is the political and economic context in which they are used.

Our study of the redevelopment process in Chicago concludes that the process we have been describing favors private real estate developers who have little incentive to develop affordable housing for very poor people.[31] These projects are made possible by the creation of submunicipal TIF districts that depend on rising property values to make them work.[32] City government, therefore, needs plans from developers that will increase property tax yields. The urban planning process, in practice, is highly fragmented and proceeds through a series of deals between the developers and city officials in submunicipal fiscal enclaves in different parts of the city. According to one city planner involved in urban redevelopment during the Harold Washington administration,

> The reason there was little affordable housing built [in redevelopment projects] is that it is hard to do. . . . There was not any way to say [to the developer] you need to build in 20 percent low income housing. There was no tool to convince him to do that. . . . We [planners] are facilitators. . . . There are always so many

projects on the table that there has to be someone within city government who is willing to champion a particular one. That was the role I played on this. . . . The developer came to me, told me they wanted to expand; they had some property there . . . and the city had some and what they wanted was generally consistent with our thinking.[33]

Developers, for their part, are not only concerned about the profit potential of their investments, but about minimizing perceived risks. Sometimes race plays a key role in risk perception. One developer put it this way:

You get worried that if you make your radius a little bigger you are going to bring in people that are going to drive other people away. And whether it's racial or economic, people's perceptions and fears are an issue you have to deal with . . . And in a neighborhood there is such a thing as a "tipping point." You can not scientifically say where it is, but if the perception becomes that . . . some people making a decision to buy a condominium are going to say, "wow! I'm a little scared to make an investment here."[34]

Developers who have traditionally supported the pro growth alliance policies in the past continue to push them in the present. When asked about a $115,000 donation to the campaign of Mayor Richard M. Daley, developer J. Paul Beitler had this to say:

We are not out to buy a piece of Chicago. We already own a substantial piece of Chicago. The property we own pays more property taxes as a single building than most communities. . . . The only way we can make our voices heard is to support financially the best candidate who will do the best job for creating a city environment that will be fertile ground for development and business.[35]

The present system of large-scale urban development financed by TIFs facilitates the developer's desire to maximize profit potential and minimize risks in several ways. Unlike the old Urban Renewal program, the developer often has title to much of the land for proposed projects from the start. Developers initiate the planning so that they, not the city, propose the kind of development they want for the land. Second, since the value of the land at the time of purchase is much lower than after redevelopment, part of the profit potential lies in the rising property values throughout the development process itself. The city's share of those extra values goes to retire TIF bonds, which have been used to improve the land to begin with. Thus, in essence much of the city's share of rising land values brought about by the redevelopment project goes to the developer. The developer also gets a share of those rising values when he sells the land and improvements to private individuals. Third, since public funds are being used for the land development phase, the TIF financing constitutes a public subsidy to the developer, which is a further source of profit.

However, developers and city administrations now depend on TIFs. Furthermore, TIFs, like mortgage-backed securities, are part of global capital markets.

Thus, developers and city administrations do not have the power to determine on their own what is and what is not a "good project." "Keeping the markets happy" is thus a critical feature of local real estate development. The TIF bonds have to be sold and traded in international capital markets. This gives the players in those markets a say in local development priorities.

The TIF bonds used for the gentrification of the area presently occupied by Cabrini-Green Public Housing, a subject of one of our case studies below, demonstrates how this can work. After the city declared the Cabrini area a TIF district, it began the process of selling the TIF bonds so the project could get under way.[36] Large institutional investors like Allstate Insurance, Kemper Insurance, and Novine Mutual Fund had purchased such bonds in the past. Such firms add and delete investments from their portfolio to maximize return and minimize risk for their investors. But in this case Cabrini-Green residents were resisting the developer's proposal and had initiated a lawsuit to stop the process. This introduced an unacceptable degree of uncertainty for these bonds. The city wanted the money badly to begin the project so that the deal with the developer didn't turn sour. What they did was the sort of hocus pocus that demonstrates just how far the system of credit expansion and speculation through the international capital markets can go.

A financial services firm that did the underwriting for the city sought bids to obtain a letter of credit from a bank that would guarantee repayment of the bonds. Different financial institutions bid on the letter of credit by stating the terms under which they would assume this risk. One term was that a certain amount of money off the top of the sale of the bonds would go directly to the lowest bidder. In this case, the Imperial Bank of Canada was the lowest bidder but they also wanted a guarantee of a fixed interest rate, which would diminish the risk of non-payment. To meet these terms, the financial services firm let out bids for a bond insurance program (similar to the notion of an interest rate swap discussed in Chapter 3). The idea was that the successful bidder would guarantee a fixed interest rate on the TIF bonds in return for the rights to lend out the cash flow from tax increments generated by the development project. There were five bidders. The best proposal came from Nations Bank in California, a large international banking corporation. Nations Bank guaranteed an agreed-upon rate of interest for the TIF bonds and also paid the city of Chicago a fee. According to a Finance Department spokesperson, the fee was sufficient not only to offset the fee paid to the Canadian bank for the letter of credit, but also provided the city with a profit on the deal. The agreement with Nations Bank is that once the Cabrini-Green development begins to produce tax increments, Nations Bank receives the money and invests it in short-term (seven-day to fifteen-year) fixed rate investments. They use the profits from these investments to pay off the TIF bondholders while making a handsome profit.

Developers and investors are always trying to avoid risk. And one of these is the potential risk of rising interest rates. The bank in Canada sought a hedge against this risk that was met through the bond insurance program. But developers wish to avoid this sort of risk as well, which gives them a further stake in global capital markets. Money borrowed to purchase land and build housing or other improvements carries flexible interest rates. If the rates go up before the developer can sell the property and repay the loans, the costs of the project will be greater than anticipated. Developers today commonly use various innovations to hedge this risk.[37] One method is to buy financial products whose interest rates correlate with those of development loans in the financial futures markets that were described in Chapter 3. It works like this. When the developer takes out a development loan to purchase land or build structures on it, she or he also sells a future of some financial product whose interest rates tend to move with those of the loan. Because it is a future, the sale locks in the existing interest rate on that product. When the loan is paid off, the developer then purchases an identical futures product to close out her or his position in the markets. Often the developer will negotiate a loan where the lender will agree to tie flexible loan rates to the particular futures product being used for the hedge. The most common futures products used to hedge development and construction loans are either short-term U.S. government Treasury bills or notes or MBS futures from Ginnie Mae or Freddie Mac. Developers can also now hedge on interest rate fluctuation through the use of interest rate swaps, similar to what the city of Chicago negotiated with Nations Bank. There are also interest rate caps, where the developer purchases an agreement from another party in which the other party agrees to pay the difference between the existing interest rate and any increase during the life of the developer's project. The seller of interest rate caps is speculating that the costs of interest rate increases will be less than the amount the developer paid for the cap.

Housing Policy and Finance in the New World Order

The withdrawal of government from publicly owned housing, the shift in public policy to treating housing almost exclusively as an individual commodity, and the integration of housing-related credit and speculation into broader international capital markets have had profound effects on the vast numbers of citizens who are unable to afford market rate housing. Housing is now treated mainly as a commodity to buy and sell. Housing is mainly an exchange value rather than a useful place to live. While this has stimulated home ownership for some, its impact on the urban poor has been negative and shows up as a shortage of affordable housing and an increase in homelessness. At the same time, government housing policy in the United States has promoted a new form of privatized urban redevelopment and gentrification. Below we present two case studies to illustrate these points. One case, which spans both

Fordism and the present era of the new world order, describes the process of the gentrification of the south Loop area of Chicago and the efforts of community groups to oppose it. The other relates to the destruction of public housing that began in Chicago in the 1990s during the administration of Bill Clinton and the mayorship of Richard M. Daley.

Gentrifying the South Loop

Background

This case study[38] involves an effort by citizen groups to halt the destruction of viable affordable housing in the south Loop area of Chicago and to force developers gentrifying the area to include housing for poor people. It is important to see this effort in relation to the history of planning and development in the area.[39] The south Loop is an area of residential enclaves and transportation access routes to the Loop. It is made up of a number of planned unit residential developments, which house some of the highest-income, politically connected households and lowest-income, disenfranchised households in the city. For example, Mayor Richard M. Daley lives in the south Loop. Less than a mile from his home, residents of the Hilliard Homes public housing development live mostly on incomes below poverty level. South Armour Square, the location of the Chicago White Sox stadium discussed in the previous chapter, is also in the south Loop area.

There was little development in this part of the city until the 1850s, when the railroads laid their tracks through the South Side of Chicago. The railroad lines drew industrial development and a demand for workers, who in turn sought inexpensive homes near their work. By 1903, there were four major railroad terminals, located in what is now the south Loop and the Loop itself. Some of Chicago's wealthiest families also built mansions in the area but later moved out as the area declined. The most significant factor in the decline of the area was the infusion of commercial and industrial development. As industrial development grew, the old mansions that had been built by the city's elite families were converted into rooming houses or torn down to make way for factories. Proximity to the railroad terminals gave the south Loop access to Chicago's convention trade. This is still true today.

In the 1920s and 1930s, a number of public buildings were built along the lakefront in the vicinity of the south Loop. These include the Field Museum of Natural History, Adler Planetarium, the Shedd Aquarium, and Soldier Field, the stadium of the Chicago Bears. Recently, several of these public buildings have been expanded and renovated with major infrastructure improvements and highway reconfigurations that have created what the city calls a "museum campus."

The south Loop experienced a decline in population from the 1920s until the 1940s, when there was a large influx of African Americans into Chicago. After World War I, African Americans became an increasing proportion of the south Loop population. The significant rise in population, however, was not matched by a corresponding increase in housing units. The result was a tremendous concentration of African American families living in over-crowded and substandard conditions. At the end of World War II, African Americans continued to dominate this area due to heavy migration to Chicago after the war and to racial discrimination, which limited housing options. As noted in the previous chapter, Mayor Richard J. Daley pursued a deliberate pol-icy to contain African American residents in specific parts of the city through massive slum clearance and public housing construction. The near South Side of Chicago, which includes the south Loop, was an area designated for African American public housing development. In the 1950s and 1960s, hundreds of units were built there, and they were separated from the rest of the city by the construction of two interstate highways.

The south Loop is now one of the areas of Chicago to experience the ur-ban cycle of industrial prosperity, decline, and renewal as an appendage to the Loop's downtown service-sector economy. The historical landscape of the area has been transformed. Abandoned warehouses and industrial buildings that once serviced the Loop are being converted into upscale condominiums. Vacant railroad yards, once the lifeline of the city, have been transformed into secluded upscale residential communities.

Initially, the pro growth alliance's approach to the development of the near South Side was done without a lot of planning. Instead, deals were cut with development and business interests around particular projects. Up until the mid-1950s, the area had been primarily a place for the containment of both African Americans and Chinese. But after that, real estate development and other pro growth business interests began to take an interest in the south Loop. City politicians, planners, and developers, motivated by revitalizing the central city and increasing the tax base of the city, envisioned the develop-ment of the south Loop as a residential community geared toward middle- and upper-income professionals working downtown. This was spurred by the decline in manufacturing in the city and the decline in the use of railroads, which left much of the railroad yards on the near South Side ripe for redevel-opment.

In 1956, the Chicago Central Area Committee, which represented pro growth interests, was formed. In cooperation with the Chicago Department of Planning, they began to put forward a vision for the near South Side that was expressed in a formal planning document in 1958.[40] The plan called for the consolidation of the railroad terminals in the south Loop and for residential land use redevelopment in the southern portion of the Loop and into the south Loop that would create 23,000 new higher-priced housing units. The Central Area Committee followed up on this plan with a housing market analysis in 1959. They surveyed people who worked in and around the Loop to determine the demand for housing. They found that the demand was highest close to the Loop but fell off sharply as one moved south (into the African American neighborhoods). They concluded "Most of the Near South Side must undergo large-scale redevelopment if there is to be created here a suitable environment for new housing."[41]

In 1966, the Chicago Central Area Committee moved further to establish their vision of near South Side development with a policy plan.[42] The plan called for the concentration of people and enterprises in a compact development anchored with residential development; the use of highways and road improvements to promote maximum accessibility to the Loop; and a program of beautification. These conceptions were further developed in an official planning document in 1973 known as the Chicago 21 plan,[43] and a follow-up document, "South Loop New Town."[44] Essentially, Chicago 21 promoted a vision in which residential and commercial facilities would be designed to bring middle- and upper-income people back to the city. It proposed a "new town in town" concept and saw the nearby communities, many of which were low-income neighborhoods that had experienced serious disinvestment, as extensions of the central area. Outside of the Chicago Central Area Committee (CCAC), there was no citizen input into the planning process for the south Loop. But with the publication of Chicago 21, community organizations in the surrounding area became concerned about the potential of this vision to gentrify their communities. That concern about Chicago 21 is the basis for much of the conflict around current developments that is described below. According to three community activists and researchers,

> The main concept of the Chicago 21 Plan was a fortress city. It aimed to redevelop the land that circled a booming service sector downtown for middle and upper class residents. This redevelopment was to create an ever increasing buffer zone to protect the downtown investments from the growing number of poor and minority people living in Chicago's surrounding neighborhoods.[45]

City planning officials failed to understand this basis for the opposition. According to one who was active during the Harold Washington administration,

> I think that the most important thing about the South Loop is that the City of Chicago has had a policy of introducing housing to its downtown that has included six mayors. So the concept of development of the South Loop was never fought. Except, that is, for a few people worried about gentrification. The Chicago 21 Plan, I know, was controversial. I think it was a very important and forward looking plan for the city. The whole notion that there was this railroad land that could be developed offered the potential to transform the Loop to include major residential development. It turned out to be a smart move.[46]

Yet there was opposition. Different communities surrounding the near South Side opposed Chicago 21 from the beginning. Different neighborhood organizations formed a "Citywide Coalition Against Chicago 21" in 1976. As one activist put it,

The city is giving all sorts of support to building middle and high income housing. . . . I see Chicago as a working class city, and now they are trying to destroy
its fabric. In (my neighborhood) people are always looking for housing. We lose
100 units a year that are not replaced. We see the Chicago 21 plan as drawing city
services away from us.[47]

South Loop Gentrification Begins

Beginning in the 1980s, the city played an active role in the redevelopment of
the south Loop by providing private developers public subsidies for infrastructure improvement to build over 1,400 single-family homes and town houses
that make up the suburban-like enclaves of Dearborn Park. Adjacent to these
new construction developments is the Printer's Row area, which includes several blocks of warehouses and factories that have been converted into residential lofts and upscale shops and restaurants. Until the 1970s, this was the center of the printing industry in Chicago. Between 1970 and 1987, the number of
printing firms in the area declined from ninety-six to forty-five. Today only a
handful can afford the higher rents of the area. It is important to note that the
Dearborn Park development was conceived during the term of Mayor Richard
J. Daley. It was implemented, however, during subsequent administrations
including that of Mayor Harold Washington.

Dearborn Park was one of many urban renewal projects initiated by Mayor
Richard J. Daley in the 1960s to stop white flight to the suburbs through investment in the Loop and surrounding areas. In promoting the first phase of
the residential Dearborn Park development in the south Loop, one of its developers stated the following:

> It [Dearborn Park] will house families from the full economic spectrum, with a
> great majority of the housing being within the range of the city's solid middle
> class of policemen, firemen, school teachers, and loop office workers . . . [this]
> will reverse the population trends and cause an increase in the city's population
> for the first time in decades.[48]

Even during Washington's mayorship (1983–87), which had more of an emphasis on neighborhood development and affordable housing, the strength of the
downtown development orientation prevailed in its continued development
and expansion of the south Loop as a middle-income community.

South Loop projects during the 1970s and 1980s were implemented through
significant public subsidies to developers. Supplementing the urban renewal
program, the federal government under President Carter created the Urban
Development Action Grant (UDAG) program in 1978. The stated objective
was to offer a reinvestment program for the northern industrial cities, which
were experiencing job loss and economic decline during the collapse of the
Fordist era. Many of the developers in the south Loop applied for these federal
funds and received them to do the loft conversions and other redevelopment
in the Printer's Row area. In all, nine developers in the south Loop received

$38.3 million, 39 percent of all the UDAG dollars that came into the city of Chicago.[49] Although the city of Chicago had to approve and submit the applications to the federal government, developers drove the UDAG program in Chicago. The program was administered in such a way that community groups did not know about these subsidies until after they were awarded. After a study commissioned by community groups revealed the extent of the subsidies, they met with city officials during the Washington mayorship to protest any more UDAG subsidies going into the south Loop or other areas for luxury housing and other upscale development. Nevertheless, developers went back to the city during the Washington mayorship to receive more support. They received approximately $3 million in infrastructure costs for a second phase of the Dearborn Park project.

Due to the intense reinvestment in the area, south Loop housing units increased dramatically during the 1980s. In 1980, there were 4,904 housing units; by 1990, the number of units had increased by 55 percent, to 7,609 units. While the increase in units was primarily in the category of higher-income units, there was a decrease in the number of single-room occupancy hotel (SRO) units, which house single, low-income workers. From 1985 through 1990, the number of SRO hotels decreased from 11 to 7.[50] In 1980, 27 percent of the labor force in the area were executives and professionals; by 1990, that proportion had grown to 49 percent. Not surprising, the percentage of the labor force living in the south Loop who are craftspeople, machine operators, and laborers declined from 22 percent to 6 percent.

South Loop Gentrification under the New World Order

The process of south Loop gentrification continued throughout the 1990s under Mayor Richard M. Daley. But the nature of gentrification has changed and the process itself has greatly intensified, in line with the trends described earlier. This began in April 1990, when the city of Chicago passed a TIF ordinance to aid the private development of a project known as Central Station (named for the railroad terminal that used to be there). A portion of Central Station, now home to Mayor Daley, was the first residential phase of this 72-acre mixed-use development plan, adding nearly 200 homes and infrastructure. Again in August 1994, the TIF district was greatly expanded. It generated $105 million in bonds available for area improvements. Unlike the first phase of Dearborn Park in the early 1970s, the 1990s continuation of south Loop redevelopment now excludes even middle-income families. Housing prices are no longer affordable for police, teachers, or firefighters. The price of townhouses in Central Station begin at $250,000 compared to the average single-family home price of $100,000 for the city as a whole. The new developments of the south Loop are increasingly the exclusive homes of upper-income families and individuals. As the city of Chicago has poured subsidies into such upscale development, it has allowed the local public housing authority (CHA) to neglect the public housing stock in the city. This has meant an increase in vacant and uninhabitable public housing units throughout the city and also in the public housing units at the southern edges of the south Loop area.

Two Decades of Community Campaigns

The process of gentrification that began in the 1970s and continues into the new millennium has touched off a series of community opposition campaigns. The first of the campaigns was the Coalition of Central Area Communities, which opposed the policies and direction of the Chicago 21 plan in the early 1970s. This campaign was followed in the 1980s by the Chicago 1992 Committee's opposition to Chicago holding a World's Fair. The site of the proposed World's Fair was adjacent to the south Loop. In the early 1990s, another city-wide group, the Chicago Affordable Housing Coalition, organized a "Balanced Growth Campaign," which questioned the public subsidies south Loop developers had been receiving. In 1996, there was another "South Loop Development Without Displacement Campaign" to ensure that the remaining low-income residents in the south Loop would not be displaced by the continued upscale development.

The Chicago Coalition for the Homeless and the Chicago Affordable Housing Coalition organized the South Loop Development Without Displacement Campaign to target the developer of Central Station and other developers in the south Loop who were receiving public subsidies. The campaign consistently used direct actions such as rallies, and marches, targeting the mayor's office with strategic use of media to communicate their demands to a larger audience and raise the political stakes. Leading up to the 1995 mayoral elections, weekly vigils outside the mayor's home in the Central Station development and a rally at city hall initiated a series of negotiation meetings with city officials that ended in a deadlock in the fall of 1995. The assessment of the organizers for the campaign was that the city began the negotiations as an effort to diffuse the momentum of the campaign and had no intention of negotiating in good faith to resolve the issues that the campaign was raising about low-income housing set-asides and jobs for local residents. The campaign continued to put pressure on the mayor by protesting at his office and threatening to disrupt the Democratic Party Convention, which was held in Chicago in August 1996.

One issue that was a focal point of the campaign was the struggle over the destiny of the existing Single Room Occupancy (SRO) hotels. Currently over 700 SRO units remain in the area, down from 4,000 units in 1961. In 1993, a local development corporation made up of downtown churches submitted a proposal for funding to the city to rehab one of these SROs, the St. James Hotel, located between the upscale developments of Central Station and Dearborn Park. Despite the project's wide community support, the city rejected the proposal and plans to raze the building to make way for commercial development as part of the TIF redevelopment plans.

Despite consistent opposition, the city of Chicago has continued to pursue the gentrification of the area. Throughout the 1990s, there has been a boom of construction projects. Based on a 1999 list compiled by consultants working on the issuance of new TIF bonds, there were 18 private residential projects and 17 public developments since 1990. There are another 18 private residential projects under construction, and 5 private residential and 10 public works projects proposed within the TIF district.[51] The average sales price of the units is $242,633 and the average rent of the rental units is $1,468 per month. Units to be purchased are only affordable to households making at least $75,000. And an affordable rental unit would require an income of at least $65,000 (using 30 percent of gross income for housing costs as a guide).

Commercial development has followed the residential development with new restaurants, art galleries, and a large chain grocery store opening up in the past two years. The grocery store is on the site of the torn-down St. James Hotel. The city is in the process of buying and demolishing two other SRO hotels, which will mean a loss of an additional 314 units. The main success of the South Loop Development Without Displacement Campaign has been the development of two SRO buildings since 1996 and the possibility of another SRO that is planned for construction in the near future. The two newly constructed SRO hotels are owned and managed by not-for-profit groups. These hotels have 440 units. The average rent is $255. Although these newly constructed SRO units have been built in the area, there still has been an overall loss of 24 percent, or 165 SRO units since 1990.

The number of public housing units has also declined in the south Loop. The Hilliard Homes public housing development that is located on the far south edge of the south Loop has been sold to a private developer. This public housing development had 707 units that will now be converted to 654 units, with only 305 units going to households with low incomes. This is a loss of 402 units of public housing. This redevelopment is being financed through public housing loans, tax-exempt multifamily mortgage revenue bonds, TIF proceeds, and tax credits facilitated by the city of Chicago's Department of Housing.[52]

The city's planning efforts dating back to the 1957 development plan have been directed and implemented by business and real estate interests with the financial backing of government and have done little or nothing to protect the interests of current small businesses and low-income residents. As explained earlier, new financing mechanisms like TIFs, which favor luxury housing development, are a part of the new world order's expansion of credit that has accelerated the polarization of income and wealth. Now both local developers and players in the global capital markets drive urban development priorities. This has resulted in an increased pace of gentrification in the 1990s.

The Destruction of Affordable Housing: The Case of Cabrini-Green Public Housing Development

Background

As gentrification has proceeded in the south Loop and elsewhere in Chicago, the new world order shift in housing policy has resulted in the destruction of a major source of affordable housing, the public housing projects that were built by the present mayor's father to contain the African American population during the old Fordist era. As we have seen, that housing policy shift began with the introduction of Section 8 housing vouchers in the mid-1970s and has culminated with the Clinton administration's Quality Housing and Work Responsibility Act in 1998. The combination of accelerated gentrification and the proposals to eliminate public housing caused residents to organize and oppose the plans of the federal government and the city of Chicago's CHA.[53]

The organizing efforts of public housing residents were a surprise to many public housing observers and critics because public housing in Chicago has a reputation for being some of the worst in the nation. In fact, when Congress required public housing authorities across the country in 1996 to assess whether their housing units should be saved or turned into Section 8 vouchers, Chicago had twice as many "distressed" units as any other city in the country.[54] Despite Chicago's public housing stock being the worst in the country, the public housing residents wanted to fight for their chance to rebuild their communities. They did not want to be thrown into a private housing market that did not want them or did not have enough units to accommodate them.

As it became clear that Clinton administration policies would only intensify the direction set by the previous administration, public housing residents began to organize. Public housing residents from Cabrini-Green and Rockwell Gardens developments contacted the Chicago Coalition for the Homeless in the summer of 1996. The public housing residents sought the advice of the staff members of the Coalition for the Homeless in forming a new organization to protect the rights of public housing residents and to ensure the continued existence of public housing in Chicago.

This was two years before the introduction of the Quality Housing and Work Responsibility Act. Its subsequent passage and its embrace by both political parties demonstrate that the tenants' concern was well founded. In 1996, many of the provisions that ended up in the 1998 legislation were put into the HUD appropriations bill. One provision of this bill required a viability study for half of the existing 40,000 public housing units in Chicago. The viability study was to compare the costs of maintaining the existing public housing units to the cost of replacing those units with a Section 8 voucher for an apartment in the private market.

These policy changes at the federal level were the topic of discussion at a series of meetings of public housing residents and housing activists throughout the fall of 1996. At these meetings, the Coalition to Protect Public Housing (CTPPH) was formed and included public housing residents and seventy supporting community, civic, and religious organizations. It was the goal of the CTPPH to: (1) better understand the impact the federal legislative public housing changes would have in Chicago, and, (2) try to intervene in the decision-making process so that public housing residents would not be unduly harmed by the proposed changes.

Since its inception in 1996, CTPPH has organized and sponsored a number of activities to broaden the policy debate and bring attention to the changes in public housing and how they are affecting the residents. The CTPPH decided to work on numerous fronts to have an impact. Their activities included educational workshops for residents to understand their rights and the changes that are being proposed in their developments. In 1997, the CTPPH sponsored a study by a research center at the University of Illinois–Chicago. The study was to determine the reliability of the Section 8 voucher program to provide long-term affordable housing for low-income households and to do a financial analysis of the redevelopment plans for the Cabrini-Green public housing development.[55]

The CTPPH also supported the efforts of the Cabrini-Green Local Advisory Council to file a federal civil rights lawsuit against HUD, the CHA, and the city of Chicago. This lawsuit, filed in October 1996, claimed that the residents' rights were violated because the residents were excluded from the redevelopment planning process and the plans would adversely affect African American women and children who are the majority residents of Cabrini-Green.

The CTPPH also organized a number of demonstrations to call attention to the changes and the adverse effects the changes were having on public housing residents. A March 1998 demonstration and sit-in at the regional HUD offices in Chicago led to a meeting with HUD Secretary Andrew Cuomo in the summer of 1998. At this meeting, the coalition secured a commitment from the secretary that HUD would not approve redevelopment plans for Chicago public housing until a regional market study determined the availability of affordable units in the private sector. HUD, CHA, the city of Chicago, the state of Illinois, and several local foundations commissioned the study in the spring of 1999.[56] As follow-up to the discussions with Secretary Cuomo and his staff, an Oversight Committee was formed of public officials from the HUD regional office, CHA, and the city of Chicago, community and civic organizations, and public housing residents. This Oversight Committee met regularly to address public housing issues in Chicago until another committee was formed to oversee the rental market study. This committee was named the Technical Advisors Panel and was organized by a civic community group favored by Mayor Daley. This civic community group was designated the sponsor of the rental study and received the funding and fiscal responsibility for the study. CTPPH was given only one seat on the Technical Advisors Panel. The rest of the committee was comprised of representatives of the government funders of the study: HUD, the city of Chicago, the Illinois Housing Development Authority, the CHA, an expert in marketing from the private sector, and an expert in survey research from the University of Chicago.

Despite the efforts of the CTPPH, the years of neglect of the public housing stock and the more recent aggressive efforts to eliminate public housing had already taken a serious toll. In 1983, publicly owned housing was at its height in terms of number of owned and operated units. The CHA owned and operated 40,781 units.[57] By 1999, the CHA's units were down to 38,717. Furthermore, the lack of maintenance and poor management caused the vacancy rate to grow from under 4 percent to over 35 percent. The rise in the vacancy rate occurred despite a shortage of affordable housing in the city exemplified by 30,000 families on the CHA waiting list.[58] On February 6, 2000, HUD approved the CHA's "Plan for Transformation." This plan contains an ambitious demolition and development schedule that aims to reduce the 1999 stock of public housing from 38,000 units to 25,000 units in less than ten years.

The federal government, CHA, and city of Chicago continued to push these policies in an increasingly aggressive manner, while residents and the broader CTPPH continued to fight back. The difficulties of that fight back are illustrated by the case of Cabrini-Green.

The Case of Cabrini-Green

At its height, the Cabrini-Green public housing development on Chicago's near North Side had 3,591 units in 55 high-rise, low-rise, and townhouse structures. By 1999, there were only 3,193 units, a reduction of 398 units, or 11 percent. The complex now has 1,436 vacant units, a 44.4 percent vacancy rate.[59] The population of Cabrini-Green is 99 percent African American.[60] In 1997, the average income for all households in Cabrini-Green was $10,402. In 1997, nearly half of the households received income from the existing welfare program. 323 households, or 16.6 percent, were employed. Cabrini-Green, located less than a mile from the beaches of Lake Michigan, is surrounded by one of the most affluent and desirable neighborhoods in the city. Its residents are white. This fact made Cabrini-Green a prime development to begin the destruction of the public housing program in Chicago.

The resident leadership of Cabrini-Green was keenly aware of the development pressures surrounding them. Over the years, they have been in the forefront of volunteering for any and all programs to improve the conditions at Cabrini-Green as an effort to ensure its continued existence.[61] In the 1970s, they formed a Local Advisory Council (LAC), which was elected to represent tenants to the CHA Central Advisory Council. Since then they have formed four resident management corporations, published newsletters and a community paper, and organized at least eight other tenant-run organizations that include a job training center, business enterprises, and tenant services (security and substance abuse).

Similar to other communities facing unemployment and disinvestment by public and private interests, and despite the best efforts of the majority of community residents, gangs have formed, and their sporadic violent criminal activities are what make the news. In 1992, a young resident of Cabrini-Green, Dantrell Davis, was shot on his way to school. This tragic incident made national news, and many consider it a turning point when the CHA began serious discussions about the redevelopment of the area.[62]

In 1993, Vince Lane, CHA executive director, worked with the Cabrini-Green Local Advisory Council members to develop a redevelopment plan for the Cabrini-Green development. This plan was then turned into an application for the federal HOPE VI Urban Revitalization Demonstration Project to finance the improvements in the plan.[63] On May 23, 1993, the CHA and the Cabrini-Green LAC entered into an agreement concerning the redevelopment of a portion of Cabrini-Green by utilizing these federal HOPE VI resources. $50 million in federal HOPE VI funding was requested; $40 million would go to the new construction of 303 public housing replacement units on site, while $10 million was earmarked for social services. In addition, public housing development funding for another 190 replacement units was secured by the CHA.

This plan called for the demolition of three high-rise buildings containing 660 units. The plan was completed before Congress suspended the one-for-one replacement requirement. Thus, under the plan the 660 units lost to demolition would be replaced by 493 newly constructed units and 167 Section 8 vouchers. Unfortunately, the plan was not implemented before Vince Lane was forced to resign in June 1995. At this point the federal government stepped in and took over the CHA management.

In October 1995, Joseph Shuldiner, the new CHA executive director appointed by HUD, issued a new request for proposal for the Cabrini-Green redevelopment. The original plan described above, which the Cabrini-Green LAC had agreed upon with Vince Lane, was included in the new request for proposal. In addition, the request for proposal required additional market units to be developed and financed separately to create a "mixed-income" development.[64] A Screening Committee was formed in January 1996 to review the submitted proposals and to make recommendations to the CHA. The Cabrini-Green LAC was represented on this Screening Committee along with representatives from the city, CHA, and a private developer, the Habitat Company. The Habitat Company was represented on the committee because it was the court-appointed receiver for the CHA's scattered site program under the terms of the *Gautreaux v. Chicago Housing Authority* settlement. After several months of review, all of the proposals were rejected for failing to meet the requirements of the RFP and the Screening Committee meetings ended.

At this time, the city of Chicago and the CHA organized their own private meetings to discuss an alternative strategy for the Cabrini-Green area. The representatives from the Cabrini-Green LAC were excluded from this new round of meetings. When the residents became aware of these meetings, they requested that their representatives attend and participate. The city representatives refused to have the residents included and the CHA representatives refused to require that the city include them.[65] This new round of meetings resulted in a Near North Redevelopment Plan, which was announced by the city and CHA at a June 1996 press conference.

The Near North Redevelopment Plan is a comprehensive initiative, encompassing 90 acres of land for redevelopment. This includes 20 acres of CHA-owned land. In the original HOPE VI plan, only 9.3 acres of CHA land were included. The Near North Redevelopment Plan includes the construction of 2,300 units of housing, a new library, police station, new school, parks, and commercial facilities. The redevelopment is to be undertaken by private investors assisted by significant public funds and land. The bulk of the public funds, $281 million, were to be raised by the designation of the area as a tax increment financing (TIF) district.[66]

In this plan, a total of 8 Cabrini-Green buildings were to be demolished, instead of the 3 that had been targeted under HOPE VI. The additional demolition expanded the CHA land available for development from 9.3 acres to 20 acres. In 1995, 2 Cabrini buildings with 398 units were demolished. With the proposed demolition of an additional 6 buildings with 921 units, the existing housing units at Cabrini would be reduced to 2,284 units, or by 36.6 percent. Out of the proposed 2,300 units in this plan, 1,000 would be built on CHA land. This proposed breakdown of replacement units has only 700 units, or 30 percent of the total development designated as units eligible for public housing. As part of the plan, these 700 units will be acquired by CHA, who will then rent the units. CHA would use $40 million of the earlier HOPE VI funding and an additional public housing development grant to buy 493 units.

The plan called for the demolition of 1,324 units of very-low-income Cabrini-Green units, with only 350 units replaced. This is a loss of 969 very-low-income units. The plan thus calls for over 80 percent of proposed units in the redevelopment plan to be unaffordable to current Cabrini-Green residents or other very-low-income households because of income restrictions. Most of the units will be built for middle- and upper-income households making more than $44,000 a year. It is estimated that these units would cost from $120,000 to as much as $400,000 for the market rate units.[67] The proposed plan had 1,150 market units, where most of the profits for the developer would be made. It is estimated that the developer of the proposed development would make from at least $100 to $136 million profit.[68]

In response to this plan, the Cabrini-Green Local Advisory Council decided that their rights as residents and citizens had been violated in this process and they sought legal redress. On October 24, 1996, the Cabrini-Green Local Advisory Council filed suit in federal court to stop the plans by the CHA to "demolish over 1300 units of public housing as part of its strategy to 'revitalize' the development."[69] The suit charged violation of the federal Fair Housing Act and Title VI of the Civil Rights Act of 1964. Specifically, the suit charged that the redevelopment plans would adversely affect African American women and children because they are disproportionately eligible for public housing compared to the general population. In addition, the redevelopment plans broke the CHA promise not to demolish buildings before replacement units were built, and buildings that were to be rehabilitated were now being scheduled for demolition. The suit also claimed injury to the Cabrini-Green LAC because they were denied participation in the planning process, thereby effectively denying resident consultation, which is required by HOPE VI, Section 18 of the federal act and the memorandum of agreement signed by Vince Lane when he represented the CHA.[70] The suit contends,

> in their closed door meetings, the defendants [CHA and the city of Chicago] developed a plan which changes the Cabrini-Green area from a low-income public housing area to a "mixed income community" which they believe will revitalize the area. This plan will result in a community that will drastically reduce the presence of low-income African American households by substantially supplanting the current population with households making more than 50% of the median income, the majority of which will be non-African-American and non-Cabrini-Green residents. . . . The defendants have been aware of the fact that the adverse impact of their decision to permanently eliminate approximately 1,000 units of housing for families of very low income, would fall predominantly upon African-American families with children.[71]

The suit was first filed in October 1996; a pre-trial hearing was held in December. After this hearing, the federal judge determined that there was enough evidence to move forward, and a court date was set for June 1998. The judge also ordered an injunction to stop any additional demolition of buildings until the suit was settled. Beginning in the fall of 1997, the Corporation Counsel for the City of Chicago subpoenaed notes and raw data of researchers whose work was part of the basis for the lawsuit. When they resisted, they were threatened with court action against them. Actual and potential witnesses for Cabrini-Green tenants were also served subpoenas demanding personal information and they were subjected to long depositions (four to twelve hours each) that questioned their competence as expert witnesses. Many of them considered this more as harassment than as a legal strategy. The substance of the subpoenas and the atmosphere in the depositions was hostile and purposely intimidating. The unusually harsh response of the city and the CHA to the lawsuit was likely due to the fact that the suit was threatening the viability of the proposed TIF bonds.

During the discovery period of the trial, the LAC, the CHA, and city officials began meeting to try to negotiate an out-of-court settlement. The initial court date was postponed as negotiations continued. After two full years of negotiation, a settlement was reached. In the consent decree, the LAC, CHA, and the city of Chicago agreed to a final settlement of all claims alleged in the case by the LAC and by the residents who are members of or are represented by the LAC.[72] The LAC agreed to the demolition of the six buildings and the CHA agreed to provide the funding and construction of at least 895 public housing eligible units to be located on the HOPE VI site. Seven hundred of these units were designated for families earning at or below 30 percent of the Chicago area median income, while the remaining 195 units were to be affordable to families with incomes at or below 40 percent.

The demolition of the buildings had to occur in two phases. Three buildings could be demolished as soon as the consent decree was signed and approved by HUD. Under the terms of the consent decree, no further demolitions could occur until 300 units of public housing were under construction; CHA had identified the funds for an additional 400 units in the HOPE VI planning area; the sites for these units had been identified; and the request for proposal for the construction of these units had been issued. The CHA further agreed to maintain the three additional buildings scheduled for demolition in decent and safe condition until the replacement units were built and the families were relocated.

The consent decree also provided for the Cabrini-Green LAC to be a co-general partner for the development of the new public housing units. The Cabrini-Green LAC would have a 51 percent interest in the ownership of the general partnership for the development of these sites. The request for proposal (RFP) for these development sites would include language to this effect and give extra points to developers who maximize LAC participation. The lawsuit had been filed on October 24, 1996. The consent decree that included the above provisions plus a number of others was reviewed and approved by the Cabrini-Green LAC on July 28, 1998. Residents considered it an important victory and a testament to all of the hard organizing that CCTPH had done. But the victory was short-lived.

In late summer 1998, just as all three parties were going to sign the consent decree, the Habitat Company, the private developer who had been designated as receiver for the CHA scattered site program under the *Gautreaux* decision, filed to intervene. The federal judge ruled that Habitat had standing and should be included in the decisions and approval of the consent decree. The Habitat Company proceeded to object to the amount of public housing units being proposed in the consent decree based on the old *Gautreaux* ruling that prohibited new construction of public housing in segregated neighborhoods. It also objected to the provision that the Cabrini-Green LAC would have a 51 percent interest as co-general partner. The Habitat Company claimed that these provisions of the consent decree would make the redevelopment plans infeasible for private for-profit developers. The debate over the terms of the consent decree resumed with the participation of the Habitat Company. Negotiations continued until the spring of 2000, when a settlement was finally reached. The residents lost their majority position in the co-partnership and a substantial number of public housing units.

The sudden entry of Habitat into the process after two years of negotiation looked suspicious. Habitat was clearly entering on behalf of most developers with an interest in the project and maybe even the city, which had been prepared to offer developers major profits through its TIF-based land subsidies. But Habitat stood to gain substantial profits themselves. Habitat's status as *Gautreaux* receiver awards them with 3 percent of the dollars spent on new family housing construction plus overhead costs. HUD had budgeted $21.9 million for Habitat's services, but had only paid out $17.3 million.[73]

A major stumbling block in the negotiations related specifically to the *Gautreaux* case. As explained earlier, the ruling in the *Gautreaux v. Chicago Housing Authority* lawsuit of 1966 stated that no additional public housing could be built in predominantly African American areas. The Cabrini-Green LAC through its attorneys requested a waiver of this ruling and sought to have "the Cabrini-Green public housing development (designated as) a 'revitalizing area,' which would allow for the construction of low income and public housing in the area."[74] On September 28, 1999, the federal judge who ruled on the *Gautreaux* cases denied the waiver motion of the Cabrini-Green LAC. The effect of the waiver was to enable the developers to limit the number of Cabrini-Green residents who could live in the project after redevelopment.

Once the waiver motion was lost, the CHA proceeded to form a Working Group to provide ongoing direction and oversight of the Near North Redevelopment Initiative (NNRI). According to the consent decree, the following are represented on the Working Group: the Cabrini-Green Local Advisory Council (LAC), the CHA, the city, counsel for Gautreaux plaintiffs, and the receiver, Habitat. The consent decree further states that "Under the Gautreaux Receivership Order, and other applicable law, CHA or its successor, the Receiver, and the City will have final decision-making authority in their respective areas of responsibility. A representative of the City shall chair the Working Group. A HUD staff member may attend the Working Group meetings as a non-member observer."[75] Construction of units on the CHA Cabrini-Green site began in 2002. In 2001, there were eight mixed-income private projects, in various stages of development, in and around the Cabrini-Green area. These developments will have 776 units, of which 197 are designated public housing units. This means that the CHA has agreements with these developers to lease these units for public housing residents.[76]

Meanwhile, HUD, the CHA, and the city of Chicago continued their assault on other public housing developments under the terms of the Quality Housing and Work Responsibility Act of 1998. Tenant evictions have accelerated. During the winter months of 1999–2000, many tenants living in buildings without adequate heat were moved with the expectation that their buildings would be gone by spring. These actions are in accord with two CHA plans. A requirement of the Quality Housing and Work Responsibility Act of 1998 is that CHA had to complete these plans by the end of 1999. The CHA released both plans at the end of September 1999. The plans proposed to demolish approximately 16,000 existing public housing units throughout the city of Chicago and entirely privatize the property management of the units. Cabrini-Green is slated to lose an additional 968 units in the plan. The CHA plans to reduce its permanent stock to 24,400 units. Only 15,000 of these units are for families, the rest are for seniors. The CHA is estimating that 6,150 public housing families will have to be relocated into the private market over the next five years to make way for this redevelopment. This plan was submitted to the federal government in January 2000 and, as mentioned earlier, approved in February of that year.

The CHA plan received widespread opposition from public housing tenants. Residents of Robert Taylor Homes, who are next in line for displacement, held several protests in an effort to stop the evictions and relocation of tenants. Opposition from other public housing developments and civic organizations who have joined the CTPPH was voiced at five public hearings that were held throughout the city. The regional rental housing market study, commissioned by HUD, was released November 1999 in the midst of the debate about the CHA's proposed plan. Despite the fact that the study demonstrated a very tight private rental housing market and an unwillingness for most landlords to participate in the Section 8 program, the CHA only became more determined to continue on its path to privatize the public housing program. HUD and CHA officials even tried to pressure the housing market researchers to soften the language of the study. And the mayor's public relations staff issued press advisories attempting to spin the results of the study in a favorable direction. As Carol Steele of the Coalition to Protect Public Housing commented on the rental study and the CHA's refusal to take note of the study,

> The fact is the private rental market has and continues to show that there are not enough low-income units for people who need them the most. Until CHA and the public at large acknowledge that we are dealing with people and not just numbers we will continue to play a guessing game about where people will live.[77]

CTPPH has continued to voice their opposition and raise questions about the implementation of the CHA's " Plan for Transformation." However, once HUD approved the plan in February 2000, the organizing of tenants and the maintaining of public awareness and support for the residents became even more difficult. Funding sources dried up. So, with reduced resources CTPPH began to focus its organizing on the monthly CHA board meetings. CTPPH organized residents to attend these meetings to raise questions and concerns about the redevelopment process. At the meetings they consistently raised what they called a mantra of three questions about the feasibility and planning of the CHA redevelopment. Where is the money for the redevelopment? Where is the land? Where are the people going once they are displaced? As one CTPPH supporter phrased it, "After 2000, it is the goal of the organization to keep CHA and the mayor's feet to the fire to ensure they build what they promised and pressure them to build first before demolishing units." For it is the fear of many public housing residents and CTPPH that there is not enough money and land for the CHA and city to do even the scaled-back public housing development that they laid out in their 2000 plan.

Conclusions

We began this chapter by arguing that the new world order has ushered in three important shifts in housing policy in the United States: the withdrawal of government from publicly owned housing; the nearly exclusive treatment of housing as an exchangeable commodity rather than as a social and human need; and the integration of housing-related credit and speculation into broader international capital markets. These three shifts are part of both the logic and operation of the new world order generally. The operation of the new world order includes opening up new opportunities for private businesses to move their capital around the world and also into new ventures. A greatly reduced public sector helps facilitate this aim and privatization is a key mechanism to accomplish this reduction. In this chapter we contend that the specific manifestation of the operation and logic of the new world order in housing policy, ideology, and finance shifts is both driving gentrification and leaving poor people without adequate housing options.

Public housing was one of the fruits of the social movements arising out of the Great Depression during the 1930s. But as the new world order was being born, public housing suffered from neglect in the 1970s and 1980s. The withdrawal of funds during this period, as part of a shrinking commitment to public-sector social programs meant that many public housing units were not maintained for fifteen to twenty years and were allowed to deteriorate, in some cases beyond habitability. The "solution" found in the 1990s was privatization. As a result, in Chicago and many other major cities in the United States, the buildings that house thousands of low-income citizens are being torn down. The former residents of these buildings are given Section 8 housing vouchers to seek housing in a private market that cannot meet the needs of most low-income and very poor people. Meanwhile, the extensive use of tax credits has benefited large corporations as has the integration of housing into global capital markets.

A second shift in housing policy involves the destruction of the social dimension of housing as reflected in the public housing program with the admonition that housing is a commodity to be acquired through individual effort and competitiveness. In the United States housing has never been viewed fully as a social good. Despite the best efforts of housing reformers of the 1930s and the postwar period, the result was a two-tiered housing policy that was generous to middle and upper classes through tax policies that promoted home ownership, but stingy and poorly funded for those most in need.[78] As we saw in the previous chapter, in cities like Chicago, that divide was often along racial lines. Yet the housing reformers of the 1930s and 1940s were successful in forcing public officials to pay lip service to the notion that there was a social benefit in government making sure that people had a decent place to live. And that publicly stated goal provided a basis for community organizations to form and struggle toward the end of housing as a human right as affirmed in the United Nations Declaration on Human Rights.

But the strategy of the new world order requires a full repudiation of this notion, even in the form of halfhearted, underfunded housing programs. High capital mobility and limited government interference is sustained through the ideological conviction that markets do everything better. For a market to work properly, in this view, individuals must express their preferences and needs by bidding in that market. This requires individuals to be competitive so they can get what they want or need. This logic replaces the notion that societies should strive to meet certain mutually agreed-upon standards. And it stands in contradiction to the United Nations Declaration of Human Rights that considers among those rights food, health care, and housing. In the present period, even the poorly funded and run programs for the very poor are being withdrawn and cut back. These policy cutbacks have caused the Chicago Housing Authority to change its mission from providing housing for people with inadequate incomes to a very different goal: "to invest in or facilitate housing opportunities." As pubic housing buildings are destroyed and residents are forced to compete in a private market that can't possibly meet their needs, the local government is entering into public-private partnerships to develop mixed-income housing. The rationale is that lacking concentrations of poverty and with the incentive to compete for adequate housing in the private market, individuals will become more competitive.

The residents of public housing in Chicago found themselves caught up in the whirlwind of these shifts in dominant ideology and public policy. The fact that they are predominantly African American has meant that the old system of racial exclusion has given way to a new one. In the old system, African Americans were kept out of some areas and concentrated in others. Public housing was the vehicle. The new system is in many ways more insidious. Very poor African Americans are removed from their homes and given a voucher to find housing that for the most part does not exist. In an ideological/political climate where it is believed that success (or failure) can only be achieved through individual effort (or lack of effort), the unsuccessful are easily demonized and dismissed. Race is no longer considered a factor because affluent African Americans can take the place of the former public housing residents in the new upscale developments. As Cabrini-Green resident Carol Steele observed, "they were proposing for my people to be evicted and become homeless."

The notion of the absolute benefit of mixed-income communities has become the justification for the elimination of housing for the poor. Its benefits are nowhere documented. The mixed-income community concept is a peculiar manifestation of the ideological proposition that progress can only come through the efforts of competitive individuals. The notion that concentrations of poor people are not sustainable and destructive to community development has been used to generate the CHA's housing development plan. And it was used initially to justify the destruction of Cabrini-Green buildings.

In fact, the notion of a "tipping point," the product of older forms of racial exclusion, is being used with a slightly different twist. The Near North Redevelopment Initiative, the plan that preceded the Cabrini-Green consent decree, proposed to set aside 30 percent of housing for public housing residents. There is no clear explanation for the 70/30 split except for a CHA consultant who pointed to what he called "the poor predominantly African-American" character of the area and stated that it "cannot, at least during the near term, enjoy the full complement of market-rate housing demand that the Near North Primary Market Area as a whole has to apportion."[79] Essentially, the justification for the 70/30 split was how it would play to the well-to-do who could afford the market rate housing. Most of these well-heeled buyers of the 70 percent would be white, although not exclusively so. All of the 30 percent will be African American. Racial exclusion is thus alive and well. African Americans get their homes torn down to make way for wealthy whites and a handful of African American elites. It is the perceived comfort level of the white and well-off buyers that determines the number of poor African Americans who are allowed to stay in the area. What is different is that the tipping point notion comes with the trappings of the new world order ideology. It is argued that a lack of individual competitiveness is what has put the very poor in this mess to begin with. Further, it is life in an area of concentrated poverty, not race and class discrimination, which keeps them in this state. They can be competitive if they live in mixed-income communities. So, the reasoning goes, the displacement is really doing them a favor.

The notion of a mixed-income community lends itself to the privatization of public housing and carries the trappings of a market-driven approach to development. What makes this notion particularly valuable to developers, politicians, African American elites, and bureaucrats is the fact that the mixed-income community and the old tipping point notion on which it is based is a hollow and abstract concept that takes a concrete form in the political arena. The meaning of "mixed income" varies according to the class, race, and even situational perspectives of the groups and individuals who use it. From the perspective of poor people in the south Loop SROs and public housing developments or the residents of Cabrini-Green who are trying to secure their rights in the face of city of Chicago, CHA, and Habitat Corporation plans, mixed income is good if it means they can stay. But to developers, the mix of incomes is okay as long as the lower end isn't too low and the numbers don't exceed their perception of a "tipping point." Also, bringing middle- and upper-income people into a community that is predominantly poor can and has meant gentrification. Thus, the mixed-income composition disappears as the poor are driven out by high taxes and high rents. In this case the notion of a tipping point works the other way. How many upper-class people will it take to drive up land values and drive the poor out? In communities that are already solidly upper- or middle-income and white, mixed income is a non-issue. (No one is arguing that greedy rich people need the poor as role models!)

The political contention over the very meaning of mixed income was brought into bold relief at a demonstration one wintry morning in front of the south Loop residence of Mayor Daley. The demonstration was part of the Chicago Coalition for the Homeless' "development without displacement" campaign. The mayor's neighborhood is "mixed" in that it includes a handful of African Americans. But there is no room for very-low-income people who were being displaced from SRO hotels near the mayor's home. The demonstration stuck the mixed-income notion in the mayor's face. Demonstrators demanded the inclusion of the very poor, many of them homeless, in the mayor's neighborhood as they sang an old African-American song,

> Open the door, Richard.
> Open the door and let me in!
> Open the door, Richard.
> Come on Richard, why won't you open that door.

The notion of mixed income provides a convenient political screen for other agendas. The real issue is *where are poor people going to live?* As the government offers subsidies to developers and large corporatons for upscale development through TIFs and for moderate-income development through the tax credit program, public housing, without proper maintenance, is left to deteriorate. The buildings are then scheduled for demolition without first building replacement units. A spokesperson for the Chicago Coalition for the Homeless once pointed out ironically that Chicago Bulls professional basketball players were not told they would have to play in a nearby school lot because they were going to demolish the stadium. Rather, they built the new stadium first and then tore the old one down.

Moreover, the class interests that are behind the hollow mixed-income concept can solidify to upend even the most vigorous organizing efforts. Two years of negotiations between public housing residents and local and federal government officials were simply brushed aside when Habitat stepped in on the ground that they, as developers, were excluded from the process and that they objected to what the citizens and government officials had come up with. When race and class both come into play, the result is problematic for citizen organizations whose base consists of the poorest citizens. In seeking alliances, such groups find fragmentation first on race and then along class lines. The homeless, people on public welfare, and public housing residents are increasingly isolated. And government uses this isolation to push the privatization and deregulation schemes that have become the basis for their political power.

As public housing is being destroyed, new world order housing policy is being implemented in Chicago and many other U.S. cities. As the shift in housing policy takes from the poor, it gives to the rich by the creation of subsidized upscale housing. The story of the south Loop and the plans for the replacement of the Cabrini-Green public housing development illustrate this process.

The withdrawal from publicly owned housing, its replacement with mixed-income development, and the ideology that supports the total commodification of housing is part of what drives gentrification and excludes the poor. We have also argued that new world order financial mechanisms play a critical role. Housing is a specific case of the general point developed in Chapter 3 that the new world order is sustained by credit expansion and speculation. The availability of mortgage loans to well-heeled buyers who will live in the redeveloped south Loop or Cabrini-Green areas is in part due to the fact that mortgage funds have been integrated into the international capital markets. And the secondary mortgage market operations enable lenders to continuously and rapidly recycle their capital and lend it out again and again. There are no data that link the financing of Cabrini and south Loop developments to the secondary mortgage market. Rather, the point is that these developments occur in the context of a new system in which that market and the mortgage-backed securities it generates play a central role. The availability of mortgage credit for extensive new developments is generated today not by savings and loan associations or even commercial banks. Nor does the federal government play the role it did under the old Urban Renewal program. Rather, private finance generated by various kinds of investors who seek returns in global capital markets are the backbone of today's real estate finance system. So extensive is this system that an influential real estate textbook contends, as quoted earlier, that investors in mortgage-backed securities are driving up the value of urban real estate. Meanwhile, as public housing is being demolished, the only significant resources to subsidize moderate- and low-income people is through the Section 8 and tax credit program, which are not adequate for the task. Gentrification is thus part of the new world order.

Moreover, developers are also benefiting from the ability of local governments to give them subsidies through another manifestation of the general expansion of credit that is a driving force of the new world order—tax increment financing. The profits to be derived from the Cabrini and south Loop projects are in the millions, thanks to wonders of the TIF. Tax increment financing creates fiscal-geographical enclaves where development priorities lack political accountability and whose very existence depends on rising property values that offer global investors attractive, relatively risk-free profitable investments. And developers in these areas can hedge their own risks of rising interest rates by playing in the financial futures markets. All told, both developers and international capital markets are driving gentrification in such areas. These credit mechanisms plus the tax credit program that is worth billions of dollars to major corporations are what make large developments like Cabrini-Green and Central Station projects in the south Loop happen. Thus, while in the Fordist era it was the government that drove gentrification through urban renewal funds, today it is the private sector and its global capital markets.

Ultimately, however, the three shifts in housing policy—the retreat from public housing, the ideological notion that housing is an individual responsibility, and the key role of expanding credit and speculation in the gentrification of urban neighborhoods—leaves poor people without a place to live. Chapter 2 noted the general tendency in a capitalist society of a tension between commodities as use values versus exchange values. As exchange value dominates that tension, social values relating to human needs are undermined. Social struggle during previous eras had forced a public recognition of the social value of decent housing for all people. But the combination of the three shifts that have come with the new world order has turned housing into a pure exchange value, overturning the gains of the previous era.

Furthermore, the integration of housing into the international capital markets has altered the spatial dimension of the housing problem. Housing markets are no longer confined to the buyers and sellers in a particular locality. In the previous era, federal and local governments intervened in local markets. While that intervention was not always positive from the perspective of the poor, social movements could use government as a forum in which to press their demands. But today social exclusion of the poor in the area of housing is being driven in part by the concerns of big investors who decide on a daily basis the mix of diverse portfolios of financial "products." That these social priorities are being established in submunicipal fiscal enclaves highlights a spatial dimension of the shift we have been discussing. Complex political forces that are both global and sublocal now drive housing markets and public policies that structure and govern them. This has profound implications for how best to address the problem of housing the poor. There is a need to link local housing struggles with those seeking to regulate global capital flows. We return to this issue in the final chapter of this book.

One final issue involves the connection between housing on the one hand, and employment and income on the other. An implication of Chapter 4 is that the destruction of living wage jobs in the 1980s is a major factor explaining the number of people without adequate incomes for decent housing and other human needs. In the following chapter, we will see that the generation of jobs in the 1990s did not begin to make up for the losses a decade earlier. But there is an important connection to make here between housing and employment. The shifts in housing policy and the expanded role of players in the international capital markets are part of the problem of housing affordability. These forces are driving up housing costs while backing away from social housing. But the other side of affordability is the polarization of incomes. While the present era has given rise to a stratum of society that can afford very-high-cost housing, it has also generated poverty due to a lack of living wage jobs. That began with the deindustrialization described in Chapter 4. The poor who are excluded from decent housing and living wage jobs are not simply uncompetitive individuals, as the ideology of the present period suggests. Rather, they are a class of people who are bearing the costs of the current mode of accumulation. And these are the people who are increasingly finding it difficult or impossible to find a decent place to live. Housing and living wage jobs are not separate issues. Jobs, income, and living standards are thus the focus of the next chapter.

CHAPTER 7

Jobs, Wages, and Trade in the New World Order

It has been more than two decades since Chase Manhattan Bank security guards traveled from New York to Chicago in the dead of night and locked the gates at Wisconsin Steel, ushering in a decade of plant closings. During the 1990s, the United States began one of the longest periods of sustained economic growth in its history. By the end of that decade, official unemployment stood at just a little over 4 percent—the lowest rate since the early 1970s. But the reports of a hot economy throughout the 1990s masked an important reality of American life generally as well as life specifically in Chicago. Many of the former Wisconsin Steel workers and laid-off manufacturing workers generally never worked again. And most of those who did get work were unable to find jobs with comparable wages and benefits. Moreover, the next generation of workers was unable to match the living standards of their parents. The reason that both record economic and employment growth could accompany a loss of living standards for many is that the benefits of the new world order were shared very unevenly. The 1990s continued a trend that began in the 1980s. The income of both low- and middle-income families stagnated and left them worse off than they had been in the 1970s.[1] Meanwhile, those in the top income brackets enjoyed a very high rate of income growth and were also able to accumulate assets that brought in even more income.[2] But many working families failed to make wages that allowed them to escape critical hardships that involved missing meals, being evicted from their homes, disconnected utilities, and access to needed medical care.[3]

Polarization of income and wealth is in itself certainly nothing new. But the polarization that has been a hallmark of the new world order throughout the world has a different character than previously. In the case of the United States, the growing income generated by the economic growth that followed World War II was shared among income groups. The rich got richer, but so did the middle-income and even the lowest-income families. That was part of the postwar deal that characterized the Fordist period. But as we have seen in previous chapters, even the largess of the postwar boom often left out people of color and women. Polarization during that period was largely based on race and gender. Today there is still polarization based on race and gender, but the growth of polarization has become much more generalized. Over the past two decades, the rich have gotten richer and the poor, poorer.

There are three things that are different about today's more generalized polarization. First, the high incomes are fueled by a system of credit and speculation and highly mobile capital, which is a key feature of the new world order. That has been a theme developed in previous chapters. A second distinctive characteristic of today's economic polarization involves the political discourse and resulting public policies concerning employment. Because of the political power of the financiers who fuel the new world order and of the mobile corporations who benefit from that fuel, there has been a distinct political shift in the ideology of employment and the social priority given to jobs and income. Third, with highly mobile capital, many of the new jobs created around the world do not offer enough wages and benefits to allow workers to live a decent life. In the United States, many of today's jobs—both new and old—do not pay living wages or offer adequate benefits. And a growing number of jobs are part-time or temporary.

This chapter develops these last two points, tracing and critiquing the shift in the ideology, theory, and politics of employment and the employment ramifications of "free trade." I then show how this shift has affected working people nationally and in the Chicago area.

The Evolution of the Ideology, Theory, and Politics of Employment in the United States

In the late 1920s, the world economy collapsed. Unemployment reached catastrophic levels. Capitalism itself was threatened. To those attempting to end the Great Depression and save capitalism, unemployment was considered to be the greatest evil. In the United States, public policies based on this premise followed. President Roosevelt put people to work building roads, bridges, and parks. People were paid for this public work out of taxes. Where there was not enough tax revenue to go around, the needed funds were borrowed. Employment was the heart of the New Deal. While World War II rather than these job programs saved the day, the social priority of security based on living wage jobs remained and became part of the postwar deal in the United States that began a new global era. That priority was clearly set out in the Employment Act of 1946, which called for "maximum employment, production and purchasing power" to be the goal of U.S. employment policy.[4]

By the late 1970s, the postwar deal ended with the Fordist era—and so did the way we as a society thought about employment. Despite the fact that the goals of the 1946 Employment Act were reaffirmed in 1978 with the Humphrey–Hawkins Full Employment and Balanced Growth Act, U.S. policy was moving in a different direction, more in keeping with the developing new world order. By the 1980s, both the political and academic mainstream considered inflation to be the main evil. Furthermore, it was widely believed, employment could not grow beyond a "natural" rate of unemployment. Growth beyond that rate could cause prices to rise and thus must be stopped. This shift in thinking about employment included the abandonment of employment as a social goal. Instead, employment is now widely seen as an individual responsibility that can be achieved by timely investment in one's "human capital," resulting in individual competitiveness. Out of this notion evolved the idea that employment is as much a form of moral behavior as a way to make a living. Everyone now has a personal responsibility to get and hold some kind of employment. And those who can't get work or who refuse to work for less than it takes to live a decent life are seen as morally deficient. I develop this shift in thinking first in relation to mainstream theory and politics, and then spell out the policy ramifications of the shift.

Theory and Practice

It may seem odd now, but I hesitated a while before deciding to call my book *Human Capital*. . . . In the early days, many people were criticizing this term and the underlying analysis because they believed it treated people like slaves or machines. My, how the world has changed! The name and analysis are now readily accepted by most people not only in all the social sciences, but even in the media. . . . In the recent presidential campaign, both President Clinton and former President Bush . . . did not even shy away from using the term 'investing in human capital' to describe the process of improving the quality of the labor force.[5]

——Gary Becker, Nobel Laureate Economist, 1993

Theory or ideas have always played an important role in politics, public policy, and day-to-day life in civil society. The relation of theory to practice is a part of the dialectic of everyday living. Ideas are both a response to the problems posed by the social order and a part of that order. Some ideas support the existing order, some try to accommodate its strictures, some challenge it. Which ideas prevail or prove hegemonic at any particular point in time reflect the balance of political forces. Once a set of ideas becomes hegemonic, they become part of the social order and a material force in that order. But the role of ideas in the dialectic of everyday life continues.[6] This role is important for two reasons. First, it explains why certain theories seem to catch on at a particular time, dominate public discourse, and become the basis for public policies and the behavior of people. Second, ideas play an important role in social change. In this chapter I discuss the first point in relation to the shift in ideas about employment. In the final chapter of this book, I take up the point about social change.

In the 1960s, as the era of Fordism gained momentum, the United States was enjoying a sustained period of economic growth and prosperity. Throughout the decade of the 1960s, the rate of unemployment dropped from nearly 7 percent to about 3.5 percent. Inflation was holding steady at about 2 percent. During this period, economists from both Britain and the United States began studying the relationship between inflation and unemployment. Looking at data since the turn of the century, they found a regular relationship between the rate of unemployment and the rate of inflation. Lowering unemployment, they contended, would lead to rising inflation. The relationship appeared to be so regular that it was possible to plot it on a graph and estimate how much declining unemployment would "cost" in terms of inflation. This relationship became known as the Phillips Curve, named after the British economist who first discovered it. In the United States it was widely argued that society could make a determination of how far to push a full employment policy based on a clear knowledge of this trade-off. Since there was a general consensus that unemployment was a greater evil than inflation, policymakers opted for continuing growth. Losses from inflation were compensated through cost of living adjustments in wages and pensions. The dominant mechanism to achieve such growth was known as fiscal policy. Increased government spending and decreased taxes could stimulate growth that would lower unemployment. If inflation rose above what was politically acceptable, the government could reduce spending and increase taxes. Monetary policy, which was the province of the Federal Reserve Bank, supplemented fiscal policy by adjusting interest rates. Rates were kept low when fiscal policy opted for growth and lower unemployment, or they could be raised to try to help cool the economy off. Since inflation rates were quite low in the 1960s, public policy was oriented toward growth and the lowest possible unemployment.

But this consensus was called into question as the Fordist era began to unravel. In the early 1970s, the unemployment rate increased to nearly 6 percent while inflation reached 5 percent. In the early 1980s, these rates increased to over 7 percent and 10 percent, respectively. Mainstream economists who favored an expansionist fiscal policy and had accepted the premises of the Phillips Curve were in a quandary about what was happening. They knew that some fundamental changes were under way. Some argued that essentially the Phillips Curve had shifted so that the relationship between unemployment and inflation was still intact but at higher levels. But they sharply disagreed about what was causing the shift. Political leaders also understood that something was fundamentally changing and were seeking an explanation and a way to proceed.

With all of the confusion accompanying the end of an era, there was a theory waiting in the wings that profoundly changed the way we would look at employment. In 1968, University of Chicago economist Milton Friedman gave a fateful lecture to the American Economics Association. In it he argued that the use of fiscal policy to pursue a goal of full employment was futile. The Phillips Curve, he contended was only stable in the "short run." He went on to argue that because of the short run predictability of the relationship between unemployment and inflation, it was relatively easy to predict future levels of both. If employers saw unemployment going down, they would anticipate inflation and raise their prices. Workers, in turn, would anticipate higher prices and push for more wages. Eventually, these "rational expectations" would cause every level of unemployment to be associated with a higher rate of inflation. As long as unemployment was perceived as being "too low," inflation would continue to rise. This process, Friedman argued, would continue until a rate of unemployment was reached that no longer generated expectations of increased inflation. At this point the system was in equilibrium. That rate of unemployment was termed a "natural rate of unemployment" or a "non-accelerating inflation rate of unemployment" (NAIRU). The policy implication of this was clear. A national goal of full employment made no sense because if unemployment fell below the natural rate, gains would be wiped out by inflation.

Up until this time, economists generally believed that inflation came from two sources. One was when people were trying to buy more goods than the economy was able to produce. This was known as demand pull inflation. The other was when workers pushed wages up too high and employers were forced to raise their prices to maintain their profits. This was known as wage push inflation. The theory of the natural rate of unemployment introduced a third source of inflation—that generated by expectations.

The general acceptance of the NAIRU theory as an explanation for the simultaneous increase in unemployment and inflation aided the ascendancy of another part of the Chicago school economics paradigm. Friedman and others advocated monetarism. They argued that the only role for government in the management of the economy was to control the supply of money, and this role was to be strictly technical. The supply of money could be set at a level that would allow the economy to grow without inflation. That level was based on the historic relationship between the money supply and price—a relationship that was known as the monetary rule.

These theories were politically attractive at the time for several reasons. As the Fordist era began to crumble, high inflation and high unemployment made the prevailing fiscal policies unworkable. If you could slow down inflation by cutting government spending and increasing taxes or increase employment levels by increasing spending and cutting taxes, what was to be done when both unemployment and inflation were rising? Friedman's notion of a monetary rule filled a theoretical void. Moreover, his theory of a natural rate of unemployment that had been unveiled in 1968 seemed to have predicted the sudden breakdown of the historical relationship between unemployment and inflation in the 1970s.

More important, however, these theories were in tune with the needs of the emerging new world order. Mobile capital, goods, and services needed government deregulation. A goal of full employment could be used as justification to put some controls on mobility and to implement industrial policies to meet the nation's employment needs. The natural rate of unemployment theory was thus attractive to the proponents of mobile capital because it suggested that full employment as a social goal made no sense. Furthermore, inflation was most harmful to those who were fueling the new world order with credit and speculation. Modest inflation does not really hurt most people. Workers can build cost of living allowances into their wages and salaries. People on fixed incomes such as the elderly on social security can also keep up by building cost of living allowances into their retirement funds. But people who make profits by lending money and by trading stocks, bonds, and financial futures can lose out if the value of money is declining due to inflation. Thus, it is in their interest to have policies in place that put up with unemployment in order to keep inflation as low as possible. The natural rate of unemployment theory had just this policy implication. This is why it was attractive to the financiers whose political power was enhanced by the evolution of the new world order. Policies emphasizing full employment and high wages versus those that fight inflation thus benefit different constituencies. Theory in this case serves politics and not the other way around.

The Evolution of New World Order Employment Policies

The evolution of public policies grounded in these theories began with the Federal Reserve Bank. The Fed, as it is known, is an independent government agency that oversees the U.S. banking system and controls the supply of money mainly through raising and lowering interest rates. Increased rates make it more expensive for banks to lend money. Thus, when the Fed raises them it can depress lending activity and keep money out of circulation.

As I noted earlier, during the Fordist era the Fed tended to take a subordinate role to the economic policy set by the president and Congress. Monetary policy supplemented fiscal policy through the alteration of interest rates. But this changed abruptly in 1979. In that year, President Carter appointed a former investment banker, Paul Volker, to chair the Fed's board of governors. At the time the rate of inflation was over 12 percent. Volker announced that he would bring that rate down with monetary policy. He immediately moved to restrict the supply of money. By 1981, inflation was cut in half, but unemployment rose to nearly 10 percent, interest rates remained high, and the nation was in deep recession. The Volker-led Fed tried increasing the money supply at that point, but the recession continued. Interest rates continued to climb and unemployment rose to a frightful 11 percent by the end of 1982. With the high interest rates, the value of the dollar relative to other currencies began to rise. This increased the price of U.S. goods abroad and contributed to the collapse of manufacturing, which I discussed in Chapter 4. It also contributed to inflation and economic collapse in nations that were dependent on U.S. goods and were carrying U.S. debt. The resulting economic collapse in Mexico plunged all of Latin America into a depression. In 1987, President Reagan appointed Alan Greenspan to chair the Fed. Greenspan continued to focus on interest rate manipulation as the policy tool of choice. And he was very clear that inflation must be fought at every turn.

Volker's experiment with monetarism initially failed, but a major policy shift had evolved that reflected an emerging conservative consensus in theory and in politics. The Fed, which represented the interests of the banking industry and the growing strata of financiers, had declared that it would fight inflation by whatever means necessary. Even a hint of inflation would set the Fed on a path of interest rate hikes that essentially gutted the previous policy goal of full employment. Paul Volker initiated this shift only two years after the passage of the Humphrey–Hawkins Full Employment and Balanced Growth Act. The political activism of the Fed essentially cancelled an act of Congress.

Theoretical Consolidation

Eliminating the goal of full employment from government economic policy did not satisfy those still concerned about unemployment. While there seemed to be a political consensus around the proposition that fighting inflation was crucial, there was little agreement about what to do with those left out—the unemployed. The political answer that evolved was this. Employment was no longer primarily a social responsibility. Rather, it was an individual obligation. Free market policies would generate jobs for those who were competitive enough to get them. The only thing government should do was to aid the training process so that a supply of competitive workers was available. The demand for those workers would take care of itself. Following this line of reasoning, government withdrew from economic policies aimed at enhancing the demand for goods, services, and workers. Economic policy was focused instead on the "supply side" of the economy—using the supply of money to create opportunities for investment.

Rational Choices, Rational Expectations, and Human Capital

Two strands of theory emerged to bolster this evolving political consensus. They were both part of the Chicago school social science paradigm based on the concepts of rational choice and rational expectations. These are human capital theory and related theories of poverty. In 1992, University of Chicago economist Gary Becker won the Nobel prize for his work on human capital theory. This theory was grounded in the concept of rational choice that was now at the heart of Chicago school economics. Becker initially looked at the effects of individual choices about education and training, arguing that education should be seen as an investment that would pay a return to individuals in the form of future higher wages. Education, training, and work experience were considered to be forms of human capital that determined employability and wage potential. Other social dimensions of work—the positive value of co-operative labor; the role that class, race, and gender play in determining wages and employability; and the contribution of work to human development beyond monetary return—were subsumed under or explained by human capital investment. Employment relations were solely price-denominated costs and returns on "human capital." In fact, Becker used data from the U.S. slave trade, which he sees as the purest form of a market for labor. Slavery, Becker contends, is "the one example of an explicit market that trades and prices human capital stocks, rather than simply the services yielded by these stocks."[7]

While Becker's earliest formulation of his theory focused mainly on individual income gains from on-the-job training, more recent developments of human capital theory use it to explain such things as income and wealth polarization, the role of families in individual economic achievement, and the development or underdevelopment of nations.[8] Becker argues that income and wealth distribution is the result of human capital investment decisions of different individuals. Since education leads to higher wages, individuals with more education will naturally end up better off than those without. Using his philosophic and theoretical ground of rational choice, Becker contends that differences among children tend to get greater over time because of different "investment" behavior of parents in preparing their children for school and providing them with intellectual and emotional support once they are in school. These patterns, in Becker's view, are reinforced in school. The most prepared groups enjoy greater returns on their education, while the least prepared may drop out of school altogether. In this way, families, Becker contends, influence the knowledge, skills, education, marital stability, values, and habits of their children. He found that the statistical relationship between the income of parents and children is strongest in lower-income groups. "Underclass" families with low education, welfare dependence, and marital instability will tend to pass these qualities on to their children, negating the impact of formal education.

Poverty in the New World Order

As these theories gained acceptance in the political and policy arenas, they were developed further by other social scientists whose ideas particularly influenced government housing policies (discussed in the previous chapter) and employment policies (the present focus). This extension of the rational choice ideas focused on the high rates of unemployment and poverty in the nation's African American and Latino inner cities. An implication of the work of Becker and other economists who are grounded in rational choice and rational expectations theories is that rational choices and good human capital investment decisions depend on freely functioning markets. "Interference" with labor markets, such as unions pushing wages "too high" or government offering public welfare payments and minimum wages, distorts individual judgments about the costs and benefits of acquiring human capital. Conservative poverty theorists developed an argument that built on these implications. Federal government poverty programs—welfare, public housing, and even minimum wage—have actually contributed, they argue, to unemployment and poverty by destroying the incentive to work. The influence of the economic theories of the labor market and rational choice on these conservative poverty theories that have been developed by sociologists and even journalists is striking. A key aspect of their theory is that the cause of unemployment and the resulting poverty lies in the behavior of those who are in poverty. And federal programs contribute to unproductive behavior by distorting or masking the signals of the market, which otherwise could lead individuals to make better decisions.[9]

The development of these poverty theories was not limited to the politically conservative, however. One of the most prominent sociologists who has generated poverty theories grounded in the philosophy of rational choice, William Julius Wilson, is considered to be politically progressive.[10] As a matter of fact, Wilson takes issue with the conclusion of conservative theorists that federal programs cause poverty and unemployment, seeing racism as a major cause of African American and Latino poverty. Yet he accepts and reinforces a key aspect of the conservative formulation of the nature of poverty—namely, that the persistence of poverty lies in the behavior of those living in poverty. Disadvantages that can be attributed to race, in this view, can be overcome by individuals if they make the correct choices. In Wilson's formulation, joblessness is not so much an economic category as a behavioral one. While he sees African American poverty as a legacy of past discrimination, he argues that this poverty gets reinforced through social isolation and the development of a "tangle of pathology in the inner city" that includes violent crime, mother-only households, welfare dependency, out-of-wedlock births, and teenage pregnancies. In his most recent work he argues that the root cause of the tangle of pathologies he describes is what he terms "joblessness."[11] But work, to Wilson, is not primarily about either income or self-development. It is a form of socially acceptable behavior. A job is something that provides the worker with "discipline and regularity," qualities (or human capital in Becker's terms) that enable one to suffer the adversity of being poor without resorting to behaviors that reinforce that condition.

Central to Wilson's analysis is his concept of social class. This concept is also critical to both his policy conclusions and much of today's social science research on employment and poverty. Class is treated as an individual rather than a social concept. It is defined in terms of living standards or behaviors that are related to living standards. It coincides neatly with a central concept of mainstream economics: "economic man." Economic man strives as an *individual* to "maximize utility" through rational choices that are mediated by markets. Increasingly, both political science and sociology are adopting the rational choice model in their respective fields. Wilson, as a sociologist, sees "good behavior" (which includes everything from giving a good interview to marriage) as a "resource" that enables individuals to become more competitive in the world of commodity exchange. Any behavior that diminishes what one brings to the exchange relationship both in the labor market (the human capital you have to offer) and in the commodity and service markets where you bid for your wants and needs with the returns on your human capital is in these terms "aberrant" and "pathological." It is these behaviors that define you as lower-class or even underclass. By defining class in terms of exchange relations, Wilson makes social class independent of most social relations. Your class becomes an individual matter, and the only association between your class and your relationship to others is a competitive one during the act of exchange. Success in exchange relations, in turn, depends on the qualities of discipline, regularity, and self-sufficiency that Becker and others now view as part of human capital. These qualities, according to Wilson, are what you learn at a job, even if your job pays below-poverty wages and offers no benefits.

Policy Ramifications: Flexible Workers, Flexible Wages, Flexible Jobs

These theories reinforced global and domestic policies that individualized the labor process under the banner of "flexibility." In 1977, as the new world order was beginning to evolve, the OECD, an association of the most developed capitalist nations, formed a group of experts to study common economic problems. Paul McCracken, who was the chief economic advisor to President Ford at the time, headed the OECD group. Their report concluded that a lack of "flexibility in labor markets" was responsible for rising rates of unemployment throughout the world.[12] Lack of flexibility in labor markets was defined in terms of excessive wage and benefit expectations, rigid work rules that constrained the production process, refusal of some workers to do certain kinds of work, barriers to the use of temporary and part-time work, and government policies that encouraged these things. These themes continued to be developed in OECD reports throughout the 1980s and 1990s.[13] The resulting government policies were worldwide and undermined labor laws that protected union collective bargaining arrangements and government social programs that made it possible for workers to refuse poverty wage jobs as well as temporary or part-time work. These shifts in policy took root in most OECD nations, particularly the United States and Britain. The World Bank and the IMF also took them up as a part of the SAPs in the developing world. By the end of the 1990s, the notion of labor market flexibility and its policy implications were part of the new world order.

In the discussion below, I focus on three areas of U.S. government employment policy that are key aspects of a political commitment to human capital investment and labor market flexibility in the United States. These are welfare "reform," job training, and "free trade." All three of these policy areas have developed in a broader context of a political orientation in which the U.S. government has abandoned the goal of full employment; has embraced the notion that inflation is a greater evil than unemployment; and has agreed to limit the role of government, especially the federal government, in employment issues. Limiting the role of government has meant cutbacks in social programs and an orientation toward balancing the budget at the expense of such programs. This shift in domestic economic and social policy has been accompanied by a global commitment to "free trade," a name given to policies being used to enforce global labor market flexibility.

Welfare "Reform"

President Clinton's approach to welfare "reform" represented a further retreat from the Fordist era's consensus around employment as a social goal. The political consolidation of the contrary view that work is an investment in one's own human capital and thus a personal responsibility found its ultimate expression in the 1996 Personal Responsibility and Work Opportunities Reconciliation Act (PRWORA). PRWORA replaced a program established in 1935 that was the result of the demands of social movements in the wake of the Great Depression. The program established the notion of an economic floor as an entitlement. Political consensus around the meaning of entitlement was shaky from the beginning. Conservatives attacked the welfare program as contributing to a "culture of poverty" while others criticized the welfare program as a form of social control of the poor—particularly African American women, who were the largest group receiving this aid.[14] In fact, at the height of the civil rights movement of the 1960s, welfare rights became an important part of the struggle for civil rights generally. The National Welfare Rights Organization campaigned for the rights of the poor and demanded fair treatment for welfare recipients.

In the late 1970s, however, there was a political move that spanned much of the political spectrum that attacked the notion of entitlement itself and replaced it with the personal responsibility of every individual to invest in your own or your children's human capital. The move began with a number of state programs developed in the United States that experimented with the concept of "welfare to work." The federal government granted waivers from the traditional welfare program to implement demonstration programs aimed at getting people off welfare and into jobs. Several of these programs—especially the Wisconsin Works Program (W2)—emerged as models for the welfare reform legislation of the 1990s.

Despite serious questions about the success of W2 and similar local programs,[15] President Clinton announced in his state of the union address in 1996 that he was close to "ending welfare as we know it." The result was PRWORA. Its name alone demonstrates the political shift away from entitlement toward personal responsibility. PRWORA places limits on the length of time an individual can receive welfare benefits and requires individuals to work for the benefits they receive. In practice, state and local welfare-to-work programs work hand in hand with the activities of the one-stop job training centers. As we will see later in this chapter, the practical effect of both PWRORA and the new job training program, known as the Workforce Investment Act (WIA), is to force people into employment "opportunities" that fail to pay living wages and benefits. The jobs of most PWRORA and WIA workers are the ultimate expression of "labor market flexibility." The ability to hold out for living wage employment and decent benefits is gone so employers have the flexibility to offer lower wages and work rules of their own choosing. All of this is justified by the notion that people in these flexible jobs are learning important behavior—gaining human capital—that will put them and their children in a better position in the future. Their human capital is further enhanced by being taken out of "welfare dependency," which teaches them only indolence and masks the market signals that would set them on the road to good behavior.

Job Training

New world order job training programs work hand in hand with welfare "reform." And, like PWRORA, the 1998 Workforce Investment Act funnels workers into a world of flexible jobs with flexible wages. Job training programs in the 1960s were a response by both Presidents Kennedy and Johnson to the demands of civil rights advocates for a fair distribution of employment opportunities. In 1962, Congress passed the Manpower Development and Training Act (MDTA) that targeted job training and other employment services to hardcore unemployed people—mostly people of color. This commitment began to be undermined in 1973, when President Nixon introduced the Comprehensive Employment and Training Act (CETA). CETA took much of the job training initiative out of federal government hands by turning its administration over to state and local governments and private industry. The negative impacts of this shift on people of color were softened somewhat because the federal government still had an expansive fiscal policy designed to stimulate the demand for workers. In 1982, the Kennedy–Johnson commitment to targeted training for the hardcore unemployed was further undermined by the passage of the

Job Training and Partnership Act (JTPA). JTPA purged the last remnants of the Great Society and War on Poverty influence from job training through the elimination of a key public service employment program. Moreover, JTPA was the first of President Reagan's "new federalism" programs (or "devolution" as we call it today).[16] More administrative and oversight authority went to the governors of states and to private industry councils that were dominated by private businesses. Most important, JTPA was enacted on the heels of the formal abandonment of the goal of full employment. Job training was being pursued without any program to stimulate the demand for workers. Job training had now shifted from a societal to an individual responsibility as devolution took hold. The result was that the main recipient of federal training funds had shifted from the urban poor to private business. Corporations, rather than poor people, would decide how to use public funds for "human capital investment." And this shift came at a time when big business was focused on the benefits of its increasing mobility. JTPA was job training without jobs. The idea of job training as an investment in human capital for future returns rather than a mechanism to employ those mired in unemployment had taken hold. But the investment of public funds was, at the same time, greatly reduced. JTPA was not only job training without jobs, it was also job training without funds. Between 1978 and 1984, dollar allocations for job training adjusted for inflation declined by over 70 percent.[17]

Throughout the remainder of the 1980s and much of the 1990s, the JTPA program continued in this general direction. But in 1998, new legislation consolidated further the new world order view of employment as an investment in one's own human capital and hence a desired form of behavior and a personal responsibility. The Workforce Investment Act (WIA) of 1998 contains as a central feature the notion of "work first" that calls for "providing the shortest and least expensive servicing first, using the labor market itself as the test of employability."[18] The act sets up "one-stop" employment service centers that focus on providing information about available jobs and "prevocational job readiness training" (learning how to dress, get to work on time, be nice to your employer, etc.). If work is still not found, job training needs are assessed and a voucher is given to the unemployed person that can be used to find suitable training services. Again, the emphasis is on getting a job as quickly as possible. The hierarchy established by the one-stop centers using the "work first" model tends to place people where the need for preparation and education is the lowest, which will be reflected in the level of pay and benefits as well. Workers will be forced into flexible labor markets with no control over working conditions or hours and little protection if the job is lost other than another trip to the "one-stop" for more counseling.

"Free Trade" as an Employment Program

Welfare "reform" and job training programs are part of the programmatic expression of the new world order's ideological and theoretical shift with regard to employment from a national priority to an individual responsibility to participate in flexible labor markets. This shift occurred as public policies at national and international levels were enacted that were designed to enhance the mobility of capital, goods, and services globally. NAFTA, WTO, and the IMF/World Bank structural adjustment programs were the result. But they proved to be very controversial in the United States. Workers, who throughout the 1980s and 1990s lost living wage jobs and who were now being forced to take two or sometimes three jobs to stay out of poverty, viewed the rise of "free trade" with alarm. Would not the rise of such "open markets" result in further loss of employment and income? What did it mean to compete with workers in developing nations who were being paid in some instances less than $4 per day and who were being forced to live and work in frightful conditions?

The answer offered by political leaders and many academic advisors was that the rising tide of "free trade" would lift all boats. Greater production efficiency worldwide, it was argued, would enable employers to hire more people and pay higher wages. Using this logic, "free trade" has become the one exception to the government's abandonment of demand side macro economic policy to achieve higher levels of employment. "Free trade" became President Clinton's jobs program.

The theory behind the notion of "free trade" is this. Each nation in the world can produce some goods more efficiently (meaning at a lower cost per unit of output) than they can produce others. If nations specialize in producing what they can do most efficiently and trade with other nations, global production will be more efficient. The greater efficiency will mean that the workers in each nation will be employed in activities in which they can be most productive and earn the highest wages. Their employment and wages are thus enhanced through trade. If, on the other hand, nations try to protect domestic firms that are producing things inefficiently by imposing tariffs and other barriers to trade on the imports from other nations, the world will suffer because some production will be less efficient than it could be. It will cost relatively more to produce the things people of the world want and need.

Trade agreements and structural adjustment programs have clearly contributed to the growth of flexible labor markets that have lowered production costs. Yet, in the United States throughout a period of high economic growth in the 1990s workers' wages were stagnant and the distribution of income became more unequal. One reason for this is that "free trade" under its current manifestation in trade agreements and SAPS encourages mobile capital. Thus, there is no guarantee that the fruits of lower labor costs of global firms result in investment in any particular place. Rather, capital moves to areas of low cost or to be near markets. Second, the industries most involved in "free trade" are not competitive but tend to be dominated by a few giant firms. This means that there is no market discipline that compels these firms to pass on cost savings through greater efficiency to workers in the form of higher wages or to consumers in the form of lower prices. Finally, "free trade" also includes provisions to prohibit government regulation of firms in terms of how they use investment and discourages actions such as worker and environmental protection laws that cut into profits.

Local Collisions

The policy mix that has evolved from the ideologies and theories of rational choice, rational expectations, human capital, and free trade have led to local collisions at a community level. Inflation-fighting monetary policy; job training without jobs or adequate funds; welfare "reform" that stresses job placement rather than income support; the retreat from both public housing and demand side employment policies in the context of labor market flexibility and "free trade" have hurt those with the least resources. This entire mix of policies with their associated ideologies, theories, and politics is the aspect of the new world order that most impacts local employment, wages, and income. This mix has only truly been to the benefit of those at the very top. That is the explanation of the growing polarization of income and wealth throughout the 1980s and 1990s. It can be seen starkly in neighborhoods, communities, and workplaces across the United States where the cold data on income and wealth polarization becomes transformed into very human local collisions. My interviews reported in previous chapters with Wisconsin Steel workers and the statements of the public housing residents who are being tossed out of their homes with no assurance that there will be another place to live show this human dimension of the global decisions and local collisions. To illuminate the impact of the shift in the ideology, theory, and policies relating specifically to employment, I am going to examine three aspects of these local collisions in Chicago and the state of Illinois: wages and living standards; the impact of trade policies; and worker rights.

Chicago Area Living Conditions: A View from the Bottom

By the end of 2000, the peak of the business cycle, Chicago's unemployment rate seemed very low—a bit over 4 percent. Politicians, government officials, and many academics saw the low rates in cities like Chicago as proof that the strategy of tight money and flexible labor markets was working. Yet the use of the unemployment rate and the numbers of jobs created as indicators of prosperity masks some very important local collisions. The unemployment rate counts everyone who has a job, no matter how meager the compensation. It also bases the rate on a labor force consisting of employed people plus those who are actively looking for work during the period in which the unemployment rate statistic is based. It thus excludes the so-called "discouraged workers" who have given up looking for work, including those whose unemployment compensation benefits have expired. The unemployment rate excludes part-time workers (working less than twenty hours a week) who want to be working full-time. Also, official unemployment rates vary by race. African American and Latino rates are in some instances double the official rate. Discouraged and involuntary part-time workers are also disproportionately African American and Latino. Furthermore, unemployment for entry-level workers—those without skills or experience—is much higher.

In the state of Illinois in the mid-1990s, it was estimated that there were roughly six people looking for every available entry-level job.[19] This figure has undoubtedly gone up as persons on welfare have been forced to move into the job market and the economy slides into recession. It's hard to estimate the number of people who are effectively out of work or work less than they want to. But in Chicago it is likely to be a significant number. One estimate made in 1997 when the Chicago area unemployment rate stood at 5.5 percent concluded that this rate goes up to 17 percent when you add in discouraged workers and involuntary part-time workers.[20]

Neither unemployment rates nor new jobs numbers address the relation of employment to income. The income distribution in Illinois mirrors the figures reported earlier for the nation. For the two decades beginning in 1980 the poorest families in the state of Illinois have lost ground while the richest have gained ground. The income of the richest 5 percent of Illinois families gained 42 percent during the past two decades, while the richest 20 percent gained 26 percent. But the poorest 20 percent lost one percent of their income. As a result, the top 20 percent of the population has 43 percent of the state's income, while the lowest 20 percent has only 5 percent of the income.[21]

Added to the problems of the lack of entry-level jobs and income polarization is the fact that there is a shortage of jobs that pay a living wage. Chicago-specific research has estimated living wages by calculating a minimal family budget for a single parent with two children—the situation of the average person on public assistance. In 1999, the living wage was estimated to be $35,307 a year, which is nearly $18 per hour.[22] This is far above the official "poverty level wage" of $11,522, or $5.75 per hour. While entry-level jobs at all wage levels are in short supply, the shortages become greater if we want people to earn enough to live on. Estimates suggest that in the late 1990s more than 200 workers were available for every job opening that pays a living wage. And even at the official poverty wage rate there are seven workers for each available job.[23] Surveys conducted of Illinois welfare recipients who were forced off of the welfare rolls as of January 1999 as part of welfare "reform" reveal that 64 percent were living on incomes below the federal poverty level and one-third were living in "extreme poverty," which is only half of the poverty level.[24] These statistics translate into serious hardships that can and have threatened life itself. It has been estimated, for example, that 13 percent of individuals living in households whose income is at or below 200 percent of the rate of federal poverty did not have enough food to eat and 17.5 percent missed meals.

Thirteen percent did not receive needed health care and 36 percent lacked health insurance. Twenty-five percent were unable to make housing or utility payments, while 4 percent have had utilities disconnected.[25]

The phenomenon of the "working poor" is in part due to the growth of labor market flexibility for low-wage workers. Many of the jobs being generated that are suitable for Chicago's poorest citizens are considered to be contingent. This means that they are either temporary or part-time. It is very difficult to come up with consistent measures of contingent work because the number of people employed in such jobs and the kinds of work they do vary from day to day. Also it is an industry that is polarized between high-end professional employment for managers, lawyers, and accountants and the low end, which includes factory, retail, service workers, and secretaries.[26] Nationally, 20 percent of all the new jobs created are temporary.[27] Between 1990 and 1997, temporary employment in the United States grew by 144 percent. That is five times the rate of growth of employment as a whole. In Chicago that growth was 105 percent. Approximately 3.6 million workers are employed in this industry in Chicago.[28] A study by the Federal Reserve Bank of Chicago revealed that half of the decline in manufacturing employment between 1991 and 1993 was offset by temporary workers.[29] This study also revealed that temporary workers are paid lower wages than permanent full-time workers doing similar work. Only 25 percent of temporary workers received health benefits when they worked at establishments with more than 100 workers, but 80 percent of the permanent workers at those establishments received health benefits. Also, temporary workers were twice as likely as permanent workers to be unemployed a year after they were hired.

Another type of contingent worker is the part-time employee. Nationally, part-time workers (who are not included in the temporary worker numbers) constitute 17 percent of the workforce, or over 23 million people.[30] In the fastest growing sectors of the economy—service and retail industries—part-time workers constitute 30 percent and 40 percent of the workforce, respectively. Wages and benefits tend to be lower for part-time workers. Women part-timers, for example, earn 23.7 percent less per hour than female full-timers and only 25 percent of them get health benefits. As a result, many workers today work at more than one job. Some of these are part-time or temporary, while others are full-time and permanent.[31]

In Illinois, trends showing that temporary and part-time work and multiple job holders are replacing those in permanent living wage jobs are quite striking. Since 1990, the number of employees working in temporary jobs increased by over 65 percent. In 1995, there were 125,000 workers in that industry. Twenty-eight percent of all jobs gained in Illinois between 1991 and 1994 (nearly 65,000) were temporary jobs through the personnel supply industry.[32] In 1994, over a million Illinois workers constituting 23 percent of all employed workers worked part-time. Twenty percent of these workers were African American, 13 percent were Latino, and 40 percent were women.[33]

In the Chicago metropolitan area there are 150,000 part-time and temporary workers who earn less than a living wage.[34] These Chicago area workers are disproportionately African American and Latino. Although these two groups constitute only 26 percent of all workers in the area, they make up 55 percent of low-income contingent workers.

Since 1985, the number of day labor agencies in Chicago that serve the low end of the temporary help industry have increased by 70 percent.[35] There are now over 300 such agencies clustered around Chicago's poorest neighborhoods. Peck and Theodore, who surveyed the managers of these agencies, described them as

> shabby offices with boarded up windows, beyond the reach of formal regulation. . . . Workers are subjected to a process of "hyper-commodification," in the sense that they are traded in a price-oriented basis almost as if they were an undifferentiated, industrially-produced commodity. . . . Unequivocally, the main task for the temp agencies in this most exploitative segment of the market is to "meet the order." Satisfying clients' needs, preferences and even prejudices, is paramount.[36]

Workers line up in these hiring halls at 5:00 A.M. or earlier. They are dispatched by 6:00. Those not hired may sit around, hoping for something to show up. There is often another rush for second shift work around noon. Some may work a few hours, others for weeks. They are at the mercy of the employer for more work through a given agency. Many agencies send a card with their workers asking if the employer wants this worker back. If the answer is no, whatever the explanation, that worker will not be able to get placed through the agency again and must seek out another. In this segment of the labor market, the worker is vulnerable and expendable.

An interesting survey at Chicago homeless shelters shows an important connection between temporary work and poverty.[37] A survey of 510 homeless women and men was conducted at Chicago homeless shelters on a single night in October 1999. Seventy-five percent of the people interviewed had worked as temporary workers during the year. Eighty-two percent made less than $5.50 an hour at their most recent job. Those who worked regularly earned less than $9,000 per year. Nearly all of those surveyed stated that they would prefer regularly scheduled jobs but this was the only type of job they could get.[38]

I talked to a man who had been homeless for several years. He had only recently been able to get himself a room and get off the streets and out of the shelters. He had served six years in the Marine Corps. "Essentially they taught me to blow things up. There is not much of a market for that in the U.S.—not a legal one anyway. So I pumped gas when I came home." He also worked as a laborer in a factory. But bouts with alcoholism, the loss of a loved one, and the closing of several gas stations in the early 1990s eventually put him out of work and he became homeless. He survived by what he called "canning." "That's when you go through the garbage in search of aluminum.

I made a good buck but when you do that people look at you funny and steer clear when you come into the grocery to buy food."

But the price of aluminum dropped from 75 cents a pound to 25 cents. Then a nun at a homeless shelter helped him with his alcoholism and put him in touch with a man who had good contacts with a temporary help agency. His first job was filling in for someone on vacation in a cheesecake factory. So the job lasted only two weeks. He got a good rating from the cheesecake factory, so the temp agency sent him to another factory job. The pay was $5.25 an hour. The temp agency told him that he could buy health insurance through the agency for $16 a week. But he would have to pay that for a year before the insurance would take effect. He laughed. "I told him to forget about that!"

The new job was 17 miles from the homeless shelter. He had no car and the commute required three buses and a thirty-minute walk, which took three hours each way. "That's six hours commuting and eight on the job for $42. Fourteen hours! But it was the best deal I could find." After several months on the job, the company offered to make him a permanent worker at a pay rate of $7.25 an hour. He took it. Also the man who had set him up at the temp agency, the friend of the nun at the homeless shelter, gave him an old car for one dollar. He was thinking he had turned the corner. He said he had been sober for four months. He had a job and a car and a place to live in a rooming house. He had been on the "permanent" job for less than a month when the company announced they were going to invest in more productive machinery. They laid him off. He told me he was going back to the temp agency for more work.

Trade Jobs and Wages

The man I talked to had dropped out of high school. He got his GED in the Marines, but learning to "blow things up" was not a wise human capital investment on the part of the military from his perspective! So, how will things change for this man and those who follow in his footsteps in this era that I have called the new world order? Let's say he was able to get more effective training. In this circumstance will "free trade" lift his boat so that he can lead a decent life? We have now had more than a decade of flexible labor markets and "free trade" policies. So we can get a good idea of the answer to this question by looking at the employment and wage picture in Chicago by industries and firms engaged in trade.

Between 1980 and 1999, employment in the nine leading export industries in the state of Illinois experienced a net loss of over 200,000 jobs.[39] The process of capital flight and industrial reorganization that the employment numbers reflect also had negative wage and benefit impacts for many workers. Average manufacturing wages in Illinois rose between 1979 and June 2000 from $7.02 per hour to $14.40. Adjusting for inflation during the period, however, the purchasing power of these wages actually fell by 15 percent. But this is only part of the story. Part of the wage trend associated with the new world order's restructuring is the effect of the relative shift in employment between manufacturing and service industries. In 1979, 27 percent of the Illinois workforce was employed in manufacturing and 17 percent were in service industries. As of June 2000, only 15.7 percent of the Illinois labor force was employed in manufacturing while 30.8 percent was in service industries. Wages in the service industries tend to be lower than those in manufacturing. The wage differential is largely due to the strength of industrial unionism that began in the 1930s. Nationally, in 1998, 44 percent of service workers earned less than $8.50 an hour, while only 4.7 percent of production workers earned this little. For production workers, 47 percent earned between $11.25 and $15.74, which is close to the living wage range. Only 17 percent of service workers earned this much.[40] As of January 1998, the average hourly wages in five Illinois manufacturing industries that were the top employers in 1979 ranged from $12 to $15.50. Service industries of comparable importance to state employment in 1998 paid from $6.50 to $12.50.[41]

Another aspect of trade is imports, which tend to be ignored by advocates of "free trade" policies. This is a significant oversight. Throughout the 1990s, the United States ran an increasingly widening trade deficit; the value of its imports from other countries has exceeded the value of its exports. When this deficit is added to the fact that during the same time frame more income from investments flowed out of the United States than has flowed in, there is also a widening current account deficit—the money and value of goods and services that flow out of the United States is greater than what is coming in. The shortfall is larger than it has ever been in history both in dollar terms and as a percentage of the U.S. economy.

A detailed look at the impact of the trade deficit on industries and firms in the state of Illinois was very revealing not only about the effect of imports but also about the very nature of trade itself. A detailed study was made of employment trends in industries that were key employers in the state of Illinois and faced stiff import competition in the mid-1990s.[42] Findings based on industry data were supplemented by case studies of key firms within industries. Thirty-four industry groups were analyzed. The results were mixed. While nineteen industries lost jobs, fifteen actually gained jobs and there was a net gain across the thirty-four industrial groups analyzed.

A closer examination of these results, however, demonstrated that the employment changes in many industries had more to do with capital mobility than trade, and that job gains in one section of the state were often offset by losses in other Illinois locations. The dynamics of job gains and losses, moreover, suggest that there is no evidence of any consistent link between trade and employment. All of this points to the fallacy of trying to link trade with employment or to use trade as a jobs program as current U.S. policy does. Two brief cases illustrate the point.

Zenith Corporation announced on December 18, 1996, that it was laying off 1,200 workers, one-quarter of its U.S. workforce. Two-thirds of the jobs eliminated were in the Chicago area. Zenith, at the time, exported roughly 10 percent of its U.S. production. Yet, throughout the 1980s, Zenith began moving production out of the United States, mostly to Mexico, where twelve of its twenty-eight plants, offices, and retail outlets are located. About 12,000 of Zenith's 18,100 employees were in Mexico. In an earlier period, many of these workers were in the United States making goods for export. During the production shift to Mexico, Zenith eliminated 700 jobs in the Chicago area alone. In 1998, Zenith declared bankruptcy under Chapter 11 and in the reorganization ceased to manufacture anything in the United States. It also sold some of its Mexican plants. By 1999, Zenith was a subsidiary of L.G. Electronics of Korea. It is currently a marketing shell that buys television sets from L.G. Electronics and other firms such as Phillips and markets them under the Zenith label. Presently there are only twenty-one production workers in Illinois who work for Zenith. The Zenith story is not simply one of a firm losing to import competition. Rather, Zenith was a highly mobile firm that found itself overextended in a saturated market (color televisions) that was dominated by foreign firms. As it continued to lose money, Zenith eventually chose to close or sell production facilities and become a marketing shell. That decision resulted in the loss of jobs.

A second case involves the printed circuit board industry. Circuit boards are used by other industries—particularly computers and communication equipment—to make their product. U.S. firms face serious competition both from imported products and in their export markets. Until recently, computers, which are mainly produced in Asia, were the main user of this product. Now, however, various kinds of communication equipment, such as personal digital assistants (PDAs) and Internet access devices such as modems, use circuit boards. In recent years, supply to the automotive and consumer product markets has also been on the rise. U.S. firms export more than a quarter of their production, and over 60 percent of these exports go to Canada and Mexico. But the industry depends both on exports and domestic markets for survival. Foreign firms that make printed circuit boards have embraced offshore manufacturing to lower costs of production. U.S. printed circuit board companies, on the other hand, have not followed suit.[43] U.S. companies have instead, relied on developing process improvements that yield high volumes at lower costs.

Foreign producers in the United States are numerous. This is attributed to the narrow profit margins in this industry that makes it imperative for these firms to be the first to market leading-edge products that focus on high-end technology.[44] Domestic companies provide technologically advanced manufacturing and related services. As a result, there are increasing trends toward global alliances that allow firms in this industry to expand into new businesses and broaden their market penetration.

These global and domestic alliances have resulted in overall employment gains in this sector. In Illinois, the industry gained 2,467 jobs between 1991 and 1997. The job gain in Illinois is attributable to 3Com, which bought U.S. Robotics (a modem design and manufacturing firm) and set up its Midwest headquarters in Rolling Meadows, Illinois, during that period. Illinois now employs nearly 10,000 workers in 121 separate production facilities. Examining recent developments with 3-Com and U.S. Robotics reveals both the international character of the circuit board industry and the unstable nature of employment in this industry in Illinois. U.S. Robotics was a significant player in the international modem industry and employed 4,000 workers. On June 11, 1997, U.S. Robotics was sold to a large U.S.-based network services and manufacturing firm, 3Com, which closed U.S. Robotics' Skokie, Illinois plant but continued to maintain three other plants in Illinois. In this process, 800 jobs at U.S. Robotics were eliminated. 3Com, in response to a $9 million plus incentive package from the state of Illinois, agreed to expand the modem business at a new site in Rolling Meadows, Illinois. It is widely claimed that the deal merely preserved the employment base and growth potential that U.S. Robotics gave Illinois.[45] As a quid pro quo, 3Com agreed to keep a total of 3,500 employees in the state through 2004.

However, before the expiration of the deal, on June 7, 2000, 3Com, Accton Technology Corporation (a Taiwan-based network design and manufacturing firm), and NatSteel Electronics (a Singapore-based contract manufacturer) entered into an alliance to recreate U.S. Robotics into a fully autonomous company. As part of the deal, 3Com sold off its Mount Prospect manufacturing plant to NatSteel and transferred all of its 1,200 employees associated with the plant to NatSteel. In return, NatSteel received a three-year supply agreement to manufacture broadband modems and other communications equipment for 3Com. In addition, 200 of 3Com's employees were transferred to the new U.S. Robotics, pulling up its employment base to 250. 3Com assured the state that it would continue to maintain a presence in Illinois.

This study of 3Com and U.S. Robotics reiterates the point made earlier that trade does not occur in a vacuum and the trade-employment link is not as intuitive as "free trade" theories suggest. Although the printed circuit board industry faces tremendous import competition, there has been an increase in jobs in Illinois due to mergers and acquisitions. However, these job gains have not occurred without a price. In the acquisition of U.S. Robotics, 800 jobs were lost. Furthermore, there was a price paid by the state government to retain jobs in place that U.S. Robotics had already created for the region. And the future stability of those jobs is in doubt.

The employment trends and activities of industries and firms that face import competition combined with how export industries have fared in terms of employment and wages demonstrate that facile claims that exports create job growth and imports destroy jobs have little basis in reality. The mobility of capital in the new world order and the concentrated ownership of the firms that move their capital around the world give global corporations considerable market power. Such conditions place organized labor and workers' rights under increasing pressure.

Worker Rights and the Decatur, Illinois "War Zone"

Gains in employment, wages, and working conditions have historically been the fruits of labor organization, and not the market or trade. When President Ronald Reagan fired 11,000 air traffic controllers in 1982, and permanently replaced them, he began a general attack on organized labor in the United States. That act gave a political signal to employers that it was now okay to replace striking workers. While there were never laws that prevented employers from permanently replacing striking workers, the political climate would not permit it. The implicit assumption that workers would still have a job after a strike was part of the postwar deal with organized labor that exchanged a share of growing profits for a more cooperative approach to labor relations. President Reagan ended the deal with the replacement of the air traffic controllers and employers began to follow suit, which weakened labor further. Moreover, that act coincided with the nationwide destruction of manufacturing jobs discussed in Chapter 4.

In its weakened condition, organized labor was in no position to contest the deterioration of policies governing labor relations, let alone the employment policy changes described earlier. Also, the 1990s began a period in which corporations routinely launched major attacks against all efforts to organize unions. These attacks used both legal and illegal tactics, including captive audience meetings, discharges for union activity, threats, and surveillance.[46] And they had a significant negative impact on the success rate of union-organizing drives. The average annual number of new union members gained through organizing drives dropped from about 300,000 in the mid-1970s to less than 100,000 by the mid-1990s.[47] Even after successful organizing drives, firms used the same aggressive tactics to resist collective bargaining and other efforts by unions to improve conditions at the workplace. Nationally the combination of all of these forces caused a significant decline in the membership and hence political influence of organized labor. Between 1982 and 1996, union members as a percentage of all wage and salaried workers in the United States declined from more than 20 percent to 14 percent. The drop for private-sector workers went from nearly 19 percent to 10 percent. By 2000, only 9.5 percent of private-sector workers belonged to unions even though unions added 265,000 new members in 1999, the best organizing effort in more than a decade.

In Chapter 3 I argued that this attack was an integral part of the new world order since a destruction of claims on the value produced by global capitalism was needed to survive the collapse of the Fordist period. This is why there is such resistance to including workers rights clauses that guarantee the right to organize and bargain collectively in so-called "free trade" agreements like WTO and NAFTA. The attack on and subsequent decline of organized labor has been reinforced by the mobility of goods, services, and capital across borders. Much of this has been explained in terms of competitiveness both domestically and abroad with firms based in other nations. Thus worker rights and trade are integrally related. In an era of high mobility, the threat to move production, the claim that unionization or better wages and working conditions will make firms uncompetitive and force them to close, and the actual movement of capital in the wake of a successful organizing drive have become key tactics in resisting union organizing and defeating union collective bargaining strategies.[48] All of these developments have reduced the influence of labor over wages and working conditions while encouraging more aggressive anti-labor behavior on the part of the major global corporations.

These developments have very place-specific consequences. One such place is Decatur, Illinois, where intense labor struggles during the mid-1990s caused local workers to call their community the "Decatur war zone." In the 1990s, three global giants—Caterpillar (U.S.); Tate & Lyle (Great Britain); and Bridgestone/Firestone (Japan)—all prevailed in bitter labor disputes. While the strikes were nationwide, a focal point was Decatur, Illinois, where all three corporations had key operations. At the height of the strike activity 3,800 workers representing nearly one-third of the manufacturing workforce of Decatur were on strike or lockout.

Caterpillar was a major and active proponent of "free trade" policies. They served as team captain for the state of Illinois's contribution to the national lobbying organization USA*NAFTA. Caterpillar claimed that NAFTA would spur export growth and thereby create jobs. But even prior to NAFTA, Caterpillar had been expanding its exports to Mexico and around the world while cutting its domestic workforce in half. In 1990, Caterpillar proposed a U.S. contract that would impose a lower pay scale for new employees, health care cuts, the loss of job guarantees, and wage freezes for nearly one-third of the workers. In 1991, U.S. workers went on strike, but were forced back to work in 1992 after Caterpillar threatened to permanently replace the strikers. Thereafter, workers attempted to continue their struggle through "in plant strategies" that began to cut into productivity. The company responded by suspending workers and a second strike ensued in 1994.

During the course of the dispute, the National Labor Relations Board charged Caterpillar with twenty-six unfair labor practices, alleging that Caterpillar broke the law by "failing to bargain in good faith and by harassing, intimidating, and coercing its employees in a variety of attempts to prevent them from exercising their rights." The strike continued until workers were forced to return to work in December 1995 without a contract (having voted down an offer made by the company in November that was nearly identical to that proposed in 1991). After union workers returned to the job, the company imposed new rules, banning the use of terms such as "scab" or the display of union slogans on personal clothing or lunch boxes. During the first month after the imposed return to work, eighty-eight union workers were fired or suspended for violating these rules. One worker was fired for refusing to shake the hand of another worker who had crossed the picket line during the strike.

Commenting after their victory over labor and their record profits, CEO Donald Fites (who received a 25.4 percent pay increase over a two-year period, bringing his compensation to $1.8 million) stated: "U.S. workers should tread water while workers from other nations catch up (in wage levels)." Caterpillar's chief financial officer, Douglas Oberhelman added, "Today, I have a better idea of what it must feel like to win the Super Bowl, the World Series and an NBA championship ring all in the same year."[49]

A few years before the first Caterpillar strike, Tate & Lyle, a British sugar processor with a history of corporate takeovers designed to dominate market niches, took over Decatur's A. E. Staley Company. The motivation for the Staley takeover (Staley tried unsuccessfully to resist the raid) was to eliminate a competitor and dominate a lucrative niche in soft-drink sweeteners. Staley and Archer Daniels Midland (ADM), which has a plant down the road from Staley in Decatur, controlled most of this market.[50] ADM at the time of the Staley takeover owned 7 percent of Tate & Lyle. After the takeover, a pipeline capable of transporting raw material was constructed between the two plants. Shortly after the takeover, the company began to impose work rule changes, including dress and appearance codes, attendance standards, work relief time, and a new performance appraisal system. Harsh discipline was meted out for violations, including sixteen discharges. Unsafe working conditions increased dramatically after the takeover. OSHA cited Tate & Lyle's Staley operation with 298 safety violations in 1990, one of which resulted in the death of a worker. In this atmosphere, the company proposed a contract (the old contract expired in September 1992) that included mandatory twelve-hour shifts, reduced paid health care benefits, and restricted arbitration and grievance procedures. Workers chose not to strike, but voted the contract down and launched a corporate campaign against the company. The company responded with a lockout in June 1993 and promptly dropped health care coverage.

Workers then launched militant pickets (for which they were arrested), campaigns to force companies using Staley sweeteners to cancel their orders, and even a sixty-four-day hunger strike by one of the Staley workers' leaders. In the midst of all this, an FBI mole working at ADM charged that the company had been involved in illegal price fixing. Pepsi Cola, among others, promptly sued both ADM and Staley for its losses due to fixed prices. The lockout continued until December 1995, when the lack of continued support from the union forced the Staley workers back to work on the same terms they had rejected in 1992.

Workers began a national strike against Bridgestone/Firestone, another global giant with a plant in Decatur, in the fall of 1994. The issues were remarkably similar to those in both the Caterpillar and Staley conflicts. In the summer of 1995, the strike ended after the company had hired replacement workers and announced that they would become the permanent workforce if union members failed to return to work. Workers continued negotiations with the company and launched a corporate campaign against Sears, which sold Bridgestone/Firestone products. Ultimately the strike failed and workers were forced to accept new work rules, including the imposition of two twelve-hour shifts. Five years later it was revealed that tires made during the strike period were defective. They had a serious failure rate that included several fatal accidents so all of these tires had to be recalled. Workers charged that the tire flaws were related to speeded-up production and the use of replacement workers at the time of the strike.[51]

The Decatur war zone demonstrates the relationship between corporate labor relations policies and the new world order regime, where global corporations are able to use their market power to impose new pay schemes, work rules, and flexible hiring and firing arrangements that undermine job quality. The market power and global mobility of these giants give them great holding capacity during an extended labor conflict. The now common practice of hiring or threatening to hire permanent replacement workers also undermines the ability of the workforce to contest these changes. The basis of the conflict in all three of the Decatur cases was quite similar. Both Caterpillar and Bridgestone/Firestone wished to impose two-tiered wage arrangements in which newer workers earned less money. This arrangement provides a foot in the door toward driving down wages generally. But it also breaks worker unity by creating two classes of workers. Ultimately, such programs are designed to weaken or destroy unions themselves. Second, all three conflicts involved work rule changes. In the case of Staley and Bridgestone, the companies wanted twelve-hour rotating shifts. That meant that weekly work and rest days rotate, with no overtime pay for the extra four hours of work each day or on Sundays, which would cause a substantial loss of income. At Staley there was also a provision for forced overtime after the twelve-hour shift ended. At Caterpillar the company insisted on the right to impose flexible schedules. In all cases, workers lost control over when they would work and overtime pay. Control over safety and family life that go with such scheduling was taken from the union and the workers themselves. Finally, job security was an issue in all three strikes. This speaks to the flexibility discussed earlier. The issue was particularly blatant at Staley, where the company insisted on unlimited subcontracting rights. At any time, the company can now permanently lay off any worker and subcontract the job if they find that to be "cost-effective." Workers' weakened ability to contest the terms of their employment helps explain the data on employment and wage losses and also the rise of flexibility in the form of the increased use of temporary and part-time workers.

Revisiting the Shift: Employment and Philosophy

The new world order is defined in part by a definite shift in ideology, theory, politics, and public policies that pertain to the question of employment. The United States has abandoned full employment as a social goal. That goal was the product of a social struggle that began with economic collapse in 1929 and was partly resolved by the postwar deal defined globally in the Bretton Woods Agreement and domestically in the Employment Act of 1946. The Full Employment and Balanced Growth Act of 1978 reaffirmed the 1946 act. But the full employment goal was formally abandoned in 1980, when the chairman of the Federal Reserve Bank, Paul Volker, led the Fed's board of governors in a "palace coup" in which interest rate increases and restrictions in the money supply overturned an act of Congress. From this point on, U.S. macro economic policy placed top priority on fighting inflation, even when that meant higher rates of unemployment. The shift found its further expression in the notion that employment was a matter of each individual being competitive by adapting to a regime of "flexible labor markets." A variety of public policies reinforced these notions, including a hard stance on labor unions; the decline in the purchasing power of minimum wage; the linking of unemployment compensation and welfare to work—even if that meant working for less than a living wage; the elimination of the social safety net, including public housing and public welfare; building the reform of job training and public welfare on a model of "work-first" that pushed workers into low-wage, contingent work; and the reliance on "free trade" as the sole public policy used to stimulate the demand for labor.

This shift was fully supported by the ascendancy of economic and social science theories that were in development when the Fordist era was at its height. They represented at the time a politics and corresponding ideology that was in opposition to that represented by the postwar consensus with labor in the United States. Their ongoing development throughout the previous era illustrates the role of ideas in the dialectic of everyday life. Their eventual political acceptance at the birth of the new world order and their manifestation in public policies demonstrates how ideas become material forces in society. It was not the theoretical correctness of these ideas that made them such. Rather, it was their ability to rationalize a major shift in the organization of global capitalism. And as that shift began to materialize, foundations, private think tanks, corporate-controlled media, and Nobel prizes showered the purveyors of these theories with cash and legitimacy. Thus, the theories of a natural rate of unemployment; monetarism; rational choice and rational expectations; human capital; both conservative and liberal theories of poverty; and "free trade" supported and eventually helped to drive the shift in the politics of employment.

In Chapter 2 I discussed the relationship of theory to philosophy. Philosophy determines which questions become the objects of theoretical inquiry.

It also determines appropriate methodologies and measures. Theory building in economics and other social sciences constructs logical models based on certain assumptions about today's reality. The purpose of theory is to explain what is happening and to predict what is likely to happen in the future. Empirical research attempts to find measures of the different components of the theoretical model and determine how well the model can explain and predict. If a theory is based on past individual and social behavior it can have the effect of reinforcing that behavior. Public policies may be enacted that strengthen the theory's predictive power. In this way the theory becomes a material force that is an integral part of the social order.

Think about the theoretical shift relative to employment in this way. The social commitment to public policies that emphasized growth and employment was the result of a social struggle that arose out of the Great Depression. This situation was supportive of a particular brand of social theory that included specific implications of an observed relationship between unemployment and inflation that was named the Phillips Curve. It helped policymakers choose specific government spending and taxing policies designed to reduce unemployment. When contradictions within the Fordist order caused this relationship to come apart—there was high unemployment and high inflation—there was momentarily a theoretical void. This presented an opportunity for a new theoretical paradigm to achieve recognition in the political arena. Milton Friedman's speech to the American Economics Association that used rational expectations theory and the notion of a natural rate of unemployment to explain current conditions had renewed resonance in the economics profession. But it also received widespread political and popular attention because it connected politically with the interests of an emerging political realignment that would be at the heart of the new world order. And this growing recognition of these theories in professional and political circles increased the interest of foundations, academic journals, and the corporate media that funded and popularized them. The NAIRU and related theories argued that we were experiencing high unemployment and high inflation because individuals were seeking higher wages when unemployment was in their perception "too low." Acting on the basis of these "rational expectations," it was argued, would offset any possible gains from more employment and higher wages.

Monetarism offered a clear public policy alternative to government spending and taxing policies aimed at reducing unemployment. Its emphasis on fighting inflation supported the growing political muscle of the finance sector. Human capital theory helped rationalize the political move away from a public commitment to employment by undermining its social dimension. In its place is the notion that one's employment status is the result of an *individual* investment decision. This theory turned work into a form of behavior and justified the development of today's job training programs and welfare "reform." It also paved the way for the political acceptance of labor market flexibility and an attack on organized labor. Similarly, old theories of trade were twisted to justify the new "free trade" agreements that opened the world to capital mobility while contending domestically that these agreements would lead to better jobs with better wages.

The issue here should not be confined to whether the theories are really all that logical and whether there is adequate empirical support for them. In this chapter I have raised such questions and shown that in the United States the result of nearly two decades of some of these policies has been greater income and wealth polarization and an ongoing attack on the efforts of workers to contest this result. Others have also raised serious questions about the empirical validity of the Phillips Curve and the NAIRU, which is the theoretical heart of today's thinking about employment.[52] The evidence supporting conservative and liberal notions that connect poverty with individual competitiveness is likewise thin to nonexistent.[53] And there have been many attacks, some of them cited earlier, on the notion that "free trade" supports good jobs.

Yet none of this goes deep enough. If we leave our critique at the logic of the theory and the empirical support for it, we still assume that a better theory can better explain reality. And reality for many people is simply not acceptable. What if we are unwilling to say that the reality of the public housing residents described in Chapter 6 is as good as it gets? What if we are unwilling to accept a reality that some people must work for wages that are below what it takes to live a decent life? What if we are unwilling to accept a social system in which some people spend eighteen hours including commuting to and from the job for eight hours' pay without medical benefits and still end up in homeless shelters at the end of each day? What do we do if we want to change reality? For that we need to revisit the philosophical discussion initiated in Chapter 2.

In that chapter I argued that there are at least two contending philosophies around the purpose of an economy. One view is that an economy is a means to allocate scarce resources efficiently. The other is that an economy is a means toward human self-development. This division has been reflected historically in social conflict when the "efficient" functioning of the economy truncates human development. At various historical junctures, such as the one we are presently living in, the efficiency side of this conflict is so dominant that it appears to have eliminated the human development side. Yet, because this divide represents a contradiction, social movements will begin to emerge that will call today's theories into question and realign the politics that offer them political support.

Value, Values, and Jobs

As discussed in Chapter 2, mainstream economics assumes a society without social classes in which economic man pursues self-interest in a world of markets. Theories that are based on this philosophic proposition are not completely invalid; they do describe part of reality. The problem is that they are one-sided and ignore the contradiction and hence conflict that is embedded in them. This one-sidedness appears in part as an equation of money price with value. The concept of a natural rate of unemployment is based on the notion that each *individual* will assume that rates lower than the NAIRU will mean inflation and will act accordingly. And thus there is nothing to be done but to stop trying to push unemployment below that rate. Human capital theory reduces employment and wages to simply the return on individual investments in training and education. The individual calculations, in these theories, are based entirely on money considerations. And the people who are still unemployed after the magic equilibrium rate of the NAIRU theory is reached are simply out of luck. The only thing they can do is to compete hard so they can stay out of that position.

Acquiring human capital follows as the means to compete and poverty theorists like William Julius Wilson, *assume* the validity of human capital and rational expectations theories in their own explanation of human poverty. But the issue becomes philosophically whether the world is so one-sided. If the point of organizing an economy is to make life better for everyone, then a broader range of values enters the picture. It isn't that people don't make the kinds of calculations that rational expectations assume—some undoubtedly do. It isn't untrue that some people with better education, training, and experience ("human capital") get better jobs with higher wages—some do.[54] But if those calculations and competition based on human capital leave out groups of people based on their class, race, or gender, which they do, then there is a social dimension to economic development that economic man does not address. And if an economy is about human development rather than "efficiency" based on money price, that social dimension must be addressed as well.

If human development and dialectics are the philosophic ground for economic development, one can argue that an economy must be organized so that everyone has adequate housing, health care, employment, and income. And labor must be integral to the process of human development. If this is not the case, there is a need for change that runs deeper than a critique of the logic and empirical support for today's dominant theories.

The evidence presented in this and previous chapters suggests that the one-sidedness of these theories represents a class bias that is amplified by social structures, rules, and institutions that define a particular mode of accumulation such as the new world order that we presently live in. That bias was evident every time the Fed tried to slow the economy at the hint of inflation, dampening the demand for labor. It continues to be evident in the notion of flexible labor markets that means keeping wages and the costs of dismissing workers low and their work time flexible by forcing them to accept part-time or temporary work with low benefits. The bias is in "free trade" agreements that offer full mobility of capital, goods, and services to corporations even when it means lower living standards, worse working conditions, deteriorating environmental conditions, and the undermining of human and labor rights globally. Ultimately, this bias shows up as a polarization of wealth and income that was described earlier.

Time, Space, Place, and Jobs

The ideological, theoretical, and political shift pertaining to employment that has been the subject of this chapter also has a spatial dimension that has altered part of our perception of time and place. The social organization of time is an integral part of the process of human development in any era. Chapter 2 argued that a specific mode of accumulation—a system of rules, institutions, public policies, theories, and ideologies designed to accumulate social surplus—defines the era in which we live. Further, each mode of accumulation has a profound influence on the prevailing concept of time. Time has thus been a dimension of each era in the history of capitalism. In each era the social construction of time may take different forms in different societies depending on both the role that society plays in the global mode of accumulation and on the strength of cultural/social conceptions of time that prevailed in previous eras. This implies that the social construction of time contains multiple contradictions that shape the nature of social struggles over the terms of any particular mode of accumulation. Historically, people's movements over the length of the working day and the speed of the assembly line have been manifestations of the contradiction between the prevailing conception of time and the social quest for human development.

In the new world order, the speed of the movement of capital and information is a critical aspect of both the mobility of capital and the expansion of credit and speculation that fuels it. Thus the notion that "time is money" takes on heightened significance these days. In this context, the individualization of employment, which has been an emphasis in this chapter, plays an important role in the dialectic of human development. The need for each individual to be efficient, productive, and hence competitive is a matter of life or death. For those at the upper end of this polarized society, this need is satisfied by each individual being tethered to the job by a variety of electronic gizmos—cell phones, beepers, laptop computers, and the constant need for "multitasking." While this is undoubtedly alienating as a truncation of broader human development, the upper-enders are well compensated. And they can try to soften the contradiction by purchasing luxuries, expensive furniture, cars, homes, and fine dining. At the lower end, however, the alienation is intensified. The "fortunate" among the lower-enders work two jobs for the price of one. For the rest, things only get worse. Temp workers structure their days around the demands of the hiring hall. It's not only spending eighteen hours to work eight paid hours, but the activity of each day is now determined by the temp agency manager. No other considerations will be tolerated. And if you are homeless on top of that, the shelter or the search for a safe spot in the streets structures the remaining six hours of your day.

Human capital and related theories of poverty that justify programs that treat work as a form of behavior fail to consider this time-denominated feature of their one-sided theories. In a previous era when workers struggled for a limited working day, they posed the question, "When is my time my own?" In the Fordist era, when automation offered the technical capacity to increase productivity by increasing the speed of the assembly line, the pace of production began to take control of the time-human development relation. Social movements on the shop floor directly challenged this control, as workers refused to be reduced to so many appendages of their machines. Would they run the machines, or would the machines run them?[55] Today, those questions appear to be moot. The new world order is saying to one and all: "time is money." A class struggle to contest that has yet to be launched.

A change in an era also changes the relation of space and place to human development. This was also discussed in general terms in Chapter 2. Global capital mobility through deregulation makes labor market flexibility possible. This mobility also structures labor markets on a global scale so that being competitive involves workers competing for jobs around the world. The availability of cheap and productive autoworkers in Mexico, for example, means that large automobile corporations will locate there. This also means that U.S. autoworkers compete with Mexican autoworkers not in terms of their respective human capital but through the whipsaw process of bidding down wages and environmental and labor standards. U.S. workers' demands for better pay and working conditions are driven not by the standard of living they aspire to or even their contribution to the company's profits but to how much they can get without driving more production out of the country. The complexity of the changing spatial dimension of worker competition is illustrated by our case studies of industries and firms in the United States that face import competition.[56] The same firms that are major exporters are also importing and exporting to themselves while moving capital and production around the world. These machinations seek to find the most advantageous location for the expropriation of surplus values.

Ford and Bridgestone/Firestone, "American" and "Japanese" companies, produce cars and tires all over the world. Bridgestone controls the rubber plantations in Asia where their raw material is made. They export some of this to their plants in Illinois and then export the tires to Mexico and other locations in the United States to Ford. Ford produces cars with these "Japanese-American" tires in Mexico. The "Mexican-American-Japanese" cars are then exported to the United States and other locations. Trade and capital mobility define this spatial dimension of production. This space, in turn defines the geographical boundaries of the labor markets within which U.S. autoworkers and tireworkers must be competitive. It also determines the content of the comparative advantage each nation has to produce particular goods and services.

Public policies that include the structural adjustment programs of the IMF and the World Bank and "free trade" agreements like NAFTA and WTO create the conditions under which the spatial dimensions of production are defined. U.S. monetary policy, labor policy, job training policy, and the new welfare legislation constitute constraints/limits on how workers in the United States can operate in these markets. In this way both commodity markets and labor markets are socially constructed according to the dictates of the mode of accumulation that I have called the new world order. Being competitive in this order is thus not simply the return on some human capital investment, but is the outcome of the global politics through which labor markets are constructed. What drives these politics is the need of the global capitalist system to accumulate surplus value. There is thus nothing "natural" about the construction of markets as all of the dominant and acceptable theories assume. The role of competition in their formation is the competition among blocs of capital for surplus value produced by workers around the world.

Economic and poverty theories of rational choice, rational expectations, human capital, and flexible labor markets deny the relevance of the social-political construction of markets. They also ignore the significance of the spatial dimension of these markets. Yet the particular form of the spatial-social-political construction of labor markets in the new world order defines the conditions of employment and wages in any particular place. This construction, and not individual human capital investments or rational expectations, establishes the parameters for employment opportunities and the wages and working conditions of the available jobs. The impact of education and training works within these parameters and defines the limits of how much training adds to the employment opportunities and living standards of different groups of workers.

Since these limits are socially constructed and defined, only social organization can provide the counterforce necessary to challenge them. Yet, the shifts in the nature and structure of commodity and labor markets—especially their spatial and place-related dimensions—means there must also be a shift in the way such a challenge can be made. In part, this is due to the fact that labor markets now have a global dimension, which requires a form of multinational solidarity that does not yet exist. Also, the shift in the nature of production has been accompanied by the ideological, theoretical, and political shift that has been discussed in this and the previous chapters that places limits on what sorts of aspirations are "practical" and therefore acceptable.

Furthermore, there has also been a shift in the nature of place in its most local sense that includes a city like Chicago and the places in which the people of Chicago now work. In the Fordist era, the large mass production factory was the place of work of many of Chicago's people. In this place, the social character of production was evident. It was clear to production workers that cooperative labor and not individuals created the surplus value that provided the pool for both profits and better wages and working conditions. Cooperative labor still provides that pool, but that fact is obscured in part by production's global spatial dimension. It is further obscured by the fact that the workplaces of Chicago workers are shifting to places where the social dimension of production as a whole is hard to see. The conditions of many service-sector jobs, while vital to the broader production system, obscure the social character and cooperative nature of the work. It is not as easy for aides in a hospital, store clerks, janitors, and cashiers in a grocery store—all of whom are easily replaced without disrupting production—to see that the fruits of their labor are the product of the cooperation of many different workers. It is thus difficult to see the class dimension of their labor. This social dimension of labor is completely obscured for the homeless temp worker, who must go to the agency day after day to earn enough to survive. For these workers, the economists' notion of economic man competing as an individual with every other individual appears as *the* reality. But the fact remains that the system that places these individuals in this position continues to depend on cooperative labor. And that fact has historically and continues to be the basis of successful social movements that have challenged the terms of each era in the history of the capitalist system.

Because of the shifts in the changing time-space-place context of production and the ideological, theoretical, and political shifts that have generated the new world order and become a part of it, the nature of organizing itself must shift. Organizing in the United States can no longer build on gains made during the Fordist era. They are no longer part of the system. The old deal is off. But neither can the forms of organizing and the organizing agenda accept the ideological and theoretical ground of the new world order as a "practical" basis for contesting its terms. If the purpose of an economy is human development rather than efficiency, the new ideological and theoretical consensus places unacceptable limits on what can be achieved. The local collisions in Chicago that have been the subject of this section of the book and the resulting critique of the theory and practice of the new world order still leave the question of how best to combat the new world order if we seek to change reality rather than accommodate to it. That will be the subject of the concluding chapters of this book.

CHAPTER 8

Organizing to Combat the New World Order

At the end of the previous chapter, I argued that ideological, theoretical, and political shifts as well as changes in the nature of the time-space-place context of production that encompass the new world order necessitate a change in the nature of organizing. Generally, previous chapters have demonstrated that the new world order has imposed inequalities throughout the world. The question becomes, How can millions of people negatively affected by these inequalities successfully contest them?

Thus far I have argued that the new world order is a global system for the accumulation of capital that includes mobile capital, goods, and services; flexible production; and flexible labor markets fueled by debt and speculation. This system has been institutionalized at an international level through the redirection of global institutions such as the IMF, WTO, and GATT (now WTO) and the creation of new ones such as NAFTA. This system has also been institutionalized nationally through public policies that include economic policy and specifically urban policies that impact housing, employment, and economic development. And these public policies, as the previous chapter demonstrated, have been bolstered by changes in theory grounded in ideology and philosophy. These elements constitute a global system. And it is a system that has led to growing inequalities among and within nations throughout the world. The contradictions embedded in inequality also appear nationally in the United States as economic and urban policies create serious local collisions with the poor and the working class whose standard of living is under attack. This book has been focused on such local collisions and how citizens are fighting back—especially in Chicago.

The relationship between the new world order and its local collisions establishes a new context for organizing. But this new context presents a problem.

The local collisions relating to economic development, housing, and employment discussed in this book did not begin with the new world order. As the case of Chicago demonstrates, these problems were very much a part of urban life under the Fordist era. However, the motor that generates such problems, and hence effective means to contest them, are very different today. In the case of housing, the issue during the Fordist era was the equitable sharing of resources. The federal government financed public programs that led to the development of suburban white communities, gentrified neighborhoods in the central city, and massive public housing. Again, organizers took on the inequities that resulted from these programs. And their target was often big city mayors and the federal government. In the new world order, however, gentrification and the elimination of housing for the poor are driven by the fact that housing is now integrated into the new global system. Publicly owned housing is falling to the wrecking ball and the privatization of government housing programs. Housing finance is now privately generated through globalized capital markets. And these shifts are accompanied by the reduction of housing to a pure commodity, undermining the notion that housing is first and foremost a place of shelter and hence a social good or human right.

During the Fordist era, the problems of employment and low wages in cities like Chicago were occurring in a context of an economic policy that stressed growth in the demand for workers. Full employment was a national social goal. At the time the United States was a dominant economic power in the world. And capital was firmly entrenched on U.S. soil. Inequality in this context involved the extent to which U.S. prosperity came at the expense of other nations and also the extent to which all racial groups and classes shared in that prosperity. Most demands of activists were directed at governments and corporations for a fair share. Also, toward the end of the Fordist period those demands became increasingly inclusive of other peoples of the world. As we have seen, however, today's urban policy context has changed drastically. Mobile capital is at the center of the new world order, which has destroyed living wage jobs and trade unions. There has been a full retreat from the goal of full employment. Work itself has been individualized as the fruit of human capital investments rather than national and local economic policies.

The impetus for these changes comes from a variety of sources. International institutions, national and local governments, and transnational corporations are all important players. The international finance sector is particularly important. And, as we spelled out in the previous chapter, new ideas consistent with the needs of the new world order have become a material force in the dialectic of everyday life. Urban policy and hence urban life, in short, is developing in the context of a global system that I have termed a new world order. Hence, these changes require new approaches to organizing to contest the inequities of the new system.

In the United States two lines of resistance to the various manifestations of the new world order have developed. On the one hand, there is a developing "anti-globalization movement" that is focused on global institutions—the IMF, World Bank, WTO, NAFTA—and those who hold the debt in the developing world. The protests against unsustainable debt in many developing nations have grown into an international movement. The movement, called Jubilee 2000, was initially led by religious organizations but has broadened significantly and is currently led by an association of indebted nations called Jubilee South. Their demand is for cancellation of external debt. Protests over the intolerable working conditions in the sweatshops of the developing world have given rise to international boycotts of firms that refuse to adhere to core labor rights standards. These protests and boycotts have been taken up by students at universities in a number of nations, including Canada and the United States. In addition, there have been national campaigns against changing U.S. congressional rules that would inhibit the ability of Congress to deliberate on U.S. participation in the WTO and the expansion of NAFTA ("fast track rules"). During the past decade, opposition to the policies of NAFTA, WTO, IMF, and the World Bank have become popular political issues in the United States as well as Canada, Mexico, and many other nations throughout the world.[1] Opposition to these institutions has resulted in massive militant street demonstrations that first appeared in the developed world in Seattle, Washington, in December 1999 as a protest over a proposed expansion of WTO authority. They have continued wherever trade ministers gather, forcing them to meet in isolated locations or with a display of repressive state police power. These demonstrations have included advocates of labor rights, including the AFL-CIO unions in the United States, advocates of other human rights, including women, environmental activists, students, and young anarchists.

The other line of resistance is more local in nature. In the United States that includes opposition to the destruction of public housing and gentrification as described in Chapter 6. It also has included direct confrontations with transnational corporations over abuses locally. The "Decatur war zone" described in Chapter 7 is an example. There are many more examples of workers throughout the 1980s and 1990s fighting against plant shutdowns and attacks on unions and new labor organizing efforts. There has also been weak but yet significant opposition to welfare reform policies and immigration policies, and there have been efforts in some locations to organize temporary workers.

Some of the players in these two lines of resistance are the same. Unions in the AFL-CIO, for example, have been important players in the struggles against NAFTA and the WTO. Local coalitions of community and labor groups that are affiliated nationally with Jobs With Justice participate in both resistance on the global front and the local struggles. Yet, for the most part, there is a distinct disconnect between these two lines of resistance. Groups involved in housing issues locally do not see the shifts discussed in Chapter 6 at the heart of their efforts to stop the destruction of public housing and the gentrification of their neighborhoods. While many labor groups feel that "globalization" is destroying their jobs and wages, that understanding does not extend to the systemic nature of the new world order that includes everything from NAFTA to national economic policy and specific programs like welfare "reform" and job training that treat work as a form of good behavior rather than as a way to make a living and develop oneself. Nor has resistance at any level led to a fundamental challenge to the ideas that have become a critical limit to the sense of what is practical in today's new world order.

There are two interrelated reasons for this disconnect. One is that the efforts to oppose the global institutions lack a clear focus on the systemic link of the global to the local. At times this results in alliances or tactics that actually undermine or conflict with work on issues at a local level. The other reason is that organizing within the United States is based on models of organizing more appropriate to eras prior to the new world order and this undermines both an analysis and approach to action that makes the global-local link. In the remainder of the present chapter, I present a case study of the fight against NAFTA in the United States that offers insights into the inability of the global movements to make the global-local link and in fact at times undermine local social movements. In the following chapter I use the vantage point of the NAFTA case study to examine shortcomings of local organizing. I then conclude with some ideas about how we might launch a more effective challenge to the new world order by linking global and local.

Opposing NAFTA/Forming a Hemispheric Social Alliance

In October 1991, I attended a remarkable meeting of Mexican, Canadian, and U.S. activists in Zacatecas, Mexico. The purpose of the meeting was to explore the possibilities for trinational resistance to NAFTA, which was being negotiated in that city. My own interest in this meeting stemmed from the work I was doing in Chicago with local labor and community organizations that had been hit hard by the decline in living wage jobs, the result of the loss of factory jobs in the 1980s described in Chapter 4. The meeting was initiated by a coalition in Canada known as the Action Canada Network (ACN).[2] ACN was fresh from a three-year struggle against the Canada-U.S. Free Trade Agreement (CUFTA), which was signed in 1988. It was a coalition strongly grounded in the Canadian labor movement through the Canadian Labour Congress but also included a variety of economic justice, faith-based, human rights, environmental, and women's groups. The Mexican contingent that hosted the Zacatecas meeting was led by an independent trade union coalition known as the Authentic Workers Front (FAT). The Mexican coalition that emerged is called the Mexican Action Network on Free Trade (RMALC). The United States had no existing coalition. ACN went to Washington, D.C., prior to Zacatecas and met with a variety of progressive policy organizations, as well as D.C.-based labor, religious, consumer, human rights, and environmental groups. Some of the organizations that met with ACN were already discussing how to oppose the formation of the WTO, which was also in negotiations. In response to the call from Canadians and Mexicans, these groups formed a loose association known as the Mobilization on Development, Trade, Labor and the Environment (MODTLE). The awkward acronym was a response to a *Wall Street Journal* article that referred to the emerging opposition to NAFTA and the WTO in the United States as a "motley crew." Prior to the Zacatecas meeting, MODTLE, ACN, and RMALC organized forums in Washington, D.C., and later Seattle to present a trinational view of the potentially negative impacts of NAFTA and then made plans for a larger meeting in Zacatecas in October.

The meeting in Zacatecas was the first effort to establish some formal principles for trinational cooperation to oppose NAFTA. From the start it was clear that government and business leaders involved in the official negotiation process did not want this effort to succeed. The NAFTA negotiations were closed. The discussions were secret and held under heavy guard. Zacatecas, the site of these official negotiations, was not very accessible. There was only one flight a day from Mexico City or a very difficult all-day car trip from that city. The Mexican activists were determined to hold a shadow meeting there anyway. My trip to Zacatecas was my first experience of travel in Mexico. I flew into Mexico City, where I had a long four-hour layover. The waiting room in the Mexico International Airport is literally an enclosed room. There was a large sign on the wall stating that this was the place to wait for the plane to Zacatecas. When I entered, I was the only person in the room. But I was soon joined by three men in dark suits and dark glasses who sat in the opposite corner of the room for about a half hour, talking quietly and continuously looking in my direction. Then one of the men (still wearing dark glasses even though we were inside) came over and sat next to me and asked me where I was going. I glanced up at the sign on the wall that said Zacatecas in big letters and pointed to it.

"What is your business there?"

"I'm going to a meeting."

"What sort of meeting?"

I could see the other two men laughing on the other side of the room.

"And who might you be?" I asked.

He motioned to the other two and they walked over. I was feeling a little nervous, to say the least. He smiled and said, "We are journalists." At this point one of the men took my picture. I handed them my university faculty business card and smiled. They returned to the other side of the room. When other activists from the United States and Canada arrived, they received the same B-grade movie treatment. When the Mexican representatives of RMALC came, they told them to go away, which they did. When we arrived in Zacatecas, RMALC had arranged for us to hold our meeting in a public auditorium. But when we went there, the door was locked and a caretaker announced that they were rehabilitating the structure, the seats had been removed, and the building was closed. We met instead at a nearby assembly hall in the law school of the Autonomous University of Zacatecas.

At the meeting Victor Quintana, then chairman of the Chihuahua Peasants Association, declared to a cheering audience of 300 Mexican, Canadian, and U.S. activists, "We came to Zacatecas with Villa in 1914 to fight for democracy. And today we demand democracy once again." In contrast to the closed-door, tight security meetings of government officials down the street from us, our meeting was remarkable for its openness to debate and full discussion. One very full day was devoted to an airing of the issues with an open mike and a ten-minute speaking limit. From Mexican society came the horrors of structural adjustment since their 1982 debt crisis and concerns for labor conditions, the environment, human rights, women's rights, indigenous rights, the status of peasants and small collective farms, and immigrants to the United States. For most, debt relief was a precondition to the development of any new agreement. From Canada there was a full report on the negative impacts of CUFTA and a demand that CUFTA be abolished before anything new was considered. The U.S. contingent mostly listened. We were at the bottom of our learning curve.

The following day was spent in smaller breakout groups around particular concerns—women, labor, the environment, and many others. That night the forum organizers took the notes from the open discussion and breakouts and hammered out sixteen points of unity. Meanwhile, the rest of us gathered for a noisy street march behind a mariachi band, which ended with raucous singing and chanting at the hotel where the official trade ministers were trying to sleep. The next day we debated and finalized the points of unity and marched to the official NAFTA negotiating site, where each national delegation attempted to present the "Declaration of Zacatecas" to our respective trade ministers. Of the three, only the U.S. Trade Representative, Carla Hills, refused to see her country people.

The outcome established a ground for a trinational vision of an alternative to the project that had been articulated by President George H. Bush as an "initiative for the Americas," and which had been institutionalized in CUFTA. The Mexicans put great emphasis on how unequal levels of development within the region made domestic economic policy vulnerable to external pressure, especially from the United States. Thus, a trade agreement had to neutralize this. Debt cancellation was one aspect. Others involved measures to erase trade imbalances that included temporary/emergency tariffs and quotas, rules of origin that specified domestic content of goods produced in Mexico, and the regulation of foreign portfolio investment. The Canadian position supported these propositions but had a much more detailed approach to a continental accord that protected aspects of national sovereignty, and included programs for manufacturing, agriculture, energy, services, intellectual property rights, environmental sustainability, worker and human rights including women and migrants, and cultural sovereignty. The discussion and debate resulted in a five-page "Declaration of Zacatecas" that addressed these issues in sixteen specific points. We called on our governments to include these points in a final agreement.[3]

The U.S. coalition (MODTLE), at this point, consisted of a number of separate groups with different missions. Many of us had never worked together before. We had no position papers prior to Zacatecas and participation in the discussions there mainly responded to proposals and ideas coming from the other nations. When we returned to the United States, we set up a mechanism to communicate and determine how to carry these ideas forward.

It was immediately apparent, however, that there were tensions among groups that made up MODTLE. Some were focused on building a broad multinational coalition based on the common principles developed at Zacatecas. Others were more focused on the needs of a legislative campaign to defeat NAFTA in the United States. Prior to the Zacatecas meeting, two of MODTLE's constituent groups, the Institute for Agriculture and Trade Policy (IATP) and Public Citizen, formed a separate entity to do legislative work around the emerging trade agreements—both NAFTA and WTO. They called themselves the Fair Trade Campaign (FTC). An organizer for the FTC explained to me that this activity was what he termed a "classic public interest campaign." The idea, he explained, was to activate existing groups around an issue, in this case opposition to NAFTA and WTO. The role of organizers was to provide information, advise on tactics, package media materials, and help orchestrate media-oriented events. The FTC was not, he stressed, attempting to build an ongoing organization. Winning on a particular issue drove all other considerations.

There were two key implications of this approach to organizing. One was that to win the issue, the work necessarily had to be directed toward national legislation. Second, the FTC was open to anyone who would oppose NAFTA and WTO. This included a significant number of people and organizations that identified themselves as part of the political right. Their reasons for opposing NAFTA were isolationist and at times anti-Mexican. While the leadership of the FTC had more of an internationalist outlook, their effort to keep such a disparate coalition together, including accepting funding sources that belonged to the political right, was at times antithetical to the effort to develop a trinational vision and movement. As one FTC organizer put it:

> Our job is to organize the trade issue as broadly as possible. We try to bring in any group with an interest in this issue from the protectionist right to the political left. It is very hard to keep all these groups at the table. At times this may conflict with a tri-national orientation.[4]

Three months after the Zacatecas meeting, the Fair Trade Campaign began to organize support for a congressional resolution introduced by Congressmen Henry Waxman and Richard Gephardt that stipulated that Congress would not support any trade resolution that would jeopardize U.S. environmental, labor, public health, or consumer safety standards. The Waxman–Gephardt resolution was generated after the Mexican government challenged the validity of the U.S. Marine Mammal Protection Act of 1972 as an unfair trade practice under existing GATT rules. The United States had used the Marine Mammal Protection Act to justify banning imports of Mexican tuna because it was caught under conditions that threatened the lives of dolphins. The GATT declared that the United States was unfairly restricting trade. The Fair Trade Campaign claimed that this was exactly the sort of thing that would happen much more frequently and over many other kinds of issues if either NAFTA or WTO became law.

However, some Mexican activists who opposed NAFTA argued that the tuna-dolphin controversy as framed by Fair Trade Campaign and the Waxman–Gephardt supporters was being unfair to Mexican citizens because the technical methods specified for protecting dolphins were beyond the capability of Mexican fishermen. Moreover, alternative methods for protecting dolphins that were being used by Mexicans were just as effective. The issue of methods for tuna fishing was quite technical. It was clear, however, that the organizing priorities of the Fair Trade Campaign made delving into these technicalities impractical. Moreover, some FTC supporters who opposed NAFTA didn't care about offending Mexicans. Two environmental groups who were part of the broader MODTLE grouping came down on opposite sides of the issue. The Sierra Club vigorously fought for the preservation of the Marine Mammal Protection Act, while Greenpeace sided with the Mexicans. Greenpeace had been represented in Zacatecas and had an international constituency, while the Sierra Club had more of a U.S. focus. The dispute between the two environmental organizations was quite contentious. FTC, for its part, went ahead with their campaign to muster support for Waxman–Gephardt. There was no mention, except from the more internationalist groupings within MODTLE, of broader trinational principles. Despite these tensions and concerns, there was a general consensus within MODTLE that Waxman–Gephardt should be supported.

That spring, due to the concerns expressed by the more internationalist part of MODTLE over Waxman–Gephardt and other proposals, we decided to separate the legislative work within the United States from the trinational work. As a result, two distinct groups were created. Citizens' Trade Campaign (CTC) would focus on the legislative front, while the Alliance for Responsible Trade (ART) would lead trinational efforts. A number of organizations decided to join both coalitions, but some groups went with one or the other. In Chicago, I tried to bridge the divide by helping to organize the Illinois Fair Trade Campaign that had both legislative and international agendas. The Illinois group involved a handful of union leaders and individual citizen activists who had experience lobbying legislators on a variety of issues. Beyond the unions there was little local organizational involvement. For these reasons legislative campaigns pursued by the CTC involving calling and visiting congressional representatives and senators dominated our work. Nationally, CTC had a strong citizen base that was built around Public Citizen's public interest research groups (PIRGs) around the country, while ART was more grounded in Washington, D.C. policy groups.

As CTC continued to organize around Waxman–Gephardt, ART moved the trinational agenda by participating in the organization of another international meeting, which was held in Mexico City in January 1993. Prior to the meeting, we received a secret draft of the text of negotiating positions for NAFTA. That text had been leaked and sent to representatives of the trinational coalition. I participated with ART, ACN, and RMALC in developing a citizen's analysis of that text. This analysis was discussed at length in Mexico City. In this meeting a major point of contention arose. As we attempted to articulate an alternative to the leaked text, a number of individuals—mostly from the United States and Mexico—argued that we should propose the insertion of a social clause in the text that would spell out basic human, labor, and environmental standards. Representatives from Canada and Quebec argued vehemently against this proposal, contending that we had to first defeat NAFTA and then consider alternatives that would constitute a different model of development. Tony Clark, a leader of the Action Canada Network, called the approach proposed by the United States a "politics of accommodation."

The argument of those proposing the social clause had to do with both the difficulties and opportunities posed by the election of President Clinton. Clinton had indicated that he was going ahead with the Bush agenda on trade. Yet, the AFL-CIO and a number of environmental organizations had campaigned hard for Clinton and Gore. Thus, some of our contingent argued that it would be difficult to turn around and attack the Clinton administration across the board on this issue without losing the support of organized labor and much of the environmental movement. Moreover, it was now possible to influence the terms of NAFTA by negotiating side agreements that addressed labor and environmental issues through a social clause. Members of both the U.S. and the Mexican delegations were divided on this issue. Some representatives of RMALC tended to side with Canada, although they were less vehement and indicated that some accommodation might be needed to defeat NAFTA in the United States, which was crucial. My view of this division is that it revealed a deeper disagreement over how critical to our united effort against NAFTA was our ability to defeat it in the United States. Furthermore, we were divided on how much we were willing to pay in terms of accommodation to the principles behind NAFTA to defeat it. This dispute also heightened the tension between the internationalist and domestic legislative focus among U.S. activists.

Despite the fact that the dispute was not fully resolved, the meeting ended with a determination to find common ground and push forward an agenda to develop an alternative to the model represented by NAFTA. A declaration summarized points of unity that moved slightly beyond the Zacatecas document.[5] It stressed the need for a democratic process to negotiate a regional agreement and it laid out principles to be used in the area of energy and natural resources, agriculture, foreign investment and financial services, intellectual property rights, and the role of the state and public services.

For the next ten months much energy in the United States was devoted to the campaign to defeat NAFTA. CTC had by this time formed chapters throughout the nation. I participated in their monthly phone conferences that included lengthy briefings from Public Citizen staff that identified the positions of key congresspersons and senators and suggested ways to swing them to the anti-NAFTA side. Initially, the effort was to defeat legislation for special "fast track" rules. The debate over the rules change became a major battleground. Nevertheless, "fast track" passed, but not by much. Then the battle shifted to the vote on NAFTA itself. There were rallies across the nation. Local congresspersons and senators were visited by CTC delegations. At this point much of organized labor was allied in the struggle, as were the forces of Ross Perot's United We Stand America and Pat Buchanan's followers on the far right. Many of these forces found themselves working together to lobby local congresspersons. Everything was now focused on the vote in Congress. The division over the use of a social clause came up once again as President Clinton negotiated weak side agreements on labor and the environment. Some environmental organizations left the anti-NAFTA forces, but for the most part the coalition led by CTC held. The vote was close, but in late November NAFTA became law.

While all of the U.S. organizing around trade issues in 1993 was focused on the vote in Congress, the efforts to build a trinational alternative vision to NAFTA continued. After the January meeting in Mexico City, I participated in a process in which ART and RMALC began articulating areas of agreement and disagreement. We would write these areas down, bracketing areas of disagreement. RMALC would respond.[6] An initial product of this dialogue was a discussion paper that was prepared jointly by ART, CTC, and RMALC. It was also endorsed by ACN.[7] The paper came out of a meeting held in Washington in March. It was the fifth trinational meeting in a two-year period. While this discussion paper was widely circulated in Washington policy circles and on Capitol Hill, it never became an integral part of the campaign against NAFTA nationally or even within my own Illinois Fair Trade Campaign.

Following the NAFTA vote, President Clinton announced his intention to expand NAFTA to other nations of the hemisphere, beginning with Chile and Brazil. He also indicated that he wanted to bring the Uruguay Round GATT negotiations to a close by creating a new WTO. The coalitions in all three nations were in some disarray at this point. This was particularly true in the United States, where the emphasis for an entire year had been on the defeat of NAFTA in the U.S. Congress. CTC began to shift its campaign apparatus toward an effort to defeat WTO.

At this point I participated in a meeting to reflect on the past two years of organizing held in Madison, Wisconsin, in October 1994. ART, CTC, and persons outside these coalitions but interested in trade issues participated, including people from fourteen nations. Detailed notes of the discussions were prepared and distributed following the meeting.[8] I was struck by several points of debate at the meeting. A number of participants argued that the single-minded focus on the NAFTA vote undermined grassroots movement building and produced top-down decision making about the conduct of the campaign that excluded people outside Washington. Individuals in groups relating to neither ART nor CTC from regional economic justice and anti-poverty networks, as well as many women and people of color, expressed that they felt left out of the process. In addition, there was considerable concern that the effort to unite left and right to defeat NAFTA tended to downplay issues that were divisive in this context—particularly immigration. At the same time, most people agreed that the effort of the past two years had put the issue of "trade" on the political map in the United States and had forced decision makers to see worker rights, equity concerns, democracy, and the environment as part of that issue. In addition, many pointed out that our efforts had resulted in new international alliances that could be built upon in the future.

Following the Madison meeting, CTC continued and intensified its legislative campaign against GATT/WTO. Meanwhile, ART, while cooperating with the CTC campaign, continued its work in building a broader trinational alliance by amending our trinational statement of alternatives and forging a joint effort to monitor the effects of NAFTA. Our discussions over the amended document exposed another point of contention. Some U.S. participants in the process advocated the use of a provision of U.S. trade law—the Generalized System of Preferences—as a basis for labor rights and environmental standards enforcement. Many Mexicans objected on the ground that they would be turning over enforcement of such standards to a non-democratic, U.S.-dominated body. They indicated that they didn't trust the U.S. government to apply these standards fairly. The U.S. laws punish governments that violate certain standards by employing trade barriers against their products. A compromise that eventually appeared in the document was that punishment should be directed at companies rather than at governments.

The expanded joint position paper now included a substantive new section on immigration that had been hammered out during a trinational workshop in Madison. The new statement established freer labor mobility as a goal of a just and sustainable trade and development initiative. We proposed the creation of a process that would work toward more open borders. The objective of development, in this view, would be to make it possible for people to earn a living wage without having to leave their homes, but that at all times there must be rules in place that protect the human rights and economic well-being of migrants. A second activity of ART during this period was the development of a trinational monitoring effort of the impacts of NAFTA. Each national coalition released a report on NAFTA's first year in early 1995. In May of that year there was another trinational meeting in Chicago to further coordinate the monitoring effort. A second set of reports was issued in early 1996.

In the meantime, the U.S. Congress adopted rules establishing the WTO after another close vote. CTC then began to work with sympathetic congresspeople to develop legislation that would establish benchmarks that would have to be met for NAFTA authorization to continue. Again, the effort was to try to attract the widest political spectrum in order to pass the proposed bill. The resulting "NAFTA Accountability Act" directed the president of the United States to monitor NAFTA performance each year. And if the benchmark goals were not met, to renegotiate the agreement. The benchmarks included an overall trade deficit no greater than 10 percent, positive balances in particular agricultural commodities, and positive balances in manufacturing. In January 1996, I joined four other members of ART in sending a letter to the sponsors of the bill arguing that the bill had too narrow a national focus. The letter pointed out that the implication of the across the board trade balance benchmarks was that Mexico and Canada would have to have negative balances. The letter argued instead that benchmarks should be regional—show gains for people in all three nations. In addition, we pointed to the fact that the NAFTA Accountability Act ignored labor issues. This intervention heightened tensions between ART and CTC, and it pointed up the conflict between CTC's legislative focus that required broad political spectrum support and the effort of ART to build a multinational alliance.

Similar tensions surfaced again in December as the Teamsters Union sought a court order to block a provision of NAFTA that would allow Mexican trucks to operate in the United States. The court action was accompanied by a campaign that included flyers and picketing at the border in Texas. Some members of the CTC actively supported these activities. Eventually, President Clinton intervened and agreed to delay opening the borders to Mexican trucks. A number of Mexican activists from RMALC were angry. Despite the fact that the Teamsters had been supportive of Mexican union organizing efforts, this action was not preceded by any consultation with Mexicans. Mexican activists felt that some of the literature was unnecessarily inflammatory and decidedly anti-Mexican. In the end, representatives of the Teamsters met with their Mexican counterparts and agreed to tone down the rhetoric, which smoothed over the controversy.

With the NAFTA battle over and without a clear mission, CTC had mostly dissolved by 1996. Public Citizen carried on much of the work of CTC. They cooperated with ART's monitoring efforts through their "Global Trade Watch" division. In Canada, the continued opposition to NAFTA was being coordinated by an organization called Common Frontiers. They worked closely with the Canadian trade union federation, the Canadian Labour Congress (CLC). CLC sponsored a major effort to bring together national reports on NAFTA's third year from each of the three NAFTA nations. The reports were distributed to the three national networks and presented in Toronto at a special CLC meeting in March 1996. They documented a range of negatives for people in all three nations.

At the CLC meeting, concerns were raised about Patrick Buchanan's campaign for president and the fact that he had been an ally in the anti-NAFTA struggle. I participated with others in the drafting of a letter for ART that denounced Buchanan's "racist and nationalistic solutions to the trade issue."[9] The letter specifically criticized his stance on immigration, his call for a flat tax, and his opposition to an increase in the minimum wage. It also argued that there was a need for a positive alternative vision of relations among nations and laid out some principles taken from our trinational document. The letter was circulated among progressive organizations who signed on and it was then distributed to Congress and contacts around the nation.

Shortly after President Clinton began his second term in 1997, he announced he would pursue the expansion of NAFTA to the other nations of the hemisphere. His proposed Free Trade Area of the Americas (FTAA) was an elaboration of President Bush's Initiative of the Americas. In June he introduced legislation that would give him fast track authority to begin FTAA negotiations. The AFL-CIO, which had supported President Clinton's reelection, announced that they would fight him on fast track. CTC immediately began to mobilize the anti-NAFTA coalition it had built and jumped into the fight. For six months all energy on trade issues went into the effort to defeat fast track. The negative impacts of NAFTA on jobs, wages, and the environment had been documented through the monitoring activity since NAFTA's passage. These findings became the meat of the anti-fast track campaign. By November it became clear that President Clinton would not be able to get the needed votes and he pulled his legislation out of consideration. Polls showed that the negative votes would come from both liberals and the right wing, and from both Democrats and Republicans.

This was the first major legislative victory for the anti-NAFTA forces. The reasons for the victory were complex.[10] Basically, it was clear that concerns associated with "trade" had become a major political issue. As the battles against previous fast track legislation, NAFTA, and WTO continued, more and more groups around the nation were becoming involved in different ways. Local labor unions had increasingly joined this work, giving more credibility to new AFL-CIO leadership's efforts. There had been a great deal of international work that went beyond ART's trinational efforts that brought more forces into the struggle. International and trinational meetings of environmentalists, teachers, labor unions, economic justice coalitions, and human rights activists had blossomed. There had been international educational conferences on globalization put together by new formations such as the International Forum on Globalization and the Open World Conference. Students were organizing in opposition to sweatshops. There were worker-to-worker programs, where U.S. workers visited their counterparts in Mexico. Religious and human rights organizations throughout the world had launched a campaign, Jubilee 2000, to cancel the debt in the developing world without structural adjustment conditions. Labor unions were now having regular international discussions of "neo-liberal" policies through the established international organization of trade union confederations, the International Confederation of Trade Unions (ICTFU). In this hemisphere, these meetings were held under the auspices of the ICTFU regional federation, the Inter American Regional Workers Organization (ORIT).

The ORIT meetings began to focus on the proposed FTAA. In the fall of 1997, there was an important breakthrough in this regard. ORIT called for a meeting in Belo Horizonte, Brazil, where trade ministers were beginning the process of negotiating the FTAA. Traditionally, the unions rarely worked with non-union organizations. But this time, in addition to all the hemisphere's major trade union federations, ART, RMALC, Common Frontiers, and their counterparts in Chile, Brazil, and a number of other Latin American nations also participated. The subject of the meeting was how to launch the most effective campaign to defeat FTAA throughout the hemisphere while putting forward a people's agenda for hemispheric cooperation. Out of this gathering came the first joint union-NGO statement on the FTAA process, marking a dramatic shift in the unions' previous reluctance to enter into formal alliances with NGOs.

A decision was made in Belo Horizonte to hold a "People's Summit of the Americas" to correspond with the Presidents' Summit to be held in Santiago Chile, in April 1998. The organizations at Belo Horizonte also resolved to launch a cooperative effort to draft an "alternatives" document to facilitate debate and begin the process of developing a detailed alternative that its members could fight for. While the older trinational document had established a basis for such an effort, thirty people from nine nations participated in the drafting of a much more comprehensive fifty-page document. For the People's Summit, forums were organized on labor, environment, women, indigenous peoples, human rights, government officials, ethics, education, agriculture, energy, and social/economic alternatives. Each forum had its own multinational organizational structure. Most of them commissioned position paper drafts in addition to the larger alternatives document that were distributed in advance of the summit in order to facilitate a deeper discussion.

Over 1,000 activists from every nation in the hemisphere attended the people's summit. Debate was lively and intense. After the summit I participated in a continuations committee that worked to incorporate points made in the debates into a new draft document through a process that involved electronic communication. ORIT, Common Frontiers, RMALC, and ART coordinated this process.[11]

The formulation of alternatives in the new document went far beyond what had been developed in the trinational "Just and Sustainable Development and Trade Initiative." The new document turned NAFTA on its head. While NAFTA makes market access its highest principle, we proposed a system of cooperative national sovereignties where labor rights, women's rights, indigenous rights, and human rights along with environmental sustainability are the highest principles. Market access must accommodate itself, we argued, to these principles. The new document contained detailed proposals, standards, and conceptions concerning human rights, environment, labor, immigration, the role of the state, investment and finance, intellectual property, sustainable energy, agriculture, market access, enforcement, and dispute resolution. The detail contained in the document is remarkable in that it represented a consensus among participating networks throughout the hemisphere. That detail directly reflected the nature of ongoing work of all the networks in opposing various aspects of the new world order.

As this process unfolded, the CTC network began to come back together and resolved to focus its work on slowing down globalization through legislative initiatives. Between 1991 and 1993, this emphasis meant trying to stop NAFTA. Now it meant trying to organize opposition to various efforts of the Clinton administration to expand the new world order to other venues. They included WTO, fast track, the Multilateral Agreement on Investment (MAI), and a "NAFTA for Africa" initiative called the African Growth and Opportunity Act. With the exception of fast track and the MAI, these efforts failed on the legislative front. But they did widen the scope of the opposition, which partially explains the size and militancy of the Seattle demonstration in November 1999.

ART never focused on legislation, although it did join CTC at particular junctures. Rather, ART continued to build first a trinational alliance and then a hemispheric one. It has also tried to broaden its membership base by including more organizations outside Washington. ART's international work continued to deepen. After the Santiago People's Summit, the coalition of organizations that had met in Brazil to initiate the Alternatives for the Americas document and plan the people's summit formed a formal association called the Hemispheric Social Alliance (HSA). A chair was elected and a representational organizational structure was created. HSA meets twice a year. Its work is to intervene in the negotiations of the FTAA with counterproposals contained within the alternatives document. It is also committed to fostering solidarity around the activities of its constituents and promoting popular education around the alternatives proposal.

In October 1999, HSA sponsored another meeting to intervene in a trade ministers' negotiating session that was being held in Toronto. More debate was held over the content of the alternatives document, and a new writing committee was formed to make further revisions prior to the next President's Summit in Quebec City in April 2000. A new document was produced for the summit that included a new chapter on women and substantive revisions to other chapters.

The summit in Quebec matched Seattle in terms of the militancy of protests and the breadth of a growing anti-globalization movement. Chicago activists participated in Quebec both as part of ART and as street demonstrators. Rank-and-file members of labor union locals were there. Chicago Jobs With Justice (JWJ), a coalition of community and labor organizations, supported the actions and turned out its members. JWJ nationally also joined the anti-globalization forces. While not widespread, participation from Chicago began to include those whose sole focus had been on the local collisions imposed by the new world order—affordable housing, employment, welfare rights, living wages. This is beginning on a national scale. But, by and large, the globalization work is conceptually and organizationally separate from activity around the local collisions. The question of how to bring these activities together remains unanswered. Throughout 2001 and 2002, ART began a program of outreach and education in the United States that was done in conjunction with activities of other members of the Hemispheric Social Alliance. The alternatives document continued to be refined and was presented again at the World Social Forum in Porto Allegre, Brazil, in 2002.

Some Conclusions

This case offers a vantage point from which to explain the disconnect between opposition to the global decisions that NAFTA and now the proposed FTAA represent and the local collisions represented by poverty, homelessness, and underemployment in urban areas at a local level. The case reveals four kinds of tensions that have been generated by the work of ART and CTC that represent impediments to a more fully integrated movement. These tensions are both within the United States and between the United States and other nations in the hemisphere. And they can be viewed as problems to be solved in future organizing work at the local level.

A key tension within the United States was between efforts focused on the legislative arena and those directed toward building a multinational move-ment. Efforts of CTC to build a right-left alliance were directed toward the objective of slowing down or halting advances in the development of the new world order. An important mechanism used to meet this objective was to block key legislative benchmarks like the votes on fast track, NAFTA, WTO, and the African Growth and Opportunity Act (a "NAFTA for Africa" bill). An-other mechanism was to put forth legislative proposals that would undermine the ability of the U.S. government to implement these initiatives. This was the point of the Waxman–Gephardt resolution and the NAFTA Accountability Act. Most of these efforts went down to defeat. But the fact that the votes were always close reflected a growing political awareness of the importance of "trade" that resulted in some compromise and the slowing of the initiatives as participation in opposition of various kinds grew. But this clearly came at the expense of integrating this work with the efforts to build a multinational movement.

At times conflicts generated by work on the legislative front boiled to the surface, such as the controversy over the Marine Mammal Protection Act enforcement, the anti-Mexican propaganda on the trucking issue, and the failure of the legislative campaigns to link "trade" to inequality and immigration. A more subtle manifestation of the tension is the fact that much of the work of the Hemispheric Social Alliance, including the specific proposals included in the alternatives document, is not supported by a significant number of organizations and individuals who are part of the U.S. legislative alliance. That includes some fundamental principles that can be traced back to the Zacatecas Declaration and are at the heart of the Hemispheric Social Alliance itself, such as a commitment to the reduction of inequalities within and between nations; the unconditional cancellation of external debt in nations like Mexico and Brazil; and the notion that market access should be tempered by policies to harmonize social and environmental standards upward. This aspect of the tension highlights the limits of the legislative strategy itself.

A second tension within the United States relates to the inclusiveness of the organizing project. This tension applies to both the legislative strategies and those focused on building a multinational movement. The legislative focus lent itself to a hierarchical approach to organizing, where issues, propaganda, and media strategies were decided by a thin stratum of organizers based on their assessment of what will move votes in the U.S. Congress. This style of organizing necessarily downplayed inclusiveness—a point that was raised during our meetings in Madison.

Both the emphasis on a legislative campaign and the resulting top-down style of organizing influenced which issues to stress and the nature of propaganda. These were based on the need to maintain a right-left coalition rather than to attract regional and local economic and environmental justice coalitions and minorities. Ignoring or downplaying immigration and issues relating to inequality was not a mere oversight, but a necessary part of a strategic focus on winning congressional votes. It undermined the ability to link the globalization work with organizing around local urban issues such as those in Chicago. The destruction of public housing and gentrification described in Chapter 6, for example, are specific manifestations of inequality. A legislative campaign against NAFTA that downplays inequality for the sake of securing congressional votes is thus not going to be attractive to housing activists. Moreover, such an emphasis precludes an analysis that demonstrates the link between local housing issues and global capital mobility. A similar point can be made about employment. Limiting opposition to NAFTA or other global institutions to legislative campaigns precludes a fundamental challenge to the abandonment of full employment and living wages as national social goals. The jobs issue tends to become reduced to the question of whether "jobs were lost to NAFTA," rather than challenging the notion of flexible labor markets and the reduction of employment to an individual human capital decision. The latter are more at the heart of the loss of jobs and wages and are both global in impact and fundamental to any challenge to a new world order.

A third tension concerns both inter- and intranational relations. It involves the extent to which practicality means we have to accept some of the premises of the new world order. In terms of the discussion in Chapter 2 about permanencies, there were tensions over where to draw the boundaries for the entire organizing project and how this would be decided. This tension took several forms. One example of this division applies to the efforts of ART to build a multinational movement in this hemisphere. From the beginning there were those who felt the best we could do was to win concessions that would make the new world order model more palatable. The Canadians were particularly vocal that we should not do this. ART tended to support the idea of winning concessions. Compromises on the issue were made in the alternatives document, but the issue has not gone away. If provisions of the alternatives document get onto the table in the FTAA negotiations, some will be more willing than others to compromise on provisions that don't make it onto the table. The relation of this tension to the local collisions described throughout this book is similar to the points raised with the other tensions. Drawing the boundaries of the organizing project short of a full challenge to the new world order's ideological, theoretical, and political shifts will necessarily exclude the impact of these shifts on the local issues in the realm of affordable housing and living wage employment.

One final tension relates to the problem of building an international movement with unequal partners. The fact that the United States is far more powerful politically and economically than other nations in the hemisphere means that activists in other nations will view solutions that depend on the U.S. government with suspicion. An example was the proposal from the United States to use the General System of Preferences to enforce basic worker rights. Mexicans and Canadians objected. The coalition has yet to find a satisfactory way to handle enforcement and dispute resolution.

These tensions are suggestive of the difficulties of finding a clear direction for efforts to contest the terms of the new world order. Organizing efforts within the United States that bring together both the global and local dimensions of the new world order must face these tensions to be successful. In the final chapter of this book I build on this vantage point to propose an alternative approach to organizing that encompasses both global and local.

CHAPTER 9

Implications
and Directions

Previous chapters have demonstrated that the political, economic, and ideological factors that have generated global institutions and rules for a new world order are the same as those that are generating local collisions in areas like housing and employment. Both global decisions and local collisions are an integral part of a new world order. For that reason, an effective movement to contest the terms and results of the new world order must unite movements aimed directly at global institutions and rules with those at a local level that are dealing specifically with their local impacts. In Chapter 8 I noted that in the United States two lines of resistance to the new world order have formed. One is more oriented toward global institutions and the other in various localities is aimed at affordable housing, employment with living wages, and other urban policy issues. The problem is that these lines of resistance are not well connected. Nor are they based on an analysis that demonstrates that problems that these two lines of resistance address are generated by a common system.

In the previous chapter I used the case of the struggle against NAFTA to demonstrate how such an effort generated tensions that limited the effectiveness of the organizing project. Related tensions are also applicable to organizing efforts at a local level such as the efforts of people to resist the gentrification of their neighborhoods, the elimination of public housing, and the imposition of flexible labor markets in Decatur, Illinois (Chapters 6 and 7). Only in these cases the tensions were not represented by conflicts among organizing groups. Rather, they were tensions related to the new world order imposing limits on these local organizing efforts. None of the housing cases really challenged the systemic basis of the problem, which, as we argued in Chapter 6, was the emerging global finance system that turned housing into a pure commodity. Similarly, the "battle of Decatur" challenged the right of specific corporations to impose draconian rules in the three workplaces. But workers did not make the connection to the regime of mobile goods, capital, and services and flexible labor markets that is at the heart of the new world order. And as militant as these local struggles were, they accepted urban and labor market policies and other premises of the new world order as the limits of their organizing projects.

The lessons of both global and local forms of resistance reveal three inter-related issues. One is that the tensions around the anti-NAFTA organizing project limited the movement's capacity to link struggles across borders and the depth of its challenge to the new world order as a system. Second, its single-minded focus on "trade" legislation, the resulting top-down organizing style, and the acceptance of some of the premises of the new world order also limited its ability to reach out to people organizing at a local level by failing to make their concerns and issues central features of the organizing project. Third, the failure of local organizing efforts to grasp the connection of global rules to their local concerns and launch a more fundamental challenge with respect to issues like housing and employment also limited their ability to see what was happening globally as an integral part of their own work.

These three issues relating to the two lines of resistance in the United States have a common source. Both rely on an organizing model that was generated during the Fordist era. I argue in this chapter that this model had flaws during the Fordist era that are magnified in today's new world order. In the remainder of this chapter, I first examine the roots of modern organizing in the United States. Second, I return to the philosophic propositions developed in Chapter 2 and from that vantage point offer a critique of the dominant organizing model, discussing its limitations in the present era. Third, I offer criteria for an alternative model to organizing. Finally, I suggest how we might begin to operationalize new approaches to organizing based on those criteria.

The Roots of Modern Organizing in the United States

Most oppositional organizing in the United States today is derived from models developed by the trade union movement during the early days of the Fordist era. These models were adapted to community organizing by Saul Alinsky and his Industrial Areas Foundation. Alinsky's approach to organizing continues to be highly influential in the United States and many other parts of the world. Understanding this approach requires a brief discussion of the evolution of trade unionism in the United States.

The earliest period of trade unionism in the United States included a significant radical component that challenged fundamental aspects of the era of the capitalist system that prevailed at the time. Trade unionists in the late 1800s and early 1900s challenged the right of corporations to determine the length of the working day. Lengthening the working day was, in that era, the critical method by which the system accumulated surplus value. Thus, the movement to limit the working day to eight hours was a fundamental challenge to the system at that time. In the early 1900s, the Industrial Workers of the World (IWW) began organizing what they called "one big union" in entire industries instead of organizing individuals based on a particular skill. They saw their constituency as the working class of the world and were thus inclusive in terms of race, gender, and nationality. They organized in Mexico as well as the United States. Their vision of one big union was also to be the basis for a very different kind of society that would offer freedom from what they termed "wage slavery." The IWW effort reached its peak during a period when the organization of economies in developed nations was shifting to large-scale mass production. It was also a period of crisis and transition in which the viability of capitalism itself was being questioned. Thus, the activity of the IWW provided a fundamental challenge to the capitalist system as it was organized at the time. The IWW was all but destroyed during World War I. They advocated draft resistance, and those leaders who had not already been assassinated were imprisoned on charges of "seditious conspiracy."

In the 1930s, a new labor organization, the Congress of Industrial Organizations (CIO), renewed the effort to organize workers into a class alliance based on entire industries rather than crafts. Many of their leaders and members were communists, socialists, and anarchists who saw labor organizing as a way to defeat capitalism. Like the IWW, their tactics were highly militant. They occupied factories and formed "flying squadrons" that traveled around the United States to engage in pickets, blockades, and occupations.

World War II and the deal with labor that followed the Bretton Woods Agreement ended radical U.S. trade unionism. As Chapter 3 argued, the established trade union movement decided to buy into the promise of U.S. prosperity in a new era in which there would be expanded production stimulated by the rebuilding of Europe and Japan and the exploitation of the developing world. The Wagner Act of 1935 represented the beginning of the deal between capital and labor. The government agreed to recognize officially the right of workers to organize, bargain collectively, and strike if the corporations didn't live up to their side of the bargain. Corporations slowly and reluctantly went along. Following World War II, their side of the bargain as well as that of the government was to share the prosperity generated by the Bretton Woods Agreement with union members. Labor even reluctantly accepted later legislation (Taft–Hartley Act of 1947) that curtailed some of the rights gained in an earlier period. They also purged themselves of leftists who wished to maintain a more radical opposition to the system and merged the CIO with the more moderate American Federation of Labor. Thus, trade unionism from the late 1940s to the mid-1970s was geared to accommodate the Fordist system that prevailed at the time. The trade union movement aligned itself with the Democratic Party and focused much of its political activity on electing candidates who were supportive of the post–Bretton Woods bargain.

In the late 1950s and early 1960s, neighborhoods were declining due to the rapid decentralization of people and economic activity from the central cities. We examined this development in Chicago and described in detail the first Mayor Daley's response to it. Residents began to organize to demand that city, state, and national governments take measures to preserve their communities. Saul Alinsky and the Industrial Areas Foundation that he founded were important leaders of the community organization movement nationally and in Chicago. CIO industrial organizing had a major influence on them.[1] Alinsky came out of the University of Chicago's criminology program, which promoted the idea that crime was the result of poverty and bad living conditions. Following his studies of Al Capone's gang and later of juvenile delinquency in Chicago's "Back of the Yards" neighborhood in the mid-1930s, Alinsky launched his first organizing effort. "Back of the Yards" included the stockyards and meat-packing plants. His approach was unique at the time. He united over 100 organizations that were working for the improvement of the community into the Back of the Yards Neighborhood Council. The members of the council included churches, local businesses, and organized labor. This came at a time when the CIO was being formed and a radical union that was to become the Packinghouse Workers was attempting to organize the meat-packing plants in the neighborhood. Alinsky managed to marshal the support of the Catholic Church, the Democratic Party political machine, and the entire Back of the Yards Neighborhood Council in support of the Packinghouse Workers' organizing project. In 1939, John L. Lewis, founder of the CIO, came to Chicago to support the effort.

In the years to follow, Alinsky drew on the radical days of the CIO for many of his militant tactics, including mass picketing, sit-ins, disrupting meetings, and forcing confrontations with high-profile political leaders. These tactics were emulated by the civil rights, Women's Liberation, and anti-war movements of the 1960s and 1970s. Alinsky was particularly attracted to the ideas of John L. Lewis.[2] When a reporter once asked Lewis what labor wants, he gave a one word reply: "more." Alinsky's version of "more" was that you "organize for power."[3] That meant a seat at the table where decisions that affect people's lives are made. Alinsky had an unbending faith in American democracy and saw the end product of the struggle for "power" to be a higher degree of participation in the government or corporate decision-making process. Alinsky's formulation of neighborhood councils was to develop local leaders who represented a number of issue areas that could be combined to gain influence in the established political process. The broader rules that restrict the substance of the political process itself were never questioned. It is worth noting that Alinsky's mentor, John L. Lewis, participated in the post–Bretton Woods accommodation. In fact, when workers in his United Mine Workers Union began to raise potentially radical questions about the right of management to control the pace of work through automation, Lewis opposed them, touching off a wildcat strike in 1950.[4] Alinksy's organizing model in the 1960s and

1970s was a combination of the militant tactics of CIO organizing in the 1930s and the vision of the labor movement of the 1950s.

Thus, just as organized labor chose to accommodate the strategy of the Fordist era after World War II, so did community organizations under the influence of Alinsky. In the 1960s and 1970s, many African American neighborhoods formed Alinsky-style organizations. Their efforts were toward gaining what white workers had gained in the postwar deal—what Mayor Harold Washington of Chicago in 1983 called a "fair share."

Philosophy and Organization

This approach to organizing continues to dominate many efforts to contest some of the ill effects of the new world order in the United States. It was dominant in the work of the Citizen's Trade Campaign and the Seattle demonstrations described in the previous chapter. It has also been dominant in the struggles around affordable housing, employment, and living wages described in the cases in Chapters 6–7. In order to evaluate its potential to contest the terms of the new world order, I return to the philosophic discussion begun in Chapter 2.

Take the proposition developed throughout the book that the purpose of an economic system should be, in Marx's words, "the full and free development of every human being."[5] That proposition contradicts today's prevailing notion that the point of an economy is to promote the narrowest definition of economic efficiency—lowest cost per unit of output in various economic endeavors. This type of efficiency narrows the consideration of value to exchange value. It also excludes social costs generated by a particular economic venture such as low wages or pollution. Efficiency also has a specific ideological/political meaning in the era of the new world order. Anything that interferes with the unregulated movement of goods, services, and capital or with "labor market flexibility" is considered inefficient. Consider an editorial in the *Chicago Tribune* that was castigating Europeans over the falling value of the Euro and praising Americans for doing what needed to be done to enhance the value of the dollar. Capital flows into the United States and out of Europe, they argued, are due to the fact that U.S. economic growth is leaving Europe in the dust. And why are we doing so well? Because in the United States, "companies bloom, hire scads of people, go broke. People move on to other cities, other careers. They take risks. (Then) the entrepreneurs try again."[6]

But in Europe, they complained,

> Companies have been reluctant to hire workers until they absolutely must because of the long-term economic commitment each worker entailed. That has meant higher unemployment in Europe. Generous social benefits also have eased

the pain for the jobless and consequently giving them less incentive to look for work.

The implication of the editorial is that it is inefficient for workers to have job security and decent benefits while they are unemployed. But it is efficient for entrepreneurs to start up companies, go broke, and move on. The definition of efficiency is made along class lines. Companies doing what they want are efficient; the inflexibility of employment and social security is not. In this view of efficiency, starting up companies, going broke, and tossing the workers out of work has no cost that enters into the efficiency equation. There is no consideration of the possibility that we in the United States ought to emulate what the European labor movement has gained—greater social benefits through job security measures and decent unemployment benefits during times of economic downturn. If we leveled the global playing field on those terms, capital would not flow out of Europe and into the United States because conditions would be the same in both places.

Previous chapters have cited many other examples of this one-sided approach to economic efficiency. The cost to workers of massive deindustrialization described in Chapter 4 has never figured into the efficiency equation of the new world order. The human toll of demolishing public housing units at a time when there is a shortage of affordable housing is likewise not part of the efficiency calculation; neither is the suffering caused by forcing people to work at jobs that pay less than a living wage, forcing people off public assistance when there is a shortage of entry-level jobs, forcing people to spend much of their day in the temporary help agency and commuting to the dead-end low-wage jobs they offer.

Organizing in the era of the new world order, therefore, needs to challenge this concept of efficiency with the alternative objective of human self-development. In order to concretize this distinction, we might ask: What is it about the new world order that undermines human self-development? The argument developed in previous chapters has demonstrated that the elevation of efficiency over human development takes a specific form in the new world order that must be addressed by movements to combat its harmful effects. One key form of the efficiency criterion is unrestricted mobility of goods, services, and capital. Mobility is further enhanced through policies that promote labor market flexibility, which was the point of the *Chicago Tribune* editorial. Furthermore, the mobility of the new world order is fueled by continuous credit expansion and speculation. The crucial role of the finance sector in the system gives political strength to those who make money with money. This reinforces the tendency, discussed in Chapter 2, to separate money price from other forms of value, making other values subservient to it. The dominant role of a monetary policy that is focused solely on minimizing inflation (discussed in Chapter 7) is one consequence of the elevation of money price over other values. That entailed the abandonment of full employment and living wages as a social goal. The dogmatic insistence that basic living standards—housing, employment, food, health care—are pure individual commodities rather than social rights is another consequence. The consequences for affordable housing and employment were spelled out in Chapters 6 and 7.

In addition to mobility and the primacy of the finance sector, the individualization of everyday life is a key feature of the ideology and related theories and public policies that govern the new world order. In Chapter 2, I argued that in reality human relationships are at the heart of any society. Production of goods and services is a cooperative venture. I gave the example of the chemical plant where I worked in Chicago. Machine operators worked together with material movers and maintenance mechanics to get the product through the machine and ready for shipment. Our product was critical to the steel-making process. So the workers and management in the steel mills that were located 10 miles from our plant depended on us for their own production. All of society is like that. This is what a society is. Markets, I have argued in this book, are no exception to this. They are a social creation. The rules and regulations that govern their operation, the buying power of the money that is exchanged, and their geographical reach are all created by groups of people acting cooperatively. It is through this social process that our own self-development occurs. This is the meaning of the term "social individual." Since society is by nature social, our development as individuals is similarly a cooperative venture. We learn through our interaction with others.

The individualization of everyday life, however, promotes the illusion that society is simply the sum of the individuals who live in it. And markets in such a society are a product of nature, like trees, water, fish, and deer. Our relation to them is strictly individual. The theories and related policies of the new world order promote the illusion that markets, not cooperating human beings, make the best decisions and that each individual's relation to every other individual is strictly competitive. As previous chapters have demonstrated, the theories and public policies of the new world order have reduced food, clothing, shelter, and health care to so many commodities whose distribution is determined best by freely functioning competitive markets. It is this illusion that creates the political momentum that can undermine movements to restrict the full mobility of goods, services, and capital and the pursuit of flexible labor markets. The market illusion with its competitive individuals also allows the finance sector to reign with a free hand. Ultimately, this illusion hides the systemic nature of local issues like housing, employment, and living wages because people tend to see these issues in individual terms.

Thus, markets tend to mask the essential social character of life. And in doing so, they undermine the social character of human self-development. But markets in no way replace this social function. The individual who is forced to work two or three temp jobs to survive, the homeless individual who is tethered to the shelter and the day labor agency, the public housing resident who is put out in the streets to search for a nonexistent home are all ruthlessly torn from the social fabric of life. They are reduced to a piece of human capital and are told that the only way they can make things better is to make better investment choices in their capacity to create surplus for others! In the process, their social individuality is taken from them and they are forced into a terrifying and ruthless world of "competitive individuals" with little hope for redemption.

If the primary objective of a challenge to the new world order is to enhance human self-development and if the key road blocks to that development in this era are unrestricted mobility of goods, services, and capital, the primacy of the finance sector, and the individualization of everyday life, we must next ask ourselves, What is it about today's social movements that hamper an effective challenge to the new world order in these terms? With this understanding we can then move on to a more positive note and ask how these social movements might be more effective.

Challenging the New World Order

A problem with today's social movements that are trying to challenge the new world order in both the global and local arenas is that they are grounded in organizing models that were flawed during the Fordist era. And these flaws make them even less able to challenge the road blocks to human development of the present era of the new world order. The labor and community organizing models that evolved in the United States during the Fordist era ultimately represented an accommodation to that system. They did so by seeking to gain a share of its largesse in return for broad support of U.S. foreign policy and a guarantee of relative labor peace that enabled the system to thrive. As a result, both labor and community organizations failed to come to terms with the contradictions, that spawned national, racial, and gender-based inequities. The civil rights, community development, and anti-war movements attacked inequality at home and the war in Vietnam. But they failed to challenge the system that generated these contradictions, and thus also were unable to foresee the fact that a system based on U.S. dominance over the peoples of other nations was not sustainable. What that meant was that the basis for the militancy of civil rights, workers' rights, environmental quality, and community/housing movements was highly vulnerable to the destruction of the Fordist era and the evolution of a new world order.

Demands for a fair share and equal distribution of the largess of the global Fordist system made no sense once the American pie had been gobbled up and seemingly couldn't be replaced. Demands for workplace safety, a humane work pace, and even equal treatment on the job made no sense once the workplace was gone. Our struggles for justice (just us) at Chicago Shortening, the efforts to control the pace of work at Foseco, the struggles of the Wisconsin Steel workers, and the efforts of the Solo Cup workers to form a union now appear to be historic relics—the subject of individual memoirs, rather than a basis on which to critique ourselves and do better under the present system. Furthermore, demands for better housing and community facilities made no sense once the community was gentrified and the people who were pressing such militant demands were scattered about the region or left homeless, living in the streets and shelters. The very premise of the Fordist era was that the profits from rapidly expanding production and productivity should be shared within the United States. Once that premise was made obsolete by the unraveling of the Fordist period, Alinsky's notion of organizing for power and John L. Lewis' curt statement that labor wanted more were rendered meaningless. Likewise, trying simply to revive these same organizing models in the era of the new world order makes little sense for a number of reasons.

For one thing, these organizing models failed to challenge key tenets of the Fordist system because they were built on the premise that people can only be organized around their perceived self-interest. Basing organizing on self-interest is directly related to the organizing maxim that you always need an "organizing hook" to have a successful campaign. In practice, that maxim involves an appeal to *individual* self-interest. Such a notion places limits on the possibilities for change because it negates the social dimension of everyday life. In the new world order this limitation is profound due to the fact that the individualization of everyday life is critical to making the system work and directly undermines self-development. Conversely, the affirmation of the social individual—the centrality of human relationships in everyday life—potentially presents a profound challenge to the new world order. The declaration, for example, that housing, health care, or a living wage are human rights directly confronts their commodification under the rules of the new world order by insisting on placing them in a social context. This necessarily moves beyond self-interest or individualistic notions of power because you are trying to unite people with and without these things around the proposition that everyone should have them.

But is it possible to move beyond narrowly defined self-interest in a period where individualism is so deeply ingrained? A simple observation of all sorts of human behavior suggests that the answer to this question is clearly, yes. Most recently, we can observe the growth of student movements against sweatshops. Where is the self-interest here? Or we can look to the broad movement backed by many established churches for the cancellation of debt in the developing world. Where is the self-interest here? Historically, the same observation can be made. Most social progress has come about when the emergence of the social dimension that is so central to our lives becomes the organizing principle for change. People have been willing to die for various causes. Death can hardly be considered in one's self-interest. But even at a more mundane level, a labor strike is rarely in the self-interest of individual workers either. When we struck at Chicago Shortening in the late 1970s when the manufacturing sector was beginning to decline, there was no way any financial gain from that strike would ever make up for the loss in pay suffered during its duration. Moreover, the potential to lose the strike as well as our jobs (which is what happened) was high. And every worker knew it. In this case there was a principle at stake. The worker who joked that "there ain't no justice, just us" was summing up that principle. We had a social interest that was based on a common cause in opposing a company and a union that were colluding to thwart our collective will.

The social interest that defines social individualism has a philosophical basis that explains these departures from the John L. Lewis–Saul Alinsky notions of individualistic self-interest. As I discussed in Chapter 2, the fact that money price dominates and undermines other conceptions of value contains within it a contradiction. The historic division between use value and exchange value is the basis of class divisions that are manifested in exploitation and alienation. These manifestations have the capacity to awaken a consciousness of our social individuality. I gave the example of the chemical plant where the maintenance workers supported a relatively unskilled worker who had threatened a foreman because we understood the class-based reasons for his behavior. In more recent times I have witnessed a similar phenomenon in efforts to promote dialogue between workers in the United States and Mexico. U.S. workers who, goaded by a politician or union leader, may grumble about "Mexicans taking our jobs," are utterly transformed when they have the opportunity to talk to those Mexicans.

There is a very moving film, *From the Mountains to the Maquiladoras*, made by the Tennessee Industrial Renewal Network (TIRN) that documents a trip made by unemployed women workers from Tennessee to visit the workers in Mexico who "took their jobs." The Tennessee women visit the factory that now makes the products they used to make, talk to the plant manager about pay and working conditions, and then visit their counterparts in the filthy barrios where they are forced to live. Before our eyes the Tennessee and Mexican women begin to see themselves as part of a common class. The first reaction of one Tennessee woman was to burst into tears and cry, "I'm so ashamed of what my country has done!" But when she returned to the United States, her tears turned to anger and determination. At the end of the film, she gives a militant speech at a congressional hearing, opposing NAFTA. She calls on legislators to support basic principles of human and workers' rights and the protection of the environment. This went far beyond any notion of self-interest.

The Tennessee women illustrate a second limitation of the Lewis–Alinsky model that is specific to the new world order. Organizing for power based on self-interest almost always is confined to a particular place. Community organizing assumes that the place basis of self-interest is a geographical area that delineates a "turf" or a neighborhood. Fordist era labor organizing defined self-interest in terms of a particular workplace. At times, place-based organizations will unite to include an entire state or the United States as a whole when they seek legislation. In the early 1970s, there were debates about whether it was possible to unite community and labor organizations to encompass both types of places. Alinsky did this in his Back of the Yards work. But the labor and community movements drew apart after that. In the 1980s, more progressive elements in the labor movement formed Jobs With Justice. They tried to unite workers to support social and economic justice efforts in workplaces other than their own and today many chapters of Jobs With Justice try to unite labor and community organizations. Yet all of these efforts face the difficulties inherent in treating place in static terms.

Previous chapters and other studies have demonstrated how the new world order is reconstructing space, place, and time.[7] This reconstruction undermines the militancy that is required for meaningful social change. We have seen how global rules that promote mobility can easily shut down workplaces and open new ones on the other side of the world. We have seen how global capital markets can drive up land values in a Chicago neighborhood and in the process displace the militant residents who were at the heart of the community organization and bring in wealthy residents who tear apart the place basis of that organization. The social construction of space, place, and time is dynamic. That construction itself can be part of the organizing project. But the Lewis–Alinsky model treats these conceptions as permanent, thus limiting what is possible.

A third limitation of the prevailing organizing model relates to the issue of the extent to which certain things can change. In Chapter 2 I argued that key features of the social order appear to be permanent, and this forces movements based on self-interest to define self-interest in terms of these features. In the new world order these features include the unrestricted mobility of goods, services, and capital; labor market flexibility; expanded credit; living standards as commodities; and the individualization of everyday life. Chapter 2 also discussed David Harvey and Raymond Williams' idea that society constructs permanencies that provide necessary boundaries and starting points for everyday living and for organizing as well. But such permanencies, as necessary as they are, also place limits on what we do.

To get out of this dilemma it is necessary to redraw the boundaries of the organizing project through a different conception of what are considered to be the permanencies we are willing to live with. Any social movement and the organizing model on which it is based must address key questions relating to the issue of permanence. What are the goals and objectives of our movement? What do we consider to be changeable and what do we consider permanent (from the perspective of a particular organizing project)? In part, the answers to these questions should be informed by what we consider to be the key features of the present period. But, as Chapter 2 argued, they are also driven by the stance taken on two philosophical divides. Does change originate through institutions or people, and are things naturally static or changing?

The first question is one of locating the change agent that originates the process of change itself. Much of the current debate over policy in the political arena limits this question to which institution should be dominant, government or markets? But both of these leave out people. I argued in Chapter 2 that while markets mask social relations that are fundamental to the goal of human self-development, government must preserve the appearance that wealth comes out of exchange relations. That means that while government can be used to develop policies that can aid a social movement, the state cannot be the change agent itself because the state is organized to preserve essential elements of the social order. The organizing project must treat people as the subject of the project rather than its object (treating people as so many bodies to protest, lobby, and change laws or elect politicians).

In fairness to Alinsky, he argued that the organizer should keep an arms length relationship between government and community organizations. Accepting money from government agencies and running political candidates was once taboo. Nevertheless, the objective of such organizing was to get a seat at the table when governments (or private companies) were making decisions related to the organizing project. In the late 1960s and throughout the 1970s, many Alinsky-style activists argued for a closer relationship to government and for a more active role in electoral politics. The post–Bretton Woods labor movement in the United States established close ties with the Democratic Party by forming political action committees that lobbied and supported political candidates. This carried over to local politics through close ties between city and state labor federations and Democratic Party politicians. This evolution on both the labor and community sides began when Saul Alinsky tried to negotiate with Chicago political boss Edward J. Kelly in the 1930s. In the process he successfully brokered labor's political support for Mayor Kelly's political machine in return for the mayor's support for the Packinghouse Worker's union drive.

In many instances, today's organizing agendas are driven by strategies to change legislation. That certainly was the case with the Citizens Trade Campaign activities that I discussed in the previous chapter. And that focus created some of the tensions I referred to. That included the tension between the work of opposing NAFTA and the effort to build a multinational alliance. The narrow legislative focus also limited the role of various local social and economic justice efforts around housing and employment in the anti-NAFTA project. It also limited the scope of affordable housing organizing at the local level. The Coalition to Protect Public Housing, for example, lacks an analysis that sees the destruction of public housing in Chicago as being driven in part by global capital markets. If they did, they might see the anti-NAFTA and anti-FTAA work as a part of their own. Instead, organizers determined that a particular legislative initiative (the application of current federal housing legislation to Chicago) could be an "organizing hook," capable of mobilizing people around their perceived self-interest. The Seattle WTO organizer who was quoted in Chapter 2 as saying "we educate to organize" conceived of education as a presentation of the organizing hook. Such an organizing project is self-limiting because it is stuck with existing perceptions of self-interest. There is no room for the development of new ways of thinking. Such a limitation not only leaves out the social dimension of everyday life but also accepts the boundaries imposed by the present system as permanencies.

A second divide discussed in Chapter 2 is whether the natural state of things is permanent or changing. Assuming that things are basically static and can be changed only through external intervention lends itself to the institutional view of change where boundaries are determined by the organizers' estimate of "political climate" or "what is practical." Alternatively, if one takes the position that the basis for change can be found in the contradictions within the social order, the organizing project tends to seek to uncover those contradictions that make the system most vulnerable and focus organizing on them. Finding these contradictions can be a social process through which people identify the key barriers to their own self-development as part of a dialogue with organizers, who can situate this experience in the larger context of the new world order.

What, then, are criteria for organizing models that can challenge the new world order, potentially bringing together the two lines of resistance that have begun to form? Based on the philosophic perspectives described above and their concretization in the previous chapters, I suggest four:

- Organizing to contest the terms of the new world order must replace Lewis–Alinsky self-interest with an approach based on the alternative of social interest that is built on solidarity.
- Such organizing should transcend the limits of a static conception of space, place, and time by making a social reconstruction of these concepts a feature of the organizing project.
- The organizing model must view people as subjects of the project.
- The project should organize around contradictions identified by project subjects.

Beyond Self-Interest

An alternative organizing principle to self-interest is solidarity. But the notion of solidarity can mean different things. It does not always counterpose the sovereign consumer to the social individual. Adolph Reed Jr. has argued that solidarity, as practiced by many organizations supporting movements in the developing world, is part of the conceptual family of noblesse oblige.[8] Activities based on this conception make an appeal to people in the United States to use their privileged position to support other people in another place. Yet this sort of appeal is another form of individualism that can easily be accommodated by the new world order. Each person offers solidarity as a form of individual philanthropy. Compromises can easily be made to placate the moral sensibilities of the givers of solidarity that not only leave out the beneficiaries of this solidarity but also keep the basic system intact. It is also subject to individuals checking their busy schedules to determine how many acts of solidarity they have time for. Noble obligations can be ranked based on which the individual feels are most worthy. An easy compromise, new personal obligations, divisions within the ranks of the recipients of solidarity, or a "more worthy" cause can cause the population of solidarity groups to ebb and flow.

The fundamental problem with solidarity based on doing something for others someplace else is that it creates a division between the giver and the recipient of the solidarity that is also a fundamental political division. The providers of solidarity perceive their interests in the activity in different terms than those who are its objects. And there is often a reluctance to see the recipients of solidarity as the subjects of their own liberation struggle. This fundamental division can lead to the undoing of the solidarity group itself.

But there is another type of solidarity that does not have such a division. The principle behind early (pre–Bretton Woods) trade union organizing in the United States was that "an injury to one is an injury to all."[9] Acts of solidarity included everyone involved. When IWW workers rode the rails to participate in strikes in another part of the country, they were doing so based on their view that they had a class interest in supporting strikers. They were doing it for themselves as part of a class—as social individuals. They did not seek financial gain as individuals, nor did they participate out of moral obligation. The same was true of the "flying squadrons" in the early days of the CIO.

This form of solidarity seeks to broaden its base by enlarging understanding of the content of common interests. In Brazil, for example, the trade union movement (CUT) began in the 1970s to unite with community organizations, women's organizations, and environmental and human rights groups on the basis of class solidarity. Eventually they created a political party (Workers Party). In Mexico in the 1990s, an independent union formation, the FAT, formed a broader class alliance, the RMALC, to oppose the North American Free Trade Agreement. In the United States Jobs With Justice and the Labor Party are basically organized around this form of solidarity.

Within such a formation, it becomes possible to construct the borders of the organizing project based on an expanding notion of social justice. First, because this is a solidarity not limited by the individualism of self-interest, it is possible to go beyond seeing justice in terms of market access, thus challenging the reduction of value to exchange value and the equation of social justice with individual freedom.[10] It is also possible to move beyond redistributive forms of justice (for example, fair share) to challenge fundamental aspects of the new world order as a form of the system of production. Building solidarity that goes beyond individual self-interest can thus be at the center of the organizing project when it is built on the principle that an injury to one is an injury to all. The concrete implication of this is the conception of an organizing campaign centered on aspects of the standard of living—housing, living wage jobs, health care, and food—opposing their commodification that has turned them into pure exchange value. Such a campaign can be built on the class interest that would dictate a decent standard of living as a human right. It also can challenge any aspect of the new world order that would place limits or qualifications on those rights. Such a conception of solidarity thus meets the basic issue posed in the previous chapter: how to bring together opposition to global decisions with organizations concerned with the local collisions.

Transcending the Limits of Space, Place, and Time

Solidarity has the potential to include in the organizing project a social reconstruction of space, place, and time that breaks the limits imposed by a militancy that treats these dimensions as permanencies. This is done in part by expanding class solidarity beyond the geographical borders of neighborhood, region, or nation. If the injury of low living standards in Mexico is seen as an injury to all in a class sense, solidarity with Mexican efforts for everything from better housing to a living wage is no longer something we in the United States do for someone else somewhere else. It is central to the class interests that transcend any place. The goal of the organizing project is to create a place that is no longer defined simply in terms of geography. Spatial relationships must meet human needs rather than seeking one-sided efficiencies that leave such needs out of the calculation. The goal of organizing, of building solidarity, is for the connections that define the social individual to encompass the globe. This could lead to international projects that force the movement of capital, goods, and services to contribute to the human rights of people throughout the world. Barriers to mobility thus include a vision of the purpose of mobility. And mobility can also include the mobility of labor and a challenge to the notion of labor market flexibility. Such a project also challenges the fundamental system of credit expansion and speculation since finance can be forced to serve human needs rather than be treated as an end in itself.

Human Beings as Subject of the Organizing Project

Most organizing models today are based on the notion that dominant social institutions and structures constrain human behavior. This structuralist view of change becomes the basis for the boundaries or permanencies of the organizing project itself. The goal of organizing is to seek some form of greater justice within the constraints offered by immutable social structures, leaving out the possibility for systemic change. As Adolph Reed Jr. puts it, this vantage point "immobilizes by its tendency to view the configuration of power relations existing at a given moment as identical to the limits of possibility."[11] In this approach to organizing, people are the objects rather than the subjects of the organizing project because it is assumed that organizers, party leaders, and intellectuals understand the limits of structure and can formulate the set of demands that has the best chance of success. Yet, as I argued in earlier chapters, it is the contradiction between the innate effort toward self-development and the systemic barriers to that effort that give rise not only to organized resistance to various manifestations of those barriers but also a vision of possibilities for alternatives—something new. The perspective that sees human beings as the subjects of their own liberation gears the organizing project toward increasing the limits of possibility by facilitating the sharing of experiences with a widening network of social individuals and encouraging reflection on the meaning of those experiences.

Contradiction and Change

Dialectical philosophy suggests that overcoming contradictions is a process through which we initially seek to challenge the present order. In Chapter 2, I discussed how the tension between use value and exchange value is the basis for exploitation and alienation. As money price subsumes all other aspects of value, self-development is thwarted. Contradictions in everyday life are generated from this process. And it is the effort of people to articulate these contradictions concretely and to resist them that generates an organizing agenda that is based on people as subjects.

This notion of change has implications for how we draw boundaries that define an organizing project. Today's institutions, particularly governments, are geared toward preserving the appearance that wealth comes solely through exchange relations. In the specific context of the new world order, the state preserves the key components of the present system—individuality, the mobility of goods, services, and capital, flexible labor markets, the key role of credit expansion and speculation. The state carries out this function by constructing these features as permanencies. In this sense, the state and related social institutions and regulations are external unifiers that hold the system together. For this reason they can never be *agents* of change itself. Diverting all organizational resources into changing institutions and rules, therefore, places limits on the potential of the organizing project. There is a tendency to make rule change *the* objective of the project. That tendency was responsible for many of the tensions between CTC and ART described in the previous chapter. A single-minded focus on external unifiers—legislation, better government officials, changing the rules of the IMF or World Bank—leaves out both the people as subjects of the organizing drive and an examination of the internal processes that can suggest different boundaries for the organizing project. If people in the course of their everyday lives experience impediments to their self-development, they also experience contradictions as part of the internal processes that define their reality.

In sum, an alternative to Lewis–Alinsky organizing models is based on the notion of solidarity rather than self-interest; the social reconstruction of space, place, and time from the perspective of people being organized; viewing these people as the subjects of the project and developing project permanencies or boundaries through a participatory search for contradictions. This approach can better challenge the boundaries imposed by the new world order and bring together the two lines of resistance that are already emerging.

Directions

How can such an approach be implemented? Can we conceive of concrete activities that can more effectively combat the new world order? Can we build on work that has occurred during the past decade and that appears to be increasing in intensity as I write this? By way of conclusion, I wish to address these questions.

This book has demonstrated that in the United States the shift from Fordism to a new world order has generated a shift in urban policy. Impacts on housing, employment and wages, public assistance, and local politics were featured in Chapters 4–7. These impacts have also generated social movements that are not consciously linked to the new world order and often employ tactics that are drawn from the Fordist order. Yet, the local collisions described in these chapters demonstrate that the terms of the new world order make the problem of affordable housing and the demand for living wage job security different than it was in the previous era. This means that there is an organic link between a challenge to the development model imbedded in the FTAA or WTO and the social movements at the local level that seek affordable housing, rights for day laborers, and demands for living wages. Effectively combating the new world order, therefore, means developing this link in our approaches to organizing.

This link simply cannot be made through external propaganda, legislative campaigns, and big events such as the demonstrations in Seattle or elsewhere. It may be possible to get people active in housing and employment issues to call their congressional representative and march at a big event. That was done during the anti-NAFTA campaign. But when the vote is taken and the demonstration is over, those activists will be back to working on "their issue." And the base of the local organizing campaigns—ordinary people who are not activists, people who are in need of homes and living wage jobs—are likely never to be engaged in the bigger picture at all.

My experience with popular education suggests that through dialogue, rather than "education," it is possible to get people to articulate contradictions in their own lives and to link these to the bigger picture. Through such a process, the organic link between the new world order and the lives of ordinary people can become a part of how people think about their lives. Dialogue can concretize the four criteria for organizing discussed above. Questions can be posed that define organizing campaigns. What are the possibilities for acts of solidarity that make sense to us? Why should there be a social reconstruction of space and place and what might that look like to people living and working in a particular location? How can one become the subject of an organizing campaign? What is a contradiction? How does it play out in our lives?

If dialogue rather than education geared to the rigors of legislative campaigns or other external agendas is to define organizing projects to contest the terms of the new world order, we are talking about a long-term perspective. Such a project cannot be viewed as simply the sum of a series of campaigns and demonstrations but as an ongoing process. The process rather than the organizer will, in turn, determine the content and timing of the campaigns and demonstrations.

In exploring this further, let me first discuss the notion of popular education as dialogue and then go on to suggest how such an organizing model could be implemented. Saul Alinsky was an advocate of what he termed "popular education." In his seminal book on organizing, first published in 1946 he put it this way: "In the last analysis the objective for which any democratic movement must strive is the ultimate objective implicit within democracy—popular education."[12]

He never said "educate to organize" but insisted that education should be integral to the organizing work itself. Yet, organizing campaigns that were geared toward power generated the content of that education and power meant getting a bigger slice of the pie. In an afterward to his book that he wrote in 1969 he put it this way:

> At various universities members of the Students for Democratic Society have asked me, "Mr. Alinsky, do you know that what you are doing is organizing the poor for the acceptance of these bourgeois, decadent, degenerate, bankrupt, materialistic, imperialistic, hawkish middle-class values of today's society?" There has been a long silence when I have responded with, "Do you know what the poor of America, or I might add the poor of the world want? They want a bigger and fatter piece of these decadent, degenerate, bankrupt, materialistic, bourgeois values and what goes with it!"[13]

Brazilian educator Paulo Freire offers an alternative view of popular education.[14] To Freire, the purpose of education is not limited to helping people get "what they want." Rather, the purpose of education is to help people become creative, active, critical thinkers—new people. Contrast Freire's view of "what people want" with that of Alinsky.

> Perhaps the greatest tragedy of modern man is his domination by the force of . . . myths and his manipulation by organized advertising, ideological or otherwise. Gradually, without even realizing the loss, he relinquishes his capacity for choice; he is expelled from the orbit of decisions.[15]

Freire's pedagogy involves a process of reflection, which leads to action. Preconceived action does not determine the boundaries of that reflection. Action is the product of reflection through dialogue among teachers and students. Such a perspective leaves the door open to changing perspectives on "what people want."

Freire's ideas have been widely applied in many nations to education related to social and economic justice projects. In my own experience, a joint project with the American Friends Service Committee in Chicago has used this approach to help labor unions and community groups develop their own organizing campaigns. For example, a local of the Service Employees International Union (SEIU) asked us to help them understand the relationship between globalization and the privatization of their jobs. We began with a dialogue about the global economy by asking small groups to make drawings of the global economy and their position in it. We created, in Freirian terms, a "code" that became the basis for dialogue that eventually developed the link between the new world order and privatization in Chicago, which threatened their jobs. The process was a long one. We worked with that local for over two years!

Yet, despite its time-consuming nature, this approach can be the basis for building a movement that can effectively challenge the new world order. It is a very time-consuming and labor-intensive process. Organizers would have to hold discussions with social, economic, and environmental justice groups, community-based organizations, and local labor unions throughout the nation. These discussions would be designed to promote the educational campaign and to develop jointly workshops designed to generate critical reflection, while linking their particular situations to the larger picture of the new world order. The process of expanding understanding of local situations could involve the development of the notion of solidarity—what I earlier referred to as social individualism—by introducing other local situations and finding the links among them. The space and place boundaries of linked local situations can lead to a social reconstruction of the meaning of geography. Since this view of popular education is not separated from action, organizing campaigns will become an integral part of the process of popular education itself. But in this case the content of the campaigns and their boundaries will be the result of critical reflection rather than the assessment of organizers of what will work in a particular organizing milieu. And because the content and boundaries of organizing campaigns are the result of critical reflection, the people/students are the subjects of their own liberation.

Such an approach opens up the possibility of challenging the present social construction of value; space, place, and time and the scope of change itself. It brings alive Marx's 1857 vision of the goals of human development:

> What is (wealth) if not a situation where man does not reproduce himself in any determined form, but produces his totality? Where he does not seek to remain something formed by the past but is in an absolute movement of becoming? [16]

Notes

Chapter 1

1. Beatrice Lumpkin, *"Always Bring a Crowd!" The Story of Frank Lumpkin: Steelworker* (New York: International Publishers, 1999).

2. William Julius Wilson, *When Work Disappears: The World of the New Urban Poor* (New York: Knopf, 1996).

3. Richard J. Barnet and John Cavanagh, *Global Dreams: Imperial Corporations in the New World Order* (New York: Simon and Schuster, 1994).

4. Michael E. Porter, *The Competitive Advantage of Nations* (New York: The Free Press, 1990).

5. David Harvey, *Justice, Nature and the Geography of Difference* (Cambridge, Mass.: Blackwell, 1996).

6. Ibid., pp. 69–76.

7. Karl Marx, "Preface to the Critique of Political Economy," in *Collected Works*, vol. 29, Marx: 1857–61 (New York: International Publishers, 1987), p. 263.

8. Raya Dunayevskaya, *Marxism and Freedom: From 1776 Until Today* (Atlantic Highlands, N.J.: Humanities Press, 1982); David Forcacs (ed.), *An Antonio Gramsci Reader: Selected Writings, 1916–35* (New York: Schocken Books, 1988), pp. 18–221.

9. Perry Anderson, "Renewals," *New Left Review*, Second Series, no. 1 (January–February 2000): 5–24.

10. Branko Milanovic, "True World Income Distribution, 1988–1993: First Calculation Based on Household Surveys Alone," World Bank Development Research Group, unpublished draft paper, October 1999.

Chapter 2

1. Barry Bluestone and Bennett Harrison, *The Deindustrialization of America: Plant Closings, Community Abandonment and the Dismantling of Basic Industry* (New York: Basic Books, 1982).

2. Michael J. Piore and Charles F. Sabel, *The Second Industrial Divide: Possibilities for Prosperity* (New York: Basic Books, 1984).

3. Raya Dunayevskaya, *Marxism and Freedom: 1876 Until Today* (Atlantic Highlands, N.J.: Humanities Press, 1982).

4. Karl Marx, "Economic Manuscripts of 1857–58 *(Grundrisse),*" in *Collected Works*, vol. 28 (New York: International Publishers, 1986), pp. 411–12.

5. Stephen S. Roach, "Working Better or Just Harder?" *New York Times*, February 14, 2000.

6. David Harvey, *Justice, Nature and the Geography of Difference* (New York: Blackwell, 1996), pp. 207–326; Sharon Zukin, *Landscapes of Power: From Detroit to Disney World* (Berkeley: University of California Press, 1991); Peter Marcuse and Ronald van Kempen, *Globalizing Cities: A New Spatial Order?* (Oxford, U.K.: Blackwell, 2000); Peter Dreier, John Mollenkopf, and Todd Swanstrom, *Place Matters: Metropolitics for the Twenty-first Century* (Lawrence: University of Kansas Press, 2001).

7. Dreier, Mollonkopf, and Swanstrom, *Place Matters*.

8. David C. Ranney, "The Closing of Wisconsin Steel," in Charles Craypo and Bruce Nissen (eds.), *Grand Designs: The Impact of Corporate Strategies on Workers, Unions and Communities* (Ithaca, N.Y.: ILR), pp. 65–91.

9. Harvey, *Justice, Nature and the Geography of Difference*, pp. 210–47.

10. Lon Grahnke, "6,700 line up for 60 job openings," *Chicago Sun Times*, April 1, 1999, p. 1.

11. Harvey, *Justice, Nature and the Geography of Difference*, pp. 19–45.

12. Ibid., p.8.

13. Karl Marx, "On the Jewish Question," in *Collected Works*, vol. 3 (New York: International Publishers, 1983), p. 147.

14. John Nichols, "Now What? Seattle is Just a Start," *The Progressive* 64, no. 1 (January 2000): 17.

15. Karl Marx, "Economic Manuscripts of 1857–58 (Grundrisse)," in *Collected Works*, vol. 28 (New York: International Publishers, 1986), p. 412.

16. Raya Dunayevskaya, *Philosophy and Revolution: From Hegel to Sartre and from Marx to Mao* (New York: Humanities, 1982), pp. 12–16.

Chapter 3

1. The nature of the crisis of the mid-1970s that brought on the present era is currently being debated. Robert Brenner wrote a comprehensive view that has become a focal point of the debate. See Robert Brenner, "Uneven Development and the Long Downturn," *New Left Review*, no. 229 (1998): 1–265. Much of this debate is collected in two volumes of the journal *Historical Materialism: Research in Critical Marxist Theory*, no. 4 (Summer 1999) and no. 5 (Winter 1999).

2. Melvin Dubofsky, *We Shall Be All: A History of the Industrial Workers of the World* (New York: Quadrangle, 1974); Elizabeth Gurley Flynn, *The Rebel Girl* (New York: International Publishers, 1973); Bill Haywood, *Autobiography of Big Bill Haywood* (New York: International Publishers, 1929); Zinn, *A People's History of the United States: 1492–Present* (New York: HarperCollins, 1999), pp. 323–31; Joyce Kornbluh (ed.), *Rebel Voices: An IWW Anthology* (Ann Arbor: University of Michigan Press, 1964).

3. Beth Sims, *Workers of the World Undermined* (Boston: South End Press, 1992).

4. Michael J. Piore and Charles F. Sabel, *The Second Industrial Divide: Possibilities for Prosperity* (New York: Basic Books, 1984), pp. 106–11.

5. Joseph Collins and John Lear, *Chile's Free Market Miracle: A Second Look* (Oakland, Calif.: Institute for Food and Development Policy, 1995); Anil Hira, *Ideas and Economic Policy in Latin America: Regional, National and Organizationl Case Studies* (Westport, Conn.: Praeger, 1998).

6. From an address to the Economic and Social Council of the United Nations in Geneva in 1984. Cited in Howard Wachtel, *Money Mandarins: The Making of a New Supranational Economic Order* (New York: Pantheon, 1986) p. 137.

7. Organization for Economic Cooperation and Development, *The OECD Jobs Study: Evidence and Explanations, Part II—The Adjustment Potential of the Labour Market* (Paris: OECD, 1994).

8. OECD, *OECD Jobs Strategy: Facts, Analysis and Strategies*, (Paris: OECD, 1994); OECD, *OECD Jobs Study: Implementing the Strategy* (Paris: OECD, 1995). The evolution of "flexible labor market" strategies is discussed in detail in Nikolas Theodore, *Regulating Labor Markets in the Age of Flexibility: Fast Policy and the Political Economy of Workfare* (unpublished Ph.D. dissertation, College of Urban Planning and Public Affairs, University of Illinois Chicago, 2000).

9. Brenner, "The Economics of Global Turbulence"; Fred Mosley, *The Falling Rate of Profit in the Post-War United States Economy* (New York: St. Martin's Press, 1992).

10. "Stateless Monies: A New Face in World Economics," *Business Week*, August 21, 1978, p. 78.

11. For a detailed discussion of this subject, see Wachtel, *Money Mandarins*. Also, Arthur MacEwan, *Debt and Disorder: International Economic Instability and U.S. Imperial Decline* (New York: Monthly Review Press, 1990).

12. Doug Henwood, *Wall Street: How It Works and for Whom* (New York: Verso Press, 1998), p. 223.

13. Wachtel, *Money Mandarins*, p. 120.

14. International Monetary Fund, *International Capital Markets Reports*, 1995, 1996.

15. Lawrence Mishel, Jared Bernstein, and John Schmitt, *The State of Working America: 1998–99* (Ithaca, N.Y.: ILR Press and Economic Policy Institute, 1999), p. 275; Chuck Collins, Betsy Leondar-Wright, and Holly Sklar, *Shifting Fortunes: The Perils of the Growing American Wealth Gap* (Boston: United for a Fair Economy, 1999), pp. 45–53.

16. Robert Pollin, *Deeper in Debt: The Changing Financial Conditions of U.S. Households* (Washington, D.C.: Economic Policy Institute, 1990).

17. Collins, Leondar-Wright, and Sklar, *Shifting Fortunes*, p. 46.

18. *U.S. Statistical Abstract 2000* (Washington, D.C.: U.S. Government Printing Office, 2001).

19. Stephen Brobeck, "Recent Trends in Bank Credit Card Marketing and Indebtedness" (Washington, D.C.: The Consumer Federation of America, July 1998). Cited in Collins, Leondar-Wright, and Sklar, *Shifting Fortunes*, p. 50.

20. Henwood, *Wall Street*, p. 24.

21. The World Bank, *1999 World Development Indicators* (Washington, D.C.: World Bank, 1999).

22. James Crotty, "The Rise and Fall of the Keynesian Revolution in the Age of the Global Marketplace," in Gerald Epstein, Julie Graham, and Jessica Nembhard, for the Center for Popular Economics, *Creating a New World Economy: Forces of Change and Plans for Action* (Philadelphia: Temple University Press, 1993) p. 173.

23. Henwood, *Wall Street*, p. 27.

24. Gerald Epstein, "The U.S. as a Debtor Country," in Epstein, Graham, Nembhard, *Creating a New World Economy*, pp. 205–6.

25. Henwood, *Wall Street*, p. 74.

26. Eric R. Quinones, Associated Press, "Merger Theory: Pay Billions, Save Money, Hope for Quick Profit," 1997.

27. Henwood, *Wall Street*, p. 74.

28. "You are There," *Grants Interest Rate Observer* 18, no. 5 (March 17, 2000).

29. Analysis by Steven Galbraith, an analyst at the investment firm of Sanford C. Berstein & Company, reported in the *New York Times*, March 24, 2000.

30. "You Are There," p. 1.

31. Jefferson Cowie, *Capital Moves: RCA's 70 year Quest for Cheap Labor* (Ithaca, N.Y.: Cornell University Press, 2001).

32. Barry Bluestone and Bennett Harrison, *The Deindustrialization of America* (New York: Basic Books, 1982); Bennett Harrison, *Lean and Mean: The Changing Landscape of Corporate Power in an Age of Flexibility* (New York: Basic Books, 1994), p. 39.

33. Bennett Harrison and Barry Bluestone, *The Great U Turn: Corporate Restructuring and the Polarizing of America* (New York: Basic Books, 1988).

34. Gerald Epstein, Julie Grahan, and Jessica Nembhard, *Creating a New World Economy: Forces of Change and Plans for Political Action* (Philadelphia: Temple University Press, 1993), p. 205.

35. Sarah Anderson, John Cavanagh and Thea Lee, *Field Guide to the Global Economy* (New York: New Press, 2000), p. 51.

36. Ibid., p. 58.

37. Kate Brofenbrenner, "Final Report: The Effects of Plant Closing or Threat of Plant Closing on Right of Workers to Organize," submitted to The Labor Secretariat of the North American Commission for Labor Cooperation by Kate Brofenbrenner, director of Labor Education Research, New York State School of Industrial and Labor Relations, Cornell University, September 30, 1996.

38. Michael J. Piore and Charles F. Sabel, *The Second Industrial Divide: Possibilities for Prosperity* (New York: Basic Books, 1984), pp. 178–81.

39. Robin Broad and John Cavanagh, "No More NICs," in Epstein, "The U.S. as a Debtor Country," pp. 376–90.

40. Ibid., p. 377.

41. The Development GAP (DGAP), "Structural Adjustment Programs and the Environment: 1992 International NGO Forum on World Bank and IMF Adjustment Lending" (Washington, D.C.: DGAP, 1992).

42. Michel Chossudovsky, *The Globalization of Poverty: Impacts of IMF and World Bank Reforms*, (London: Zed Books, 1998); Development GAP, "Questions and Answers About Structural Adjustment" (Washington, D.C.: DGAP, 1992), pp. 45–74.

43. Henwood, *Wall Street*, p. 28.

44. Federal Reserve Bank of New York, *Studies of Causes and Consequences of the*

1989–92 Credit Slowdown. (New York: Federal Reserve Bank of New York, February 1994). This study and its broader implications are discussed by Henwood, *Wall Street*, pp. 153–61.

45.   The World Bank, *1999 World Development Indicators* (Washington D.C.: The International Bank for Reconstruction and Development, 1999), p. 256. Much of the data for the discussion of developing nation debt are taken from World Bank and IMF publications as well as the reports of the Canadian Ecumenical Coalition for Economic Justice. See Ecumenical Coalition for Economic Justice, "Jubilee 2000: Time for Debt Remission," *Economic Justice Report* 8, no. 4 (December 1997); and Ecumenical Coalition for Economic Justice, "Jubilee Movement Shifts the Ground Under G7 Debt Plans," *Economic Justice Report* 10, nos. 1–2. (May 1999). Also see John Dillon, *Turning the Tide: Confronting the Money Traders* (Ottawa and Toronto: Canadian Centre for Policy Alternatives and the Ecumenical Coalition for Economic Justice, 1997).

46.   Inter-Church Coalition on Africa, *Economic Justice Update*, no. 13, 1996. Cited in Ecumenical Coalition for Economic Justice, "Jubilee 2000."

47.   Hyman Minsky, *Stabilizing an Unstable Economy* (New Haven: Yale University Press, 1986), pp. 206–20. Also see a discussion of Minsky in Henwood, *Wall Street*, pp. 222–24.

48.   The following account of the Chicago Board of Trade and the Chicago Mercantile Exchange is based on Bob Tamarkin, *The Merc: The Emergence of a Global Financial Powerhouse* (New York: HarperBusiness, 1993). Additional information on the CBOT was collected by the author through interviews and data provided by CBOT officials.

49.   Ibid., p. 181.

50.   Milton Friedman, "The Need for Futures Markets in Currencies," prepared for the Chicago Mercantile Exchange, December 20, 1971. Cited in ibid., p. 185.

51.   These points are developed in greater detail by Henwood, *Wall Street*, pp. 10–82.

52.   Ibid., p. 10.

53.   These figures are all from ibid., p. 16.

54.   This is the position of finance analyst and economics professor Robert J.Shiller in *Irrational Exuberance* (Princeton: Princeton University Press, 2000).

55.   Ibid., pp. 4–13.

56.   Henwood, *Wall Street*, p. 72.

57.   Greg Ip, Gary McWilliams, and Suzanne McGee, "Portfolio Profits Boost Bottom Line, But Stir Controversy for Some Firms," *Wall Street Journal*, January 20, 2000.

58.   Ibid.

59.   Henwood, *Wall Street*, p. 51.

60.   The following account of long-term capital management is based on Diana B. Henriques, "Fault Lines of Risk Appear as Market Hero Stumbles," *New York Times*, November 27, 1998, p. 1. Also Nicolas Dunbar, *Inventing Money: The Story of Long Term Capital Management and the Legends Behind it* (New York: Wiley, 2000).

61.   Henwood, *Wall Street*, pp. 84–86; International Monetary Fund, *World Economic Outlook* (Washington, D.C.: IMF, May 1998), pp. 4–5.

62.   Tamarkin, *The Merc*, p. 211.

63.   Peter Dicken, *Global Shift: Transforming the World Economy*, 3rd ed. (London: Paul Chapman, 1998).

64. Sarah Anderson, John Cavanagh, and Thea Lee, *Field Guide to the Global Economy* (New York: New Press, 2000), p. 12.

65. For a detailed breakdown by nation, product, and service see World Bank, *World Development Indicators, 1999* (Washington, D.C.: The World Bank, 1999), pp. 200–23.

66. International Monetary Fund, *International Capital Markets Reports* (New York: IMF, 1995, 1996).

67. James Crotty, Gerald Epstein, and Patricia Kelly, "Multinational Corporations in a Neo-Liberal Regime," in Dean Baker, Gerald Epstein, and Robert Pollin (eds.), *Globalization and Progressive Economic Policy* (New York: Cambridge University Press, 1998), p. 125.

68. Ha-joon Chang, "Globalization, Transnational Corporations, and Economic Development: Can the Developing Countries Pursue Strategic Industrial Policy in a Globalizing World Economy?" in Baker, Epstein, and Pollin, *Globalization and Progressive Economic Policy*, p. 98.

69. Anderson, Cavanagh, and Lee, Field Guide to the Global Economy, p. 66.

70. Ha-joon Chang, "Globalization," p. 98.

71. United Nations Conference on Trade and Development (UNCTAD), Division on Transnational Corporations and Development, *World Investment Report, 1997* (New York: United Nations, 1997).

72. U.S. Department of Commerce, *Survey of Current Business*, February, 1997. Cited in Anderson, Cavanagh, and Lee, *Field Guide to the Global Economy*, p. 29.

73. David Gordon, "The Global Economy: New Edifice or Crumbling Foundations?" *New Left Review* 168 (March/April 1988): 24–65; James H. Mittelman (ed.), *Globalization: Critical Reflections*, International Economy Yearbook, vol. 9 (New York: Rienner, 1996); Paul Hirst and Grahame Thompson, *Globalization in Question* (London: Polity, 1986); Linda Weiss, "Globalization and the Myth of the Powerless State," *New Left Review* 225 (September/October 1997): 3–27; Kenichi Ohmae, *Borderless World: Power and Strategy in the Inter-Linked Economy* (New York: Collins, 1990); Kevin Cox (ed.), *Spaces of Globalization: Reasserting the Power of the Local* (New York: Guilford, 1997).

74. This position is developed in the work of William Julius Wilson. See the following: William Julius Wilson, *The Declining Significance of Race: Blacks and Changing American Institutions* (Chicago: University of Chicago Press, 1978); William Julius Wilson, *The Truly Disadvantaged: The Inner City, the Underclass and Public Policy* (Chicago: University of Chicago Press, 1987); William Julius Wilson, *When Work Disappears: The World of the New Urban Poor* (New York: Knopf, 1996).

75. "Jail & Jobs," *Left Business Observer*, no. 88 (February 1999): 8.

76. United Nations Development Project, *Human Development Report 1998* (New York: Oxford University Press, 1998), pp. 46–65.

77. There are many examples of these arguments. One very concise source is Organization for Economic Development and Cooperation, *Open Markets Matter: The Benefits of Trade and Investment Liberalization* (Geneva: OECD, 1998). For a discussion of the problems generated by the global system from the same perspective, see Robert B. Zoellick, Peter D. Sutherland, and Hisashi Owada, *21st Century Strategies of the Trilateral Countries: In Concert or Conflict?* A Report to the Trilateral Commission, 53 (New York: The Trilateral Commission, September 1999).

78. Branko Milanovic, "True World Income Distribution, 1988 and 1993: First Cal-

culation Based on Household Surveys Alone," World Bank Development Research Group, unpublished draft paper, October 1999.

79. "Global Shares," *Left Business Observer,* no. 93 (February 10, 2000): 5.

80. Anderson, Cavanagh, and Lee, *Field Guide to the Global Economy,* p. 67.

Chapter 4

1. Douglas Ross and Robert Friedman, "The Emerging Third Wave: New Economic Development Strategies for the 1990s,"*The Entrepreneurial Economy Review of the Corporation for Enterprise Development* 9, no. 1 (Autumn 1990); Daniel Bell, *The Coming of Post Industrial Society* (New York: Basic Books, 1974); Lester Thurow, *Head to Head: The Coming Economic Battle Among Japan, Europe and America* (New York: William Morrow), 1992.

2. Michael E. Porter, *The Competitive Advantage of Nations* (New York: The Free Press, 1990); Michael E. Porter, "The Competitive Advantage of the Inner City," *Harvard Business Review* 73 (May/June 1995): 55–71; Michael E. Porter, "New Strategies for Inner City Development," *Economic Development Quarterly* 11, no. 1 (February 1997): 11–27.

3. Barry Bluestone and Bennett Harrison, *The Deindustrialization of America: Plant Closings, Community Abandonment and the Dismantling of Basic Industry* (New York: Basic Books, 1982); Bennett Harrison and Barry Bluestone, *The Great U Turn: Corporate Restructuring and the Polarizing of America* (New York: Basic Books, 1988); Bennett Harrison, *Lean and Mean: The Changing Landscape of Corporate Power in an Age of Flexibility* (New York: Basic Books, 1994).

4. Robert Reich, *Work of Nations: Preparing Ourselves for 21st Century Capitalism* (New York: Vintage Books, 1992); Jeremy Rifkin, *The End of Work: The Decline of the Global Labor Force and the Dawn of the Post-Market Era* (New York: G.P. Putnam's Sons, 1995).

5. For a full critique of Jeremy Rifkin's book, see David C. Ranney, "Seeking New Paradigms for Economic Development: A Review Essay," *Economic Development Quarterly* 11, no. 2 (May 1997): 181–88.

6. "Mergers Nearing New High: Wall Street Buoyed by Advisory Fees," *Chicago Tribune,* September 30, 1995, Section 3, pp. 1, 3; Ronald E. Yeats, "Shining Surface of U.S. Business Hides Rising Fury," *Chicago Tribune,* October 1, 1995, p. 1.

7. Much of this section is based on two studies I did of the Wisconsin Steel closing. See David C. Ranney, "The Closing of Wisconsin Steel," in Charles Craypo and Bruce Nissen (eds.), *Grand Designs: The Impact of Corporate Strategies on Workers, Unions and Communities* (Ithaca, N.Y.: ILR Press, 1993), pp. 65–91; David C. Ranney, "Summary of Interviews With Former Wisconsin Steel Workers" (Chicago: University of Illinois at Chicago Center for Urban Economic Development, 1984). Quotations not footnoted are from personal interviews conducted by the author.

8. *Business Week,* September 12, 1977, pp. 96–97.

9. David Bensman and Roberta Lynch, *Rusted Dreams: Hard Times in a Steel Community* (New York: McGraw Hill, 1987), p. 42.

10. *Crain's Chicago Business,* November 15, 1982, p. 22.

11. Bensman and Lynch, *Rusted Dreams,* p. 50.

12. Ibid., p. 60.

13. *Crain's Chicago Business,* November 15, 1982, p. 35.

14. Ibid., p. 31.

15. Ibid., p. 34.

16. David C. Ranney, "Transnational Investment and Job Loss: The Case of Chicago," #350A (Chicago: University of Illinois at Chicago Center for Urban Economic Development, October 1992).

17. These vignettes are based on a special appendix to my report cited earlier. William Cecil, "Transnational Investment and Job Loss: The Case of Chicago, Appendix 2, Plant and Job Loss in the City of Chicago to Transnational Corporate Parents by Firm, 1980–90" (Chicago: University of Illinois at Chicago Center for Urban Economic Development, 1992).

18. Ranney, "Transnational Investment and Job Loss."

19. David C. Ranney and William Cecil, "Transnational Investment and Job Loss in Chicago: Impacts on Women, African-Americans and Latinos," #350D (Chicago: University of Illinois at Chicago Center for Urban Economic Development, January 1993).

20. Julie S. Putterman et al. "Chicago Steelworkers: The Cost of Unemployment" (Chicago: Local 65, United Steelworkers of America and Research and Advocacy Department of Hull House Association, January 1985).

21. "Displaced Workers, 1979–83," Bulletin 2240 (Washington, D.C.: U.S. Department of Labor, Bureau of Labor Statistics, July, 1985).

22. Paul Krugman, "In Praise of Cheap Labor: Bad Jobs are Better than no Jobs At all." <www.slate.com/Dismal/97-03-20/Dismal.asp>, March 20, 1997.

Chapter 5

1. Pierre Clavel and Wim Wiewel, *Harold Washington and the Neighborhoods: Progressive City Government in Chicago 1983–87* (New Brunswick: Rutgers University Press, 1991), p. 8.

2. Roger Biles, *Richard J. Daley: Politics, Race and the Governing of Chicago* (DeKalb: Northern Illinois University Press, 1995), pp. 48–50.

3. Ibid., pp. 77–78.

4. Dempsey J. Travis, *"Harold," the People's Mayor: The Authorized Biography of Mayor Harold Washington* (Chicago: Urban Research Press, 1989) p. 74.

5. Biles, *Richard J. Daley,* pp. 98–100.

6. Ibid., pp. 88–90.

7. Ibid., p. 172.

8. Ibid., p. 144.

9. John M. Allswang, "Richard J. Daley: America's Last Boss," in Paul M. Green and Melvin G. Holli (eds.), *The Mayors: The Chicago Political Tradition* (Carbondale: Southern Illinois University Press, 1987), p. 148.

10. Biles, *Richard J. Daley,* p. 205.

11. Alberta M. Sbragia, "Finance Capital and the City," in M. Gottdiener (ed.), *Cities in Stress: A New Look at the Urban Crisis,* vol. 30, Urban Affairs Annual Reviews (Beverly Hills: Sage, 1986), pp. 199–220.

12. Biles, *Richard J. Daley,* 234.

13. Paul Kleppner, *Chicago Divided: The Making of a Black Mayor* (DeKalb: Northern Illinois University Press, 1985), p. 134.

14. Clavel and Wiewel, *Harold Washington and the Neighborhoods*, p. 27.

15. Dennis R. Judd, "Electoral Coalitions, Minority Mayors and the Contradictions in the Municipal Policy Agenda," in M. Gottdiener (ed.), *Cities in Stress: A New Look at the Urban Crisis*, Urban Affairs Annual Reviews, vol. 30 (Beverly Hills: Sage, 1986), p. 145.

16. Larry Bennett, "Harold Washington and the Black Urban Regime," *Urban Affairs Quarterly* 28, no. 3 (March 1993): 423–40. Also see Judd, "Electoral Coalitions."

17. Adolph Reed Jr. "The Black Urban Regime: Structural Origins and Constraints," in *Stirrings in the Jug: Black Politics in the Post-Segregation Era* (Minneapolis: University of Minnesota Press, 1999), pp. 79–115.

18. Ibid., p. 102.

19. Judd, "Electoral Coalitions."

20. Reed "The Black Urban Regime," pp. 84–85.

21. Sbragia, "Finance Capital," p. 213.

22. Ibid.

23. Robert Mier and Kari J. Moe, "Decentralized Development: From Theory to Practice," in *Harold Washington and the Neighborhoods Progressive City Government in Chicago*, Pierre Clavel and Wim Wiewel (eds.) (New Brunswick, N.J.: Rutgers University Press, 1991), pp. 73–74.

24. Ibid., p. 73. Emphasis is mine.

25. Travis, *"Harold,"* p. 158.

26. Robert Mier, Kari Moe, and Irene Sherr, "Strategic Planning and the Pursuit of Reform, Economic Development, and Equity," *Journal of the American Planners Association* (Summer 1986): 300.

27. Pierre Clavel, *The Progressive City: Planning and Participation 1969–84* (New Brunswick: Rutgers University Press, 1985), p. 177.

28. Mier, Moe, and Sherr, "Strategic Planning," p. 300. Emphasis added by the author.

29. "Final Report of the Mayor's Task Force on Steel and Southeast Chicago" (Chicago: City of Chicago, 1986), p. 2.

30. Ann Markusen et. al., "Steel and Southeast Chicago: Reasons and Opportunities for Industrial Renewal" (Chicago: Center for Urban Affairs and Policy Research, Northwestern University, November 1985).

31. This section was written jointly with Patricia A. Wright. It appeared in a different form in David C. Ranney, Patricia A. Wright, and Tingwei Zhang, *Citizens, Local Government and the Development of Chicago's Near South Side*, Discussion Paper 90 (Geneva: United Nations Research Institute for Social Development, November 1997).

32. Press release and statement made to the Chicago Plan Commission, South Armour Square Neighborhood Coalition, December 8, 1988.

33. Mier and Moe, "Decentralized Development," p. 86.

34. *Chicago Tribune*, December 7, 1986, section 1, p. 1.

35. Arthur Johnson, "Municipal Administration and the Sports Franchise Relocation Issue," *Public Administration Review* 43 (November/December 1983).

36. Robert A. Baade and Richard F. Dye, "Sports Stadiums and Area Development: A Critical Review," *Economic Development Quarterly* 2 (August 1988): 265–75.

37. "Battle over New Comiskey Park Goes into Extra Innings," *Chicago Enterprise,* January 1990.

38. South Armour Square Neighborhood Coalition focus group discussion, February 27, 1996.

39. Plaintiffs' Statement of Additional Facts which Require Denial of Defendants' Motion for Summary Judgement, for *Dorothy Laramore, et al. v. The Illinois Sports Facility Authority*, a municipal corporation, The City of Chicago, a municipal corporation, and the Chicago White Sox, LTD, a limited partnership. December 5, 1994.

40. Ibid.

41. Focus group discussion, February 27, 1996.

42. Personal interview, March 13, 1996.

43. Dennis R. Judd, "Symbolic Politics and Urban Policies: Why African Americans Got So Little from the Democrats," in Adolph Reed Jr. (ed.), *Without Justice for All: The New Liberalism and Our Retreat from Racial Equality* (New York: Westview Press, 1999), pp. 131–35.

44. For a different view of this from Mayor Washington's Commissioner of Planning, see Elizabeth Hollander, "The Department of Planning Under Harold Washington," in Clavel and Wiewel, *Harold Washington and the Neighborhoods*, pp. 128–31.

Chaper 6

1. Gary Dymski and Dorene Isenberg, "Housing Finance in the Age of Globalization: From Social Housing to Life-cycle Risk," in Dean Baker, Gerald Epstein, and Robert Pollin (eds.), *Globalization and Progressive Economic Policy* (New York: Cambridge University Press, 1998), pp. 223–24.

2. Dennis R. Judd, "Symbolic Politics and Urban Policies: Why African Americans Got So Little from Democrats," in Adolph Reed Jr. (ed.), *Without Justice for All: The New Liberalism and Our Retreat From Racial Equality* (New York: Westview Press, 1999), pp. 123–50.

3. Alexander von Hoffman, "A Study in Contradictions: The Origins and Legacy of the Housing Act of 1949," *Housing Policy Debate* 11, no. 2 (2000): 299–326.

4. Dymski and Isenberg, "Housing Finance," pp. 219–39.

5. Neil Smith, *The New Urban Frontier: Gentrfication and the Revanchist City* (New York: Routledge, 1996), p.116.

6. Peter Marcuse, "Interpreting 'Public Housing' History," *Journal of Architectural and Planning Research* 12, no. 3 (Autumn 1995): 240–58.

7. Arnold Hirsch, *Making the Second Ghetto: Race and Housing in Chicago, 1940–1960* (New York: Cambridge University Press, 1983), pp. 122–24; Larry Bennett and Adolph Reed Jr. (ed.), "The New Face of Urban Renewal," in Adolph Reed Jr., *Without Justice for All: The New Liberalism and Our Retreat from Racial Equality* (Boulder, Colo.: Westview Press, 1999), p. 179.

8. Brian Rogal, "CHA Tenant Evictions Jump as Buildings Fall," *The Chicago Reporter* 27, no. 11 (December 1998).

9. *Gautreaux v. Chicago Housing Authority,* 296f.Supp.907 (NDIL 1969).

10. Dennis R. Judd, "Symbolic Politics and Urban Policies: Why African Americans Got So Little from the Democrats," in Reed, *Without Justice for All,* pp. 123–50.

11. Ibid., p. 129.

12. Ibid., p. 141.

13. Illinois Assisted Housing Research and Action Project, First Annual Report, 1999, Statewide Housing Action Coalition, 1999.

14. Great Cities Institute, "For Rent: Housing Options in the Chicago Region, Regional Rental Market Analysis Summary Report" (Chicago: Great Cities Institute, University of Illinois Chicago, November, 1999.

15. Nathaie P. Voorhees Center for Neighborhood and Community Improvement, University of Illinois at Chicago, 2002.

16. Larry Bennett, "The Shifting Terrain of Neighborhood Politics," in Nancy Kleniewski and Gordana Rabrenovic (eds.), *Research in Politics and Society: Community Politics and Policy,* vol. 7 (New York: JAI Press, 1999), pp. 21–41.

17. Alexander Von Hoffman, "High Ambitions: The Past and Future of American Low-Income Housing Policy," in David P. Varady, Wolfgang Preiser, and Francis P. Russell (ed.), *New Directions for Urban Public Housing* (New Brunswick, N.J: Center for Urban Policy Research, 1998), p. 16.

18. Great Cities Institute, November, 1999.

19. Ibid.

20. Ibid.

21. Chicago Housing Authority, "Draft Plan for Transformation, Improving Public Housing in Chicago and the Quality of Life," September 30, 1999.

22. Rick Lazio, January 7, 1997. From website of Congressman Rick Lazio, <www.house.gov/lazio>.

23. Rick Lazio, press release, October 5, 1998.

24. Louise Hunt, Mary Schulhof, and Stephen Holmquist, "Summary of the Quality Housing and Work Responsibility Act of 1998 (Title V of P.L. 105–276)," Office of Policy, Program and Legislative Initiatives, Office of Public and Indian Housing, December 1998.

25. Lisa Ranghelli, "The Immediate Crisis in Public and Assisted Housing: More Than a Million Affordable Homes at Risk," Center for Community Change, January 1999.

26. John Gilderbloom and Richard Appelbaum, *Rethinking Rental Housing* (Philadelphia: Temple University Press, 1988).

27. John B. Corgel, Halbert C. Smith, and David C. Ling, *Real Estate Perspectives: An Introduction to Real Estate,* 3rd ed. (New York: Irwin McGraw-Hill, 1998), pp. vi–vii. Emphasis is ours.

28. Dymski and Isenberg, "Housing Finance," p. 225.

29. Corgel, Smith, and Ling, *Real Estate Perspectives,* p. 445.

30. William B. Brueggeman and Jeffrey D. Fisher, *Real Estate Finance and Investments,* 9th ed. (Burr Ridge, Ill.: Irwin, 1993), p. 719.

31. David C. Ranney, Patricia A. Wright, and Tingwei Zhang, *Citizens, Local Government and the Development of Chicago's Near South Side,* Discussion Paper 90 (Geneva: United Nations Research Institute for Social Development, November, 1997).

32. Rachel Weber, "Extracting Value from the City: Neoliberalism and Urban Development," *Antipode* 34, no. 3 (Summer 2000): 525–46.

33. Personal interview.

34. Personal interview.

35. David Moberg, "After Harold Washington," *Chicago Reader*, March 11, 1989, p. 23.

36. This section based on personal interviews with representatives of the city of Chicago Finance Department and Mesirow Corporation, the firm that did the underwriting for this project.

37. Brueggeman and Fisher, *Real Estate Finance*, pp. 632–34.

38. This case is adapted from Ranney, Wright, and Zhang, "Citizens, Local Government and Development of Chicago's Near South Side."

39. The historic background information in this section was primarily excerpted from two sources. The first source is the *Local Community Fact Book, Chicago Metropolitan Area, 1980*, edited by The Chicago Fact Book Consortium (The Chicago Review Press, 1984). The second source is Chicago Historical Society, *Chicago: A Historical Guide to the Neighborhoods* (Chicago: Chicago Historical Society, 1979).

40. Department of City Planning, *Development Plan for the Central Area of Chicago*, City of Chicago, 1958.

41. Chicago Central Area Committee, *Chicago Central Area Housing Market Analysis*, CCAC, 1959, p. 7.

42. Chicago Central Area Committee, *Planning Principles for the Chicago Central Area*, CCAC, 1966.

43. Chicago Department of Development and Planning, *Chicago 21: A Plan for the Central Area Communities*, City of Chicago, 1973.

44. Chicago 21 Corporation, *South Loop New Town*, City of Chicago, 1974.

45. John Betancur, Deborah Bennett, and Patricia Wright, "Effective Strategies for Community Economic Development," in Philip Nyden and Wim Wiewel (eds.), *Challenging Uneven Development: An Urban Agenda for the 1990's* (New Brunswick: Rutgers University Press, 1991), pp. 203–4.

46. Personal interview, March 27, 1996.

47. Ed McCahill, "South Loop: Building for the Future," *Chicago Magazine*, December 1977, p. 161.

48. Miller, Nory, "South Loop New Town," *Inland Architect*, October, 1974, p. 8.

49. Patricia Wright, "The Impact of the Federal and State Urban Development Action Grants on Chicago: 1979–1986," 1987.

50. Patricia Wright and Thomas, Karen, "An Assessment of Single Room Occupancy Hotels in the South Loop," Nathalie P. Voorhees Neighborhood Center for Neighborhood and Community Improvement, April 1990.

51. City of Chicago, "Official Statement: $50,000,000 Tax Increment Allocation Bonds," dated February 10, 1999.

52. City of Chicago, Department of Housing, "Affordable Housing Plan 1999–2003, Quarterly Progress Report," Quarter ending March 31, 2001, p. 5.

53. This case has been adapted from David C. Ranney and Patricia A. Wright, "Race, Class and the Abuse of State Power: The Case of Public Housing in Chicago," *Sage Race Relations Abstracts* vol. 25, no. 3 (August 2000): pp. 3–32.

54. "Chicago Housing Authority: Condemned," *The Chicago Reporter* 26, no. 6 (October 1997).

55. Patricia Wright, Yittayih Zelalem, Julie deGraaf, and Linda Roman, "The Plan

to Voucher Out Public Housing: An Analysis of the Chicago Experience and A case Study of the Proposal to Redevelop the Cabrini-Green Public Housing Area," Publication #: V-155, Nathalie P. Voorhees Center for Neighborhood and Community Improvement, University of Illinois, Chicago, May 1997.

56. Great Cities Institute, November 1999.

57. Chicago Housing Authority, "1983 Statistical Report," 1983.

58. Chicago Housing Authority, September 30, 1999.

59. Ibid.

60. Chicago Housing Authority, Office of Management Analysis and Planning, "Residential Statistical Summary," 1997. All of the information in the following paragraph is from this report.

61. Bennett and Reed, "The New Face of Urban Renewal."

62. Ibid.

63. Patricia Wright, and Yittayih Zelalem, May 1997. All of the facts and details related to the HOPE VI process and Near North Plan were first researched and discussed in this technical report. HOPE VI is a federal grant program, which began in 1993 to provide dollars to revitalize the more distressed public housing developments. HOPE VI permits expenditures for capital costs of demolitions, construction, rehabilitation and other physical improvements. It can also be used for replacement housing and community and supportive services. Only public housing authorities are eligible to apply and compete nationally for HOPE VI program funding. The program encourages the public housing authorities to use HOPE VI to develop partnerships with private developers to create "mixed income" communities. Since 1993, $500 million per year has been made available through this program.

64. Patricia Wright and Yittayih Zelalem, May 1997.

65. Cabrini Green Local Advisory Council: Plaintiffs v. Chicago Housing Authority, an Illinois Municipal Corporation, and Joseph Shuldiner, in his official capacity as Executive Director of CHA; defendants, Complaint for Declaratory and Injunctive Relief, in the United States District Court for the Northern District of Illinois, Eastern Division, No. 96C 6949. p. 20.

66. A TIF allows the city to sell bonds to redevelop an area and use the extra property taxes generated by the development to pay off the bonds.

67. Paul Fischer, "Section 8 and Public Housing Revolution: Where Will the Families Go?" (Chicago: The Woods Fund, Spring 1999).

68. Wright and Zelalem, May, 1997.

69. Legal Assistance Foundation of Chicago, Press Release, "Tenants File Suit to Have Voice in Cabrini Green Revitalization," October 24, 1996.

70. Cabrini Green Local Advisory Council; plaintiffs v. Chicago Housing Authority et al.

71. Cabrini Green Local Advisory Council; plaintiffs v. Chicago Housing Authority et al., p. 26.

72. Consent Decree, Cabrini Green Local Advisory Council; plaintiffs v. Chicago Housing Authority, an Illinois Municipal Corporation, and Joseph Shuldiner, in his official capacity as Executive Director of CHA; defendants, in the United States District Court for the Northern District of Illinois, Eastern Division, No. 96C 6949. The following paragraphs summarize the main points from the consent decree.

73. Brian Rogal, "Private Firm Keeps Tight Grip on Public Housing," *The Chicago Reporter* 28, no. 10, (November 1999).

74. Order, Gautreaux v. CHA, 66C1459, September 28, 1999.

75. Consent Decree, Cabrini-Green Local Advisory Council vs. Chicago Housing Authority and Terry Petersen, City of Chicago, Richard M. Daley, 96C6949.

76. Plan for Transformation Year 3 Moving to Work (MTW) Draft Annual Plan FY 2002, released for public comment, September 1, 2001.

77. Chicago Coalition to Protect Public Housing, "Rental Study Shows Market Won't Support CHA Plans," press release, December 2, 1999.

78. Gail Radford, *Modern Housing for America: Policy Struggles in the New Deal Era* (Chicago: University of Chicago Press, 1996)

79. Tracy Cross and Associates, "An Analysis of the Potential for Market Rate Units in Cabrini-Hope VI Urban Revitalization Program, Chicago, Illinois" (Chicago: Tracy Cross and Associates, February, 1997) II, p. 22. Cited in Bennett and Reed, "The New Face of Urban Renewal," p. 191.

Chapter 7

1. Jared Bernstein, Elizabeth C. McNichol, Lawrence Mishell, and Robert Zahradnik, *Pulling Apart: A State-by-State Analysis of Income Trends* (Washington, D.C.: Center on Budget and Policy Priorities and the Economic Policy Institute, January 2000).

2. Edward N. Wolff, *Top Heavy: The Increasing Inequality of Wealth in America and What Can Be Done About it* (New York: New Press, 1995); Chuck Collins, Betsy Leondar-Wright, and Holly Sklar, *Shifting Fortunes: The Perils of the Growing American Wealth Gap* (Boston: United for a Fair Economy, 1999).

3. Heather Boushey, Chauna Brocht, Bethney Gundersen, and Jared Bernstein, *Hardships in America: The Real Story of Working Families* (Washington, D.C.: Economic Policy Institute, 2001).

4. James K. Galbraith, *Created Unequal: The Crisis in American Pay* (New York: The Free Press, 1998), p. 217.

5. Gary S. Becker, *Human Capital: A Theoretical and Empirical Analysis, with Special Reference to Education*, 3rd ed. (Chicago: University of Chicago Press, 1993), pp. xix, 16.

6. David Forcacs (ed.), *An Antonio Gramsci Reader: Selected Writings, 1916–35* (New York: Schocken Books, 1988), pp. 189–221.

7. Becker, *Human Capital*, p. 9.

8. Ibid., pp. 255–349.

9. George Gilder, *Wealth and Poverty* (New York: Basic Books, 1981); Lawrence Mead, *Beyond Entitlement: The Social Obligations of Citizenship* (New York: Free Press, 1986); Lawrence Mead, *The New Politics of Poverty: The Working Poor in America* (New York: Basic Books, 1992); Charles Murray, *Losing Ground: American Social Policy 1950–80* (New York: Basic Books, 1984).

10. William Julius Wilson, *The Declining Significance of Race: Blacks and Changing American Institutions* (Chicago: University of Chicago Press, 1978); William Julius Wilson, *The Truly Disadvantaged: The Inner City, the Underclass, and Public*

Policy (Chicago: University of Chicago Press, 1987); William Julius Wilson, *When the Work Disappears: The World of the New Urban Poor* (New York: Knopf, 1996); William Julius Wilson, *The Bridge Over the Racial Divide: Rising Inequality and Coalition Politics* (Berkeley: University of California Press, 1999) .

11. Wilson, *When the Work Disappears*, p. xiii.

12. Paul McCracken et al., *Towards Full Employment and Price Stability: A Report to the OECD by a Group of Independent Experts* (Paris: OECD, 1977).

13. OECD, *Structural Adjustment and Economic Performance* (Paris: OECD, 1987); OECD, *Measures to Assist the Long-Term Unemployed: Recent Experience in Some OECD Countries* (Paris: OECD, 1988); OECD, *Economies in Transition— Structural Adjustments in OECD Countries* (Paris: OECD, 1989); OECD, *Labour Market Policies in the 1990s* (Paris: OECD, 1990); OECD, *The OECD Jobs Study: Facts, Analysis, Strategies* (Paris: OECD, 1994); OECD, *The OECD Jobs Study: Part II—The Adjustment Potential of the Labour Market* (Paris: OECD, 1994).

14. Frances Fox Piven and Richard Cloward, *Regulating the Poor: The Functions of Public Welfare* (New York: Pantheon Books, 1971).

15. Nikolas Theodore, "Regulating Labor Markets in an Age of Flexibility: Fast Policy and the Political Economy of Workfare," unpublished Ph.D diss., Chicago, Univesity of Illinois–Chicago, 2000, p. 185.

16. Gary Orfield and Helene Slessarev, *Job Training Under the New Federalism*, Report to the Subcommittee on Employment Opportunities, Committee on Education and Labor, U.S.House of Representatives (Chicago: Illinois Unemployment and Job Training Research Project, University of Chicago, 1986), pp. 44–47.

17. Ibid., pp. 61–73.

18. Nikolas Theodore, "Workforce Investment Act: Recommendations for Illinois," Chicago Urban League and the University of Illinois Chicago Great Cities Institute, July 1999.

19. Virginia Carlson and Nikolas Theodore, "Are There Enough Jobs? Welfare Reform and Labor Market Reality" (Chicago: University of Illinois at Chicago Center for Urban Economic Development, Chicago Urban League and Northern Illinois University Office for Social Policy Research, December 1995).

20. The estimate is based on 1990 U.S. Census data. The methodology was developed in an unpublished paper, Nikolas Theodore and Jodi Pietrowski, "Hidden Unemployment in Chicago: A Look at Worker Discouragement," Chicago Urban League, March 11, 1997. Also see Danielle Gordon, "Invisible Jobless Ambush Welfare Plan," *The Chicago Reporter*, 26, no. 2 (March 1997).

21. Bernstein, McNicol, Mishell, and Zahradnik, *Pulling Apart.*

22. Heather Boushey, Chauna Brocht, Bethney Gundersen, and Jaren Bernstein, *Hardships in America: The Real Story of Working Families* (Washington, D.C.: Economic Policy Institute, 2001).

23. Carlson and Theodore, "Are There Enough Jobs?" p. 11.

24. Susan Armato, Jim Lewis, and Tim Lohrentz, "Living With Welfare Reform: A Survey of Low Income Families in Illinois" (Chicago: Work, Welfare and Families, Chicago Urban League, and University of Illinois Chicago Center for Urban Economic Development, January 2000).

25. Boushey, Brocht, Gundersen, and Bernstein, *Hardships in America*, p. 31.

26. Jamie Peck and Nikolas Theodore, "The Business of Contingent Work: Growth

and Restructuring in Chicago's Temporary Employment Industry," *Work, Employment and Society* 12, no. 4 (Decmeber 1998): 655–74; Jamie Peck and Nikolas Theodore, "Contingent Chicago: Restructuring the Spaces of Temporary Labor," unpublished, July 1999.

27. R. C. Longworth and Sharman Stein, "Temp Jobs Gaining Permanence," *Chicago Tribune*, October 11, 1995.

28. U.S. Census Bureau, *County Business Patterns*; Bureau of Labor Statistics, *Industry Staffing Patterns*; Staffing Industry Analysts, *Staffing Industry Sourcebook*; Dun and Bradstreet, *Marketplace 2000*.

29. Lewis M. Segal and Daniel G. Sullivan, "The Temporary Labor Force" *Economic Perspectives*, Federal Reserve Bank of Chicago, Chicago, March/April 1995.

30. Bureau of Labor Statistics, "Geographic Profile of Employment and Unemployment, 1994, Bulletin 2469, December, 1995; Bureau of Labor Statistics, "A Different Look at Part-time Employment," *Issues in Labor Statistics*, April, 1996.

31. Bureau of Labor Statistics, "Multiple Job Holders by State, 1994 Annual Averages," unpublished data produced from Current Population Survey microdata, 1996.

32. Calculated by the author from data contained in: *Illinois Labor Market Review*, Summer 1995, Illinois Department of Employment Security.

33. Bureau of Labor Statistics, "Geographic Profile of Employment and Unemployment, 1994," Bulletin 2469, December, 1995.

34. Nikolas C. Theodore, "When the Job Doesn't Pay: Contingent Workers in the Chicago Metropolitan Area," The Working Poor Project, Chicago Urban League, Northern Illinois University, Latino Institute, March 1995. The notion of a living wage is based on minimal purchases needed by a single-parent family with two children. See Kathleen Shankman, "Jobs That Pay: Are There Enough Good Jobs Available in Metropolitan Chicago?" The Working Poor Project, Chicago Urban League, Northern Illinois University, Latino Institute, November 1995.

35. Peck and Theodore, "The Business of Contingent Work," pp. 656–58.

36. Ibid., p. 658.

37. Nikolas Theodore, "A Fair Day's Pay? Homeless Day Laborers in Chicago," University of Illinois Chicago Center for Urban Economic Development, February 22, 2000.

38. Ibid.

39. Numbers in this section have been compiled by the author from data available from the Illinois Department of Employment Security.

40. Bureau of Labor Statistics, "Occupational Employment and Wages, 1998," press release, December 22, 1999.

41. Wage data was compiled by the author from data available from the Bureau of Labor Statistics Monthly Reports on Employment, Hours and Earnings.

42. This section is based on Nikolas Theodore, David C. Ranney and Snigdha Srivastava, "Import Competition and Employment," University of Illinois Chicago, Center for Urban Economic Development, 2001.

43. U.S. Department of Commerce, *Trade and Industrial Outlook 1998* (Washington, D.C.: U.S. Government Printing Office, 1998).

44. U.S. Department of Commerce, *Trade and Industrial Outlook 1998* (Washington, D.C.: U.S. Government Printing Office, 1998).

45. *Crain's Chicago Business* (September 15, 1997). Terry Harville, then Governor

Jim Edgar's chief economic development advisor, said: "I would say it's a save, with a *potential* for a win" (italics added).

46. Kate Bronfenbrenner, "Final Report: The Effects of Plant Closing or Threat of Plant Closing on the Right of Workers to Organize," submitted to The Labor Secretariat of the NorthAmerican Commission for Labor Cooperation, New York State School of Industrial and Labor Relations, Cornell University, September 30, 1996, pp. 4–5.

47. Ibid., p. 2.

48. Ibid.

49. Stephen Franklin, "Caterpillar's Profit Tops $1 Billion," *Chicago Tribune*, January 19, 1996.

50. This section based on a report by David Ranney and Paul Schwalb, "An Analysis of the A. E. Staley/Tate & Lyle Lockout in Decatur, Illinois," Project 404 (Chicago: University of Illinois Chicago Center for Urban Economic Development, 1995).

51. Melita Marie Garza, Lauren Comander, and Patrick Cole, "Problems at Tire Plant Alleged: Firestone Disputes Accusations by Former Decatur Workers," *Chicago Tribune*, August 20, 2000, p. 1.

52. Dean Baker, "NAIRU: Is It a Real Constraint," in Dean Baker, Gerald Epstein, and Robert Pollin (eds.), *Globalization and Progressive Economic Policy* (New York: Cambridge University Press, 1998), pp. 369–90; Galbraith, *Created Unequal*, pp. 171–82.

53. David C. Ranney, "Class, Race, Gender and Poverty: A Critique of Some Contemporary Theories," *Sage Race Relations Abstracts* 23, no. 2 (May 1998): 5–26.

54. A view of human development that places education in a critical role but places it in a broader context has been developed by another Nobel Prize winner, Amartya Sen. See Amartya Sen, *Development As Freedom* (New York: Knopf, 1999).

55. Raya Dunayevskaya, *Marxism and Freedom: From 1776 Until Today* (Atlantic Highlands, N.J.: Humanities Press, 1982), pp. 266–87.

56. Theodore, Ranney, and Srivastava, "Trade Policy and Employment: An Examination of Illinois Import-Sensitive Industries," University of Illinois Chicago Center for Urban Economic Development, unpublished discussion paper, 2002.

Chapter 8

1. For a discussion of these movements, see Jeremy Brecher, Tim Costello, and Brendan Smith, *Globalization From Below: The Power of Solidarity* (Cambridge, Mass.: South End Press, 2000).

2. The background on trinational organizing contained in this section is based in part on an unpublished paper: John Cavanagh, Sarah Anderson, and Karen Hansen Kuhn, "Tri-national Organizing for Just and Sustainable Trade and Development: Some Lessons and Insights" (Washington D.C.: Institute for Policy Studies [IPS] and Development Group for Alternative Policies [DGAP], August 27, 1998). Additional material not footnoted are from the author's own notes at trinational and national meetings and interviews.

3. Action Canada Network (Canada), Mobilization for Development, Trade, Labor and the Environment (U.S.A.), Red Mexicana de Accion Frente Al Libre Comercio

(Mexico), *Final Declaration*, International Forum: Public Opinion and the Free Trade Negotiations, Citizens' Alternatives, City of Zacatecas, Mexico, October 25–27, 1991.

4. Interview, February 1992.

5. Red Mexicana de Accion Frente al Libre Comercio, Action Canada Network, Quebec Coalition on Trilateral Negotiations, Alliance for Responsible Trade, Citizens Trade Campaign, National Rainbow Coalition, Final Declaration, TriNational Consultation on the North American Free Trade Agreement, January 15–15, 1993, Mexico City, D.F., Mexico.

6. John Cavanagh, Sarah Anderson, Karen Hansen Kuhn, "Tri-national Organizing for Just and Sustainable Trade and Development: Some Lessons and Insights," unpublished discussion paper, Washington, D.C., Institute for Policy Studies and Development Group for Alternative Policies, August 27, 1998.

7. Alliance for Responsible Trade, Citizens Trade Campaign, Mexican Action Network on Free Trade, "A Just and Sustainable Trade and Development Initiative for North America."

8. "Conference Report, Beyond NAFTA: Toward Equity and Sustainability," Madison, Wisconsin, October 6–11, 1994, Havens Center, Rm. 8117 Social Science Building, 1180 Observatory Drive, Madison, WI 53706.

9. Alliance for Responsible Trade, "Citizen Groups Respond to Buchanomics," March 1, 1996.

10. John Cavanagh and Sarah Anderson, "Ten Lessons and Opportunities from the Fast Track Victory," Institute for Policy Studies, November 13, 1997.

11. Alliance for Responsible Trade (U.S.), Common Frontiers (Canada), Red Chile por una Iniciativa de los Pueblos (Chile), Red Mexicana de Accion Frente al Libre Comercio (Mexico), Reseau Quebecois sur l'integration continentale (Quebec), *Alternatives for the Americas: Building a Peoples' Hemispheric Agreement, Discussion Draft #2*, November 1998, Alliance for Responsible Trade, c/o Development GAP, 927 15th Avenue, 4th Floor, Washington, D.C. 20005.

Chapter 9

1. Saul D. Alinsky, *Reveille for Radicals* (New York: Vintage Books, 1969). Much of the history of the Industrial Areas Foundation that is described below is based on the film *Alinsky: The Chicago Experience*, produced for PBS by the Chicago Video Project, 1999.

2. See Saul D. Alinsky, *John L. Lewis: A Unauthorized Biography* (New York: Putnam, 1949).

3. Saul D. Alinsky, *Rules for Radicals: A Practical Primer for Realistic Radicals* (New York: Vintage Books, 1972).

4. Melvin Dubofsky and Warren Van Tine, *John L. Lewis: A Biography* (New York: New York Times Books, 1977); Andy Phillips and Raya Dunayevskaya, *The Coal Miners' General Strike of 1949–50: The Birth of Marxist-Humanism in the U.S.* (Chicago: News and Letters Committees, 1984).

5. Karl Marx, "Economic Manuscripts of 1857–58 (Grundrisse)," in *Collected Works*, vol. 28 (New York: International Publishers, 1986), p. 412.

6. "The Euro's Difficult Childhood," *Chicago Tribune*, September 24, 2000, section I, p. 22.

7. Peter Dicken, *Global Shift: Transforming the World Economy*, 3rd ed. (New York: Guilford Press, 1998); David Harvey, *The Condition of Postmodernity* (Cambridge, Mass.: Blackwell, 1990); David Harvey, *Justice, Nature and the Geography of Difference* (Cambridge, Mass.: Blackwell, 1996).

8. Adolph Reed Jr., *Class Notes Posing as Politics and Other Thoughts on the American Scene* (New York: New Press, 2000), p. 207.

9. Ibid., p. 108; Kim Moody, *Workers in a Lean World: Unions in the International Economy* (New York: Verso, 1997).

10. Harvey, *Justice*, p. 361.

11. Reed, *Class Notes*, p. xiii.

12. Alinsky, *Reveille for Radicals*, p. 153.

13. Ibid., p. 229.

14. Paulo Freire, *Pedagogy of the Oppressed* (New York: Continuum, 1996); Paulo Freire, *Education for Critical Consciousness* (New York: Continuum, 1974); Paulo Freire, *Teachers as Cultural Workers: Letters to Those Who Dare to Teach* (New York: Westview, 1998).

15. Freire, *Education for Critical Consciousness*, p. 6.

16. Karl Marx, "Economic Manuscripts of 1857–58 (Grundrisse)," in *Collected Works*, vol. 28 (New York: International Publishers, 1986), p. 412.

Index